Library of
Davidson College

Monograph 60
THE AMERICAN ETHNOLOGICAL SOCIETY
Robert F. Spencer, *Editor*

The author interviewing head elder

PWO KAREN

At the Edge of Mountain and Plain

James W. Hamilton

WEST PUBLISHING CO.
St. Paul • New York • Boston
Los Angeles • San Francisco

301.29
H218p

COPYRIGHT © 1976 By WEST PUBLISHING CO.
All rights reserved
Printed in the United States of America

Library of Congress Cataloging in Publication Data

Hamilton, James W
  PWO KAREN: At the Edge of Mountain and Plain.
  (Monograph—American Ethnological Society; 60)
  Bibliography: p.
  Includes index.
  1. Karens. I. Title. II. Series: American Ethnological Society.
Monographs; 60.
DS570.K37H35 301.29'59 75-44046
ISBN 0-8299-0075-6

80-101

Hamilton—PWO Karen

To four people who had a significant influence on the result:
An Animist and a Christian,
a Buddhist and a Scientist

Foreword

"There is another People in this Country called Carianners, whiter than either [the Burmans or Mons], distinguished into *Bûraghmah* and *Pegu Carianners*; they live in the *woods*, in small *Societies*, of 10 or 12 *houses*; are not wanting in industry, though it goes no farther than to procure them an annual subsistence."

"They are remarkable for their *perfect morality*, but have no apparent Religion: When asked if they believed the *existence* of any SUPERIOR BEING, they replied, that the *Bûraghmah* and *Pegu Tallopins* [monks] told them so, but that they knew nothing about IT."

"It is customary with them to place a Duck, or Fowl, with some rice, upon the grave of every deceased person; when asked on this also, they give no reply, but that it is customary. When any person dies they abandon the house, and build another."[1]

These observations of the Karen appeared in British notices, from a letter written in 1759 by Captain George Baker to his superiors in the East India Company. The attractive character of "natural man" into which they were cast was enhanced upon further acquaintance. Colonists-to-be saw them as one of the oppressed minorities of Burma, who during the first Anglo-Burmese war gave support to the forces of General Archibald Campbell. Subsequently, they advanced to the status of a sturdy yeomanry, who responded eagerly to opportunity in the fields of education, nursing, and military service. The religious aspect paralleled the political: Adoniram Judson and his Baptist colleagues, laboring after 1826 in the jungle hinterlands of Moulmein and Tavoy, found ready converts among Karen. Though receptivity to Christianity in fact marked but a small portion of the Karen, it was the more striking and portentous by contrast to the resistance exhibited by their Buddhist neighbors. Colonial officials and missionaries alike gave special attention to this promising people, who after the Shan, were the most numerous of the indigenous minorities of Burma. The result was a voluminous literature, as uneven in quality as it was enthusiastic in tone.

One who has sampled these writings can at least sympathize with Alleyne Ireland, who during the first decade of this century noted with satisfaction "a very marked decline in the cult of the Karen." In his opinion the Karen had "attracted perhaps a trifle more than his fair share of attention" among the minorities of Burma.[2] Yet, whatever may be deemed a "fair share" of scholarly attention—which (witness the recent attention to Purum, Ambryn Islanders, and Natchez) is not meted out with the egalitarian impartiality of these institutions Professor Ireland was studying—there are reasons now for a fresh look at the Karen. The best of the early scholarship has been obtained largely through missionaries, from Mason to Marshall, and suffers less from persuasive bias than from the limitations of the anthropological perspectives of the time. Indeed, the long-term and intimate acquaintance of these savants to the people whom they described renders their reports still indispensable to us. It is new interests that dictate that their observations now be reexamined and supplemented.

In one sense, it must be conceded, Professor Ireland has a valid point, for the Karen themselves have been unevenly studied. Most of the earlier attention given to the Southern or Plains, Karen of Burma had focused upon that branch known as the Sgaw, Captain Baker's Burmese Karen, who had shown the greater attraction to Christianity. The other major branch, the Pwo—Baker's Peguan (i. e., Mon) Karen—many of whom, as Buddhists, resisted conversion, had been largely ignored. Again,

FOREWORD

most of those studies had been limited to the Karen of Burma; and it was only after the second World War that the eminent student of Burmese history, Gordon Luce, called attention to the need to examine the Karen in neighboring Thailand. James Hamilton was among the first of the American scholars to turn to that field, and it is doubly welcome that the subjects of his study are members of that neglected branch, the Pwo.

From case study such as this, one may expect to find necessary data for an ethnology of Karen peoples. Its implications, however, embrace themes of change that touch peoples everywhere in one form or another. Dr. Hamilton tells us that he selected the village of Ban Hong, in Northwestern Thailand, as the scene of his research because it was destined to be displaced by the construction of a dam; eventually he was able to return and restudy the changes that stemmed from that event. But even in the first phase of his fieldwork, it was evident that the villagers of Ban Hong were already poised between a traditional lifeway and engagement in the larger society of Thailand; and the exigencies of their economic plight were impelling them daily toward the latter. It must be added that such dilemmas have confronted the Karen before: for what passes as "traditional" has its own history. Thus, the ancestors of those villagers had founded Ban Hong in the aftermath of a displacement some two centuries earlier.

No, far from rationing studies to a "fair share" we need studies responsive to the significant questions raised by each age of scholarship. Given sufficient case studies of satisfactory penetration, we can hope to trace with some confidence the plasticity of Karen response to diverse settings, and thus to provide generalizations for comparison with other peoples. Fortunately, scholars from countries around the world have recently been at work among the Karen, and we are beginning to acquire the critical mass of data we need. The study that lies before you in this volume provides both an analysis illuminating in itself and a substantial base for future comparison.

Theodore Stern

FOREWORD

Literature Cited

[1] Reprint from Dalrymple's Oriental Repository, 1791–7, of Portions Relating to Burma.
- 1926 Letters Concerning the *Negrais Expedition*; and concerning the *adjacent countries*. June, 1759, Captain George Baker. Rangoon, Burma: Superintendent of Government Printing and Stationery.

[2] Ireland, Alleyne
- 1907 "A Report Prepared on Behalf of the University of Chicago." The Province of Burma Vol. 1, p. 64. Boston and New York: Houghton, Mifflin and Co.

Preface

> Before the flooding, I was a man; when the flood came, it was as if I had died; now, it is as if I have been born again as a young boy; I must learn again how to make a living.
>
> (Karen headman)

The above statement by a Karen headman was made during my second field trip to Thailand, ten years after I had completed the first study. The first field work was carried out between 1959 and 1961; the second, in 1969 (see Appendix A for details of schedule and procedures).

The headman's statement dramatizes what happened in the intervening years to some of the Karen villages in this study when the Yanhee Dam was completed, (see figure A, page xiii). Ban Hong, with its thirty-five houses and nearly two hundred people (see figure B, page xiv), and many of the surrounding villages have already been forced to move and disperse because of the Yanhee Dam. The dam was built on the Ping River and, has now begun to form its reservoir in an area that was once the territory of Pwo Karen (see figure 8).

This study, then, is concerned with a before-and-after analysis of the tribal Pwo Karen found in northern Thailand. I concentrate on the village of Ban Hong but also analyze relations with surrounding Karen and Thai villages and their characteristics. The emphasis of this study deals with social structure, economic organization, and culture change due to natural and cultural variations within the environment. The approach is both historical and systemic. Aspects of religion, politics, and socialization are dealt with mainly as they elucidate the central problem.

In addition to an analysis of social structure and economic organization, this study is one in cultural ecology. It focusses upon the two-pronged adaptation that Karen culture is making in its articulation with the natural environment on one hand, and its adaptation to the Thai cultural environment on the other hand.

The general problem is the following: What are the adaptive processes whereby a tribal culture becomes incorporated within a state as the state expands into tribal areas? A basic assumption is that economic change or adaption is a most important aspect of the total process. The effects considered in this study are due to the present incorporation of the Karen within the Thai state. Present-day Karen culture can only be understood in terms of this contact and the resultant changes. I attempt to present the dynamic factors of this interactive relationship because the change is still occurring and cannot be understood otherwise. The fact that the Karen are becoming dependent upon Thai markets has caused some loss of cultural autonomy. Many Thai elements are being incorporated into the Karen view and way of life as a direct result of changes in the economy.

The Karen are not peasants. They are, however, in the process of being peasantized as they adapt to, and are being incorporated into the Thai state. The change from one culture type to another has begun and it cannot be reversed. The fact that Karen culture is not a peasant culture has many implications and raises many problems of analysis. The process of economic and cultural change through adaptation to natural and cultural environment is the issue. The solution presented in this study is to analyze the social structure and the economic organization as it relates to social structure, to show that entering the Thai market system is a necessity for survival of the society, and finally to indicate how this process is changing all of Karen culture.

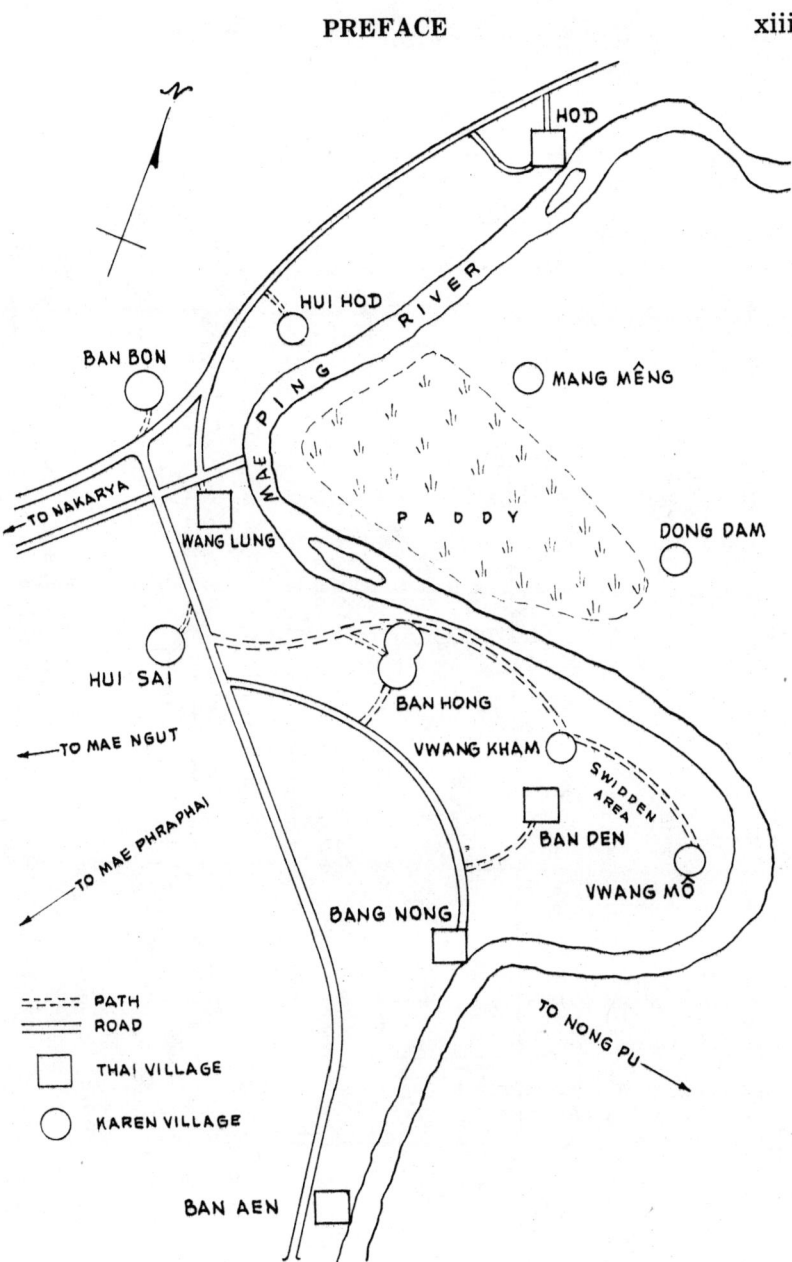

Fig. A. Sketch Map of Central Research Area

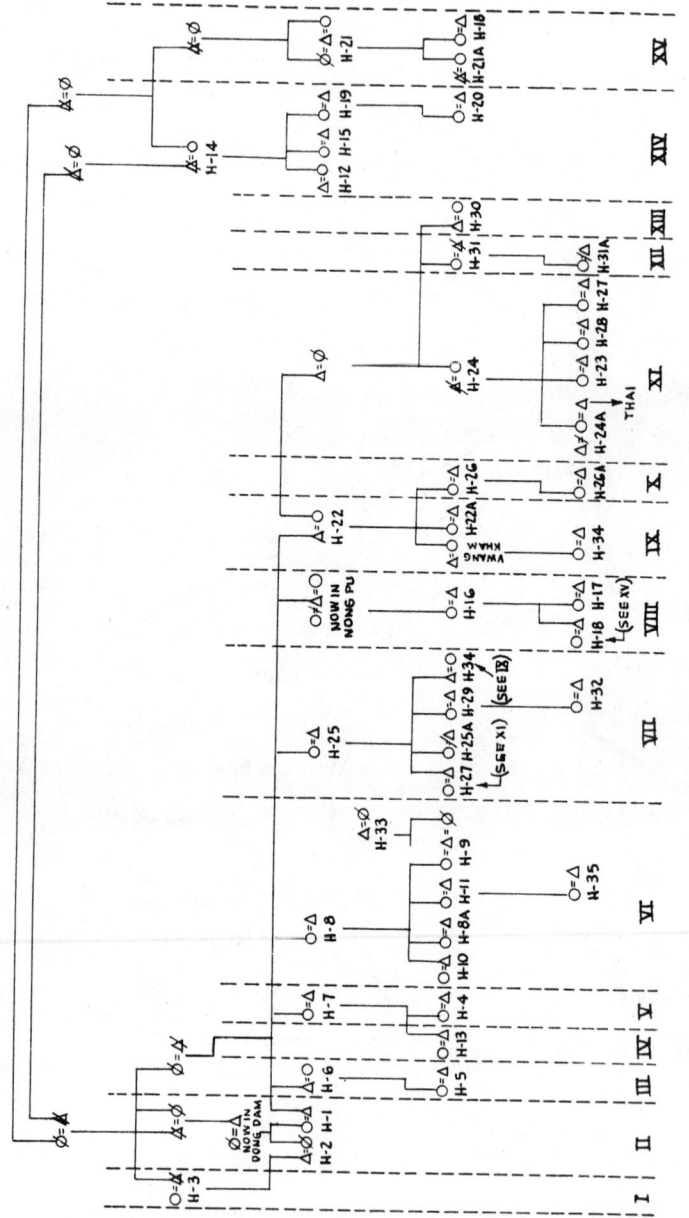

Fig. B. Village Households and Lineage Segments

PREFACE

The goals of this study are both broad and narrow, both synchronic and diachronic: First, I present a general picture of Karen society and culture with attention to time and space. This goal is an overarching one and can only be realized by reading the entire study and by keeping in mind that the ethnographic present shifts from before to after the construction of the Yanhee Dam. A second goal is to provide the details of Karen social structure and in summary fashion the entire social organization. These interests are dealt with in chapters 4, 5, and 6. Thirdly, I present an historical and organizational view of economic structure, its relationship to the rest of the culture, and its interplay with Thai economy. These concerns are found in chapters 7 and 8. My fourth goal concerns culture contact and specific changes which is dealt with in chapters 9 and 10. And finally, in the conclusion I attempt to summarize and draw inferences.

This study has been a long time in coming for two reasons. First, one cannot analyze culture change until some change has occurred, and culture change occurs slowly—for an author—even if the people concerned believe that it is happening all too fast. Secondly, my interests are professional and scholarly. I did not want my Karen friends, through anything I wrote, to become embroiled in the recently ended wars of Southeast Asia. I, therefore, hesitated about putting any data in print. Hopefully, those restraints are now removed.

*

Acknowledgements

Before turning to the Karen, I must make some acknowledgment of debt and gratitude. It is not possible to list all of the people who have aided me or who have influenced my thinking in one way or another. Only an outstanding few can be mentioned: I never knew A. L. Kroeber, but I was introduced to cultural anthropology through his work, and he has become a culture hero to me for his dedication to field research and for his anthropological breadth. While a student at the University of Chicago I became indebted to B. Malinowski and A. R. Radcliffe-Brown and a long line of their students. Structural-functional anthropology left a strong imprint on my orientation. A major theoretical debt is also owed to a group of scholars who were at the University of Michigan while I was a student there. I merely list their names here with the hope that they know the personal regard I accord them: Marshall D. Sahlins, Elman Service, Eric Wolf, David F. Aberle, and especially Leslie A. White.

While preparing for, during, and after field work, I received professional assistance from a long list of individuals. A few who gave time, advice, and knowledge are Lauriston Sharp, Robert Textor, Lucien Hanks, and John Brohm. David Aberle and Leslie White answered questions from the field, boosted my morale, and kept me going when I was ready to admit defeat at the hands of Karen "spirits." One Thai scholar, *Phya* Anuman Rajadhon, deserves special mention for his knowledge of Thai cultural history which contributed to my interpretation of the data. Others who deserve mention are Dr. and Mrs. John Bisset (M.D.) who were friends and mentors. The good doctor tried hard to deal with the health questions I raised about myself and the Karen. It was not his fault if I had to ignore his germ theory of disease! Also, for thought provoking discussion, comment, and criticism, I must single out Robbins Burling, Richard Beardsley, Theodore Stern, and Frederic Lehman.

To the Department of Anthropology, University of Michigan, and indirectly to the Ford Foundation which supplied the financial aid to the Department, I owe a special debt for the three grants awarded to me for the initial two years of field research. The Research Council of the University of Missouri was very generous in supporting the second field research ten years later as well as providing financial assistance for data analysis, technical assistance, and equipment. I hope the results of the research will justify the aid given.

There are many Thai and Karen friends who have helped: *Achan* Kua Saligupta provided a doorway into the world of Thai culture. She introduced my wife and me to the Chitra Dansuptra family who taught us the Thai way and became our family while we were in Bangkok. I will always hold a special feeling for this most unusual family. To the former Governor of Bangkok, *Luang* Krishnamara, and his family, I want to say "thank you" again. In northern Thailand, *Khru* Sant Khangaew and his wife opened their home and gave much more than friendship. Chaiyaphan Chantarasonti was my assistant, friend, and teacher. Difficult times were overcome with his Buddhist calm. The Pwo Karen friends will never be able to read these words, but they already know my deep respect for them. One man of Ban Hong must be mentioned by name; without the help and knowledge of Khung Ci, this study and my understanding of the culture would be thin indeed. If I have made mistakes it is not because he did not try to teach me. Khung Ci and I shed a tear together when I left the field.

Two graduate students deserve mention for their painstaking help: Ethel Vesper typed the manuscript and helped construct tables; Margaret Mandeville did the tedious job of proofreading and index preparation. Thank you both. There is also a group of unsung heroes at West Publishing Company that have my gratitude for reasons they know best.

It is traditional to express some debt of gratitude to one's own family for being difficult to live with during the troubled period of thinking and writing, but it somehow sounds hollow after all this time. Hats off to them anyway. I have only myself to blame for errors and omissions, but I owe my wife, Donna, much praise for her contributions of data collected and insights provided.

*

Contents

Foreword v
Preface vii
Acknowledgments xii

1. THE KAREN IN SOUTHEAST ASIA 1
2. BAN HONG IN SPACE AND TIME 15
3. ECOLOGY AND ECONOMIC ACTIVITIES IN THE YEARLY ROUND 49
4. THE GEOMETRY OF KINSHIP AND DESCENT 93
5. HOUSEHOLD, LINEAGE SEGMENT, AND WORK GROUP 119
6. VILLAGE AND VILLAGE COMPLEX 144
7. THE BAN HONG ECONOMY 173
8. MONEY AND THE ECONOMY: KINSHIP, BAZAAR, MARKET 194
9. THE WINDS OF TIME AND CHANGE: THE PAST 230
10. TEN YEARS LATER 248
11. CONCLUSION: THE BEGINNING 288

Appendixes 293
Bibliography 341
Index 351

FIGURES

1	Location of Karen in Southeast Asia	3
2	Research Area and Village Locations	17
3	Ban Hong Village	24
4	Population Distribution in Ban Hong	28
5	Kinship Terminology	96
6	Proscribed Marriage	127
7	Headman Relationships	150
8	Upper Reservoir Area	251
A	Sketch Map of Central Research Area	xiii
B	Village Household and Lineage Segments	xiv

TABLES

1	Karen Population	13
2	Linguistic Relationships	14
3	Summary of Village Demography	26–27
4	Age of Villages	33
5	Crime and Punishment	43
6	Summary of Climate During 1960	51
7	Stages of Work-Group Activities	66
8	Ownership of Buffalo, Land, Corral, and Hayloft	76
9	Pig Population	79
10	House Construction Costs	90
11	Relationship Between Marriage Partners	125
12	Lineage Connections of Segment Nuclei	133

CONTENTS

13	Socio-Economic Classes	137
14	Village Specialists in Ban Hong	156
15	Annual Expenditures of an Average Household for One Year	204
16	Estimate of Average Household Income and Assets for One Year	215
17	Days of Rain Fall	254
18	Amount of Rain Fall	255
19	Amphur (District) Population	260
20	Economic Scheduling in the Annual Round	275
21	Income	276–77
22	Various Weights and Measures	286
23	Table 23	287

*

PWO KAREN
At the Edge of Mountain and Plain

☦

South east view of central research area from a height of 500 meters. Light area in center is Karen paddy fields.

1

The Karen in Southeast Asia

INTRODUCTION

In the mountainous regions of mainland Southeast Asia are many groups of people who gain much of their subsistance by slash-and-burn agriculture. These are the tribal hill peoples known as Akha, Lahu, Maeo, Yao, Lawa, Karen, and others (for cultural summaries, see LeBar 1964). These groups have been changing and have been in more or less contact with the valley people—Burmese, Thai, Lao, Chinese, Indian—for centuries. At present, however, contact is becoming more intense as the nations of Southeast Asia expand their control into the mountainous areas of their respective domains. Some of the various hill groups are themselves moving into the valley areas, and as they do, their culture changes even more as they adapt to new ways of dealing with the natural environment and the more dominant culture of the nation-state.

One of these tribal groups living in the forested foothills and mountains of Northern Thailand is called Pwo Karen. They too have begun to filter more and more into the fertile valleys and to adopt wet rice agriculture and certain other elements of Thai culture. I spent two and one half years in Thailand studying Ban Hong, and surrounding Pwo Karen villages. My concern was to understand the culture of Ban Hong, its relations with other Karen villages, and its contacts with Thai culture. Before turning to Ban Hong, however, I will discuss the Karen in more general terms.

THE KAREN AND THEIR LOCATIONS IN SOUTHEAST ASIA

The colorful and numerous people called Karen are found in Burma and Thailand. They live mostly in the hills along the border of the two countries, but some groups have been moving into the valleys and plains as they have adopted wet-rice agriculture.

There are several subgroups of Karen with different names, customs, languages, and degrees of cultural contact. As a matter of fact, there are disagreements among specialists as to the name, origin, ethnic and racial connections, language affiliation, and population and distribution of Karen in Southeast Asia. Even the complexity of cultural development which they have achieved is disputed (see pp. 10–11).

Today, the Karen are located within the broad area between the 10th and 21st degrees north latitude, and between the 94th and 101st degrees of east longitude (see Marshall 1922:1; Young 1962:92, 101; LeBar 1964:59).[1]

The Karen groups are found mostly in the hills and now occasionally on the plains in Arakan, and stretched along the border between Thailand and Burma (Figure 1). In Burma, the northern extreme of the Karen is in the Southern Shan States, and from there extend south almost to the tip of the country. In Thailand, they are found in the following provinces (from south to north), along the Thai-Burma border: Petchaburi, Rajaburi, Kanchanaburi, Tak, Maehongsorn, Lampoon, Chiengmai, and Chiengrai (Rajadon 1957:889; Young 1962:93–101; Blanchard 1958:58–64; Seidenfaden 1958:124–125; Marshall 1922:1–4;

Marshall 1945:2–3). These provinces stretch from just south of Bangkok to the northern extremes of the country.

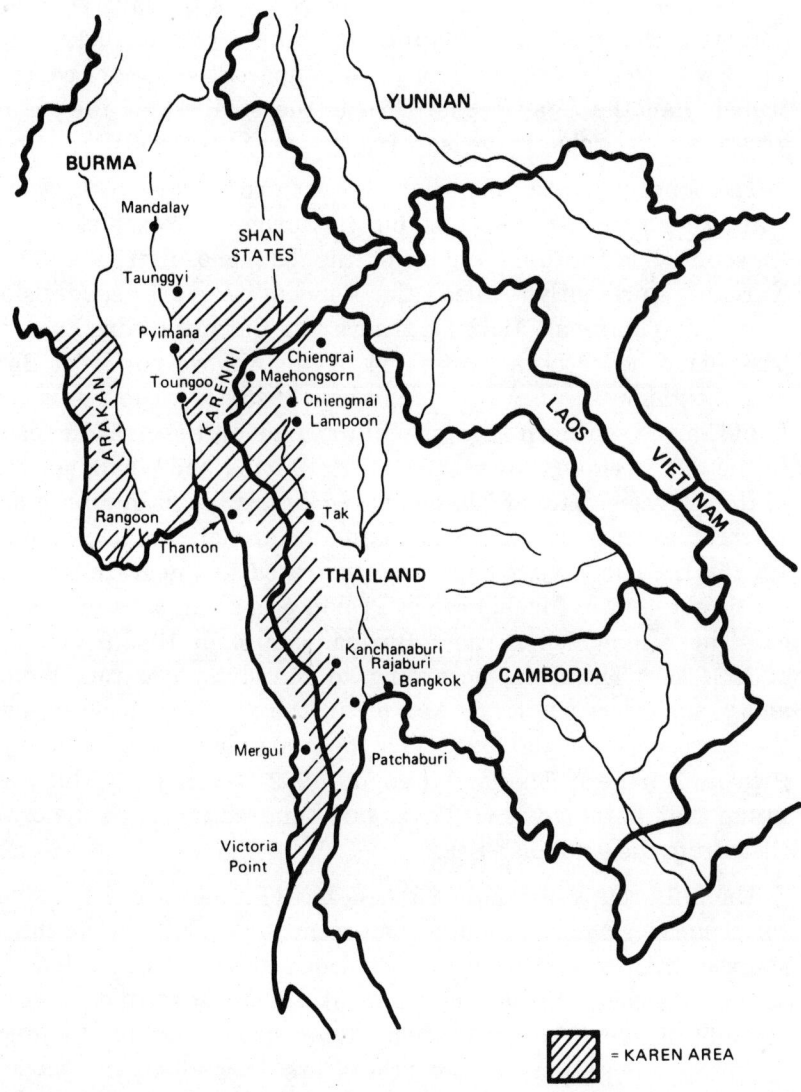

FIGURE 1   Location of Karen in Southeast Asia

DISTRIBUTION OF SUBGROUPS

The three major subgroups of Karen are Sgaw, Pwo, and Bwe (also called *Bghai,* or *Bghwe*).[2] The Sgaw is the largest group and is more widely scattered than the others (Marshall 1922:1). The Pwo group is second in size, and apparently is more concentrated than the Sgaw. The Bwe is the smallest of the major groups and is probably the least known (see Scott 1900).[3]

The subgroups are somewhat interspersed with each other and with other non-Karen groups, but in Burma the "exclusive Karen country is the hilly region of the Toungoo district and the Karenni [presently called the "kayah" state] subdivision . . ." (Marshall 1922:1), where "in the mountains the villages have never been dominated by their more powerful Burman neighbors. . . ." (Marshall 1945:2). The Sgaw are found in the southern regions of Burma along the Arakan coast, in the delta region, down the neck of Burma and Thailand, and in the northern part of Thailand. Sgaw are found in all regions where there are Karen in Thailand (Marshall 1922:1; Young 1962:93). The Bwe group is concentrated in the Karenni area of Burma, and in Maehongsorn Province, a small area of Northern Thailand which borders Burma (Marshall 1922:3; Young 1962:106). The Pwo, according to Marshall, are found only along the sea coast, from Arakan in the west to Mergui down the eastern peninsula (1922:1); there are, however, pockets of Pwo in Northern Thailand (Young 1962:102–103).[4] The Pwo group that I studied is well over one hundred miles, as the crow flies, from the Andaman Sea.

The hill groups of Southeast Asia have found ecological niches for themselves, and although they seem to overlap and be interspersed with one another, if one looks at the distributions in three dimensions rather than two, it will be seen that there is actually little overlap in location. Some groups are located high up in the mountains, while others are located on the slopes. Still others are in the foothills at the bases of the mountains, while the Burmans, Shans, and Thai for the most part, are located in the lowlands. The Karen seem to be located between 3,000 feet altitude down to the very base of the foothills. It also appears that the Karen subgroups are located at slightly different altitudes. The Bwe seem to be the highest at around 3,000 feet, the Taungthu are found slightly lower,[5] the Sgaw seem to be found mostly around 2,000 feet, and the Pwo are found below 2,000 feet. There is some overlap among Karen subgroups, however. There are Sgaw on the plains of Burma and Thailand now, but these groups are in the throes of drastic change. The Pwo group which I studied is located at about 800 to 900 feet. (Marshall does not give any data on altitude, but see Young 1962; Seidenfaden 1958:125; Ijima 1965; Hinton 1969:2).

POPULATION, DENSITY, AND SIZE OF VILLAGE

The total population of Karen in Southeast Asia is unknown, but based on various census figures and estimates, an upper limit of two million does not seem unreasonable for the combined population of Karen in Thailand and Burma.[6]

There are no accurate figures for the Karen population in Thailand, but two estimates for all Karen groups are 60,000 and 70,000 people (Rajadhon 1957:890; Blanchard 1958:49). Young (1962:93, 101) estimates that there are 45,000 Sgaw and 24,500 Pwo Karen in Northern Thailand alone. This gives a total of 71,500 people, which makes the Karen the largest non-Thai group (excluding Chinese) in Thailand by at least 26,500, using the estimates for all hill groups. It is further estimated that there are 280 Sgaw villages with 7,000 houses, and 150 Pwo villages with 3,800 houses (Young 1962:93, 101). These figures do not include Karen found further south in Thailand, so the national total may be larger than that given by Young.

In the area of Thailand where I worked, it is estimated by local Thai officials that of a total *Amphur* (district) population of

36,089 in 1960 there were 5,000 Karen, and there are many more outside the *Amphur* toward Burma. Hinton (1969:5) estimates that the Karen population in the five northern provinces has reached 200,000.

Turning to population density, the average for all of Thailand is about 114 persons per square mile, but "since only 18 percent of the total area is cultivated, there is more significance in the average density per cultivated square mile, which is near 550" (Blanchard 1958:49). However, the population density in areas where the Karen are found is much lower. During 1947, in *Amphur* Hod, where Ban Hong is located, the density range was from 0 to 17.4 persons per square mile (according to Skinner's map, 1947). This was true also for most other *Amphur* in Thailand in which Karen are found (Skinner 1947). However, the present density of the *Amphur* is 22.5 persons per square mile.[7]

The size of a Karen village may vary considerably within a range of about four houses to fifty, if both hill and plains villages are counted. The average size is about twenty-five houses, but villages in the hills have an upper limit of approximately thirty houses (see Young 1962:113; Marshall 1945, and Hinton 1969:7). There are thirty-five households in Ban Hong.

Karen villages that grow larger than 40 to 50 houses split and a daughter village forms. Sometimes the daughter village is a very short distance, perhaps a mile or two, from the parent village. I know of two examples in which a village seemed to have around 150 houses, but on closer inspection it was found that there were really four villages in near proximity. Apparently, the very small villages are relatively new ones that have split from a parent community in the recent past. One does not find a Karen village in complete isolation; there will be others not far away.

The villages located in the very low foothills or on the plains tend to become relatively permanent in location. Individuals may move, but the village becomes more or less permanent, particularly if wet-rice techniques are being incorporated into the agricultural system. If still in the hills, the village may be moved from time to time, but may remain permanent for a period of many years between moves (see Marshall 1922:129 and Hinton 1969:10ff.).

IDENTIFICATION, LANGUAGE, ORIGIN, HISTORY

The group that I studied are called Pwo (sometimes pronounced *Pgwo*) Karen, but the term they use for themselves is *phlong*, which is their word for person or people. They may, in a more formal vain, use the complex term *kêphlong* for self-reference, adding a widely used prefix. As far as I could discover, they do not use or know the term Karen, as such, unless they have come into contact with Christian missionaries who brought the term from Burma. The Northern Thai or Yuan word for all Karen is *yang*, and Keyes (1971:9) argues that it was borrowed from the Shan (a Thai language) word for the Karen. However, Lehman (1971:14) believes that the word *yang* comes from Karen usage for self-identification through the root word *nyang* which appears in many Karen languages for person.[8] Marshall, on the other hand, states (1922:8) that " 'pgha' is a general word meaning people . . ." thus giving us two words in various Karen languages for people or person. The Central Thai or Siamese use the word *kariang* for all Karen, and it presumably was borrowed by the Siamese from the Mon word for Karen (Keyes 1971:9). Marshall (1922:6) argues that the present term *karen* comes from modern Burmese *kayin*, and Rajadhon (1957:891) agrees, but says the word from Burma was *kavin*.

There is no necessary contradiction in all of this: the word *pgha* is suspiciously close to *pwo* (or *pgwo*) and *phlong*, all meaning the same thing apparently; by adding the k-prefix to *yang* there is a close similarity to *kariang* (note *kêphlong* above), *kayin* (*kavin*), and *karen*. It is certainly possible, as I can attest from my own experience, that the Shan, Mon, Siamese, and Burman through their own linguistic idiosyncrasy could have mispronounced the root *nyang* (or *k-nyang*) to give us the modern words, *jang, kariang,* and *karen,* and that ultimately these three words, as well as *pwo*, were derived from various Karen languages. If all this is correct, then the term *Pwo Karen* is a redundancy applied to an ethnic group by outsiders, but coming ultimately from their own languages. For greater detail concerning these issues, as well as the problem of inter-ethnic relationships between the Karen and surrounding groups, I urge the careful reading of Keyes (1971) and Lehman (1971) in particular, but Luce (1959a) and Jones (1961a) as well.

There is still doubt and controversy concerning the larger language affiliation of the various Karen groups to other languages (Lehman 1971:1–14). It is clear, however, that all Karen groups are closely related to each other linguistically (Jones 1961b) even though the larger affiliation is somewhat obscure. A French linguist has attempted a reconstruction of proto-Karen, and has compared present-day dialects with Burmese. He concludes that Karen should be classed as Tibeto-Berman (Haudricourt 1942; 1953). Shafer (1955) is not quite so specific; he places Karen in a separate division of Sino-Tibetan designated as Karenic (see LeBar 1964:58). On the other hand, Jones (1961a) believes that Karen is related to Thai rather than Sino-Tibetan or Tibeto-Burman (see Lehman 1971:13) and he cites Luce (1959a) as supporting evidence.[9] Nevertheless, on the basis of other cultural and historical data, location, and subjective hunch, I am inclined to agree with Haudricourt. The Karen seem more related to the Burmese than to the Thai as postulated. In spite of my belief, however, as Lehman (1971:14) points out, we are left with the "question of Karen relations very much up in the air."

The origin and history of the Karen is likewise quite confused and debated; this may be partly due, however, to a much too simplistic view of a single origin and history. The various Karen groups have had, of course, divergent contacts and influences, and have adapted to slightly different environments. Nevertheless, the term *Karen* does refer to a large group of peoples with some elements of culture in common. They are distinct from such groups as Maeo, Chin, and so on. We ought, therefore, to be able to talk in a general way about Karen origins and history. Marshall says: "Probably they originated in China and came into Burma from the north-east in about the sixth or seventh century of the Christian era. Their language and personal characteristics would seem to indicate this" (1945:1-2).

This kind of statement may give the impression that at one point all Karen picked up and moved south; this surely did not happen. The view of Hackett, who worked among the Pa-o, seems much more realistic. He concludes that ". . . the Pa-o, together with their Karen brethren, emigrated from the high plains of central Asia, the western part of ancient China, to lands to the south, and *by stages* reached the area where they are now living" (1953:37, my emphasis).

The phrase "by stages" is, I think, the crucial one for understanding Karen history. Due to a slow filtering process in a southerly direction the Karen entered Southeast Asia, and in this process many different kinds of contacts and changes occurred causing divergence among the various groups. Even so, the original location given by Hackett may be wrong; the dispersion of identifiable Karen may have begun in the hills of Southeast Asia (see Lehman 1971); we simply do not know. The Karen that I studied had a tradition of coming from Burma, and according to Rajadhon (1957:892), this is the case for all Karen in Thailand. Where they came from before Burma, they could not tell me. It is also true, of course, that at times people change their cultural affiliation and that new groups emerge in

The author, his wife, and their village house in Ban Hong.

history. One should not confuse society with culture (see Leach 1954).

There is one further argument to be discussed concerning Karen history. Perhaps it is best summarized by the statement: "Very little is known of the origin and history of Karen. According to tradition, they once had a kingdom in the region of Northern Thailand; this may have been overrun by the Mon or Thai" (Blanchard 1958:64).

Phya Anuman Rajadhon believes there is no evidence for a Karen kingdom (1957:891). And Seidenfaden says: "As regards their tradition of once having formed a large kingdom on the banks of the Mekhong, between the 20th and 22nd degree

northern latitude, this seems rather vague and may be mixed up
with the recollections of that great Kha empire which really did
exist during the early centuries of A.D. in these regions"
(1958:125).

I agree that there is no real evidence for such a kingdom. As
a matter of fact, the cultural evidence points the other way; the
political organization is rather weak and not conducive to strong
government. The headman is more advisory than authoritarian.
He can be deposed, and this happens at times (Marshall
1922:129). The economy at its best could not support all that a
state implies. The hill Karen are mainly slash-and-burn agriculturalists, and only recently are they beginning to use wet-rice
techniques, rather than the other way round (Ijima 1965).
Karen population movements point downhill, not into the hills.
The Karen may have been subject to a state (or several) at
times, and there are, of course, so-called "Karen states" today in
Burma. Such states as the Kayah have adopted and adapted
Shan or Burman political organization and often elements of
Buddhism as well (see Lehman 1971:11).

In summary, the Karen are a large, colorful, and significant
hill group, with various subdivisions occupying, for the most
part, the mountainous regions common to Burma and Thailand.
Although the term *Karen* is not used by all the groups for themselves, it may be used as a convenient term in referring to
them.[10] The history and the racial and linguistic affiliations of
the Karen still remain problematic, but the group probably came
from somewhere in the North possibly before the Burmese,
Thai, and Shan reached present-day Burma and Thailand.
Their culture, distribution, and ecological adaptation indicate
that the story of a former Karen kingdom is a myth. They are
a group originally adapted to hill life, and many are still in a
process of transition from tribal to peasant status. There may,
of course, be a great deal of difference between groups of Karen
in cases where some have been under intensive culture contact
and have changed accordingly.

NOTES

[1] Marshall places the Karen by saying:

> Their villages are now found scattered over the plains as well as the hills in Lower Burma all the way from Pyimana [half way between Rangoon and Mandalay] to Victoria Point [the southern tip of Burma] and from Arakan in the western hills of Burma to some indefinite line in Thailand. It has been reported that there are a few scattered Karen communities even as far as east Cambodia, but they have been pretty well absorbed by the more aggressive surrounding races (1945:3).

I doubt that the Karen ever lived in Cambodia as Marshall states. The present distribution would not seem to warrant such a statement.

[2] To say that there are "three major subgroups" is probably a gross oversimplification. There are many groups of Karen, and they are lumped and split in different ways leading to confusion and dispute as to how the total group of "Karen" should be subdivided. I need not enter this argument here, but see LeBar (1964:58) and Lehman (1965:-7ff.) for a discussion of the controversy. There is, however, little, if any, dispute concerning the twofold division of Sgaw and Pwo. The Pa-o (or Taungthu, as they are also called) are sometimes considered a separate major group, and sometimes, as by Marshall (1922:1) and Hackett (1953:27), are considered a subgroup of the Pwo. The Kayah may or may not be thought of as equivalent to Bwe (B*gh*we), and they may or may not be considered a distinct major group (Lehman nd-a:3, 9). These controversies revolve around factors of history, language, cultural affiliation, and native views of themselves and others. It is far from settled.

[3] In 1922, Marshall, a Baptist missionary, did a major ethnography of the Karen, concentrating on the Sgaw (mostly those in the lowlands). In 1953 W. D. Hackett, also a missionary, completed a study of the Pa-o. In 1900, Scott wrote briefly on the Karen of Upper Burma, and in 1876, McMahon wrote a book on the Karen, recording information on customs, language, and so forth. These are the major early sources on the people, and all were carried out in Burma. My own work was among the Pwo of Thailand. More recently in the dec-

ade of the 1960s, several people have done work among the Karen in Thailand. Lehman has done historical and linguistic work among the Kayah of both Burma and Thailand; Hinton carried out studies among some upland Pwo; Stern studied aspects of language and culture among southern Pwo; Ijima studied culture change among the Sgaw; Marlowe studied some specialized aspects of Sgaw culture; Keyes has been concerned with relations between Sgaw and others (Thai and Lua'); Kunstadter has done a series of studies on the Sgaw and Pwo of Thailand; Cooke et al. analyzed the phonology of the Pwo group that I studied.

[4] The Pa-o subgroup is also concentrated, but is a little more widely spread than the Bwe (including the Kayah). The Pa-o are found from Thaton, on the Gulf of Martaban, and reaching north of Tounggyi into the southern Shan State (Marshall 1922:3; Hackett 1953). Young (1962:109) reports that a few Pa-o (Taungthu) are found in Maehongsorn Province in Thailand, but Lehman informs me by personal communication that they are now gone.

[5] However, some Taungthu in the Southern Shan State live as high as 4,000 feet (personal communication from R. Burling). Young (1962:109) reports that the few Pa-o in Thailand (five villages) were located at 3,000 feet or more.

[6] Most of the compilation of the 1941 Burmese census was lost before analysis was complete (Trager 1956:166).

In 1922, Marshall gave the following breakdown of subgroups, based partly on the government census of 1911 and partly on his own estimate:

TABLE 1 Karen Population

Sgaw	500,000	(In Burma)
Sgaw	50,000	(In Thailand)
Pwo	533,054	(Thailand, Burma, and including Pa-o)
Bwe	48,816	(Thailand and Burma)
Total	1,129,870	

More recently, the 1931 census reports about 1,367,000 Karen in Burma (see Rajadhon 1957:889), and the *Encyclopaedia Britannica* gives figures of 500,000 each of Sgaw and Pwo in Burma. The Bwe are not mentioned (see also Seidenfaden 1958:125). LeBar (1964:58) mentions a total Karen population of "close to one and a half million."

⁷ The size of *Amphur* Hod has changed since World War II. The *King* (literally "branch") *Amphur* of Om Koi to the south has become a separate *Amphur*, thus reducing the size of Hod by 600 square miles to its present size of 1,600 square miles. Also, the population density has changed, with an increase in total population since 1947; thus, the population density has changed from an upper limit of 17.4 to the present 22.5.

⁸ Marshall (1922:8) says that *k-* is "a prefix often found in the names of tribes in the vicinity of Burma. . . ." Lehman (1971:14, 16, 20) uses the same argument when he says that the term for *Kayah*, that is, *(kê)ya*, is a derivative of *nyang*, and that *Kachin* comes from *ka-khyen*. Another piece of data supporting the importance of the *nyang* root is the fact that the term for the Sgaw used by the Pwo that I studied is *shiang* which clearly could derive from *nyang* (see also Hinton 1969:3).

⁹ Writing in 1942, Paul Benedict specifically separates Thai and Karen. He says (1942:600), "The proposed classification of Southeast Asiatic languages is as follows:"

TABLE 2   Linguistic Relations

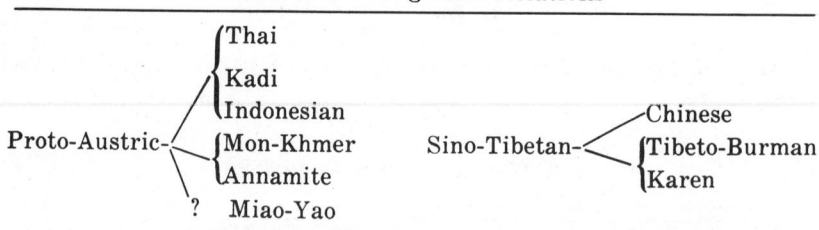

However, the general classification set up by Benedict is apparently in question (person communication from William Gedney). But, concerning Karen relations, Benedict agrees with Shafer.

¹⁰ If missionaries had contacted them first in Thailand, they might be known in the literature today as *"Jang"* instead of Karen.

2

Ban Hong in Space and Time

LOCATION AND ACCESS

The valleys of Northern Thailand cut into the hills and mountains like a series of fingers, the "palm" being the central Thai plain. Through each one of these north-south valleys flows a river toward the sea. All the rivers meet and flow past Bangkok to the south. The highest peak of Thailand is *Doi Inthanon*, which measures 8,468 feet and is about thirty-five miles directly north of *Amphur* Hod where Ban Hong is located. The valley in which Ban Hong is found averages about six miles wide for sixty miles. At the southern end, it spreads out into the broad plain that reaches all the way to Bangkok.

At the northern end of the sixty-mile strip, the valley widens into the Hod plain, which is about sixteen miles wide and thirty-two miles long. The valley then narrows and splits, with a branch on each side of *Doi Inthanon*. The eastern branch spreads out finally into the Chiengmai plain on which the provincial capital is located. The mountains on either side of the Hod plain average about 2,000 to 3,000 feet (see also Dobby 1958:259, and Spencer 1962:24–28).

The village of Ban Hong, with its thirty-five houses, is situated on the west bank of the Mae Ping River in *Muban* Hui Sai,

Thambon Hod, *Amphur* Hod, *Changwat* Chiengmai, Northern Thailand.[1]

My general research area includes nine major Karen and five major Thai villages, and is located approximately seventy miles southwest of Chiengmai city, the provincial capital and second largest city in the country (see Figure 2). The Burma border is about seventy-five miles to the west of Ban Hong and surrounding villages.[2] The economically important Ping River, from out of the north, flows past Chiengmai city, through the center of the research area, and down through Thailand, joining the Chao Phya River, which flows into the Gulf of Siam through Bangkok 500 miles to the south.

Nowadays, Ban Hong may be reached in about six hours from Chiengmai. Buses travel from Chiengmai over a road completed in about 1940 which ends in Wang Lung, a Thai village about two miles from Ban Hong. The government administrative center of the *Amphur* is Hod village, about four miles from Ban Hong.

There are several privately owned buses that leave Chiengmai daily for *Amphur* Hod. The "bus" is either a Japanese variety or it is a Chevrolet or Mercedes Benz truck which has been converted into a bus by having a large wooden structure built onto the frame, with a long wooden bench down the length of either side. These buses are used to carry people, water buffalo, pigs, sacks of rice, and many other varieties of economic goods to and from Chiengmai. They are always very crowded.

The bus leaves Chiengmai just outside the old city wall and travels south on the poorly paved road past the Chiengmai airport. After a few miles, the road is paved on only one lane as it stretches between lush rice paddies on both sides. Later, as the road turns slightly to the west, the pavement gives out altogether, turning into a gravel and dirt country road. The mountains are visible all along off to the west, but the road moves towards the mountains as one gets further from Chiengmai.

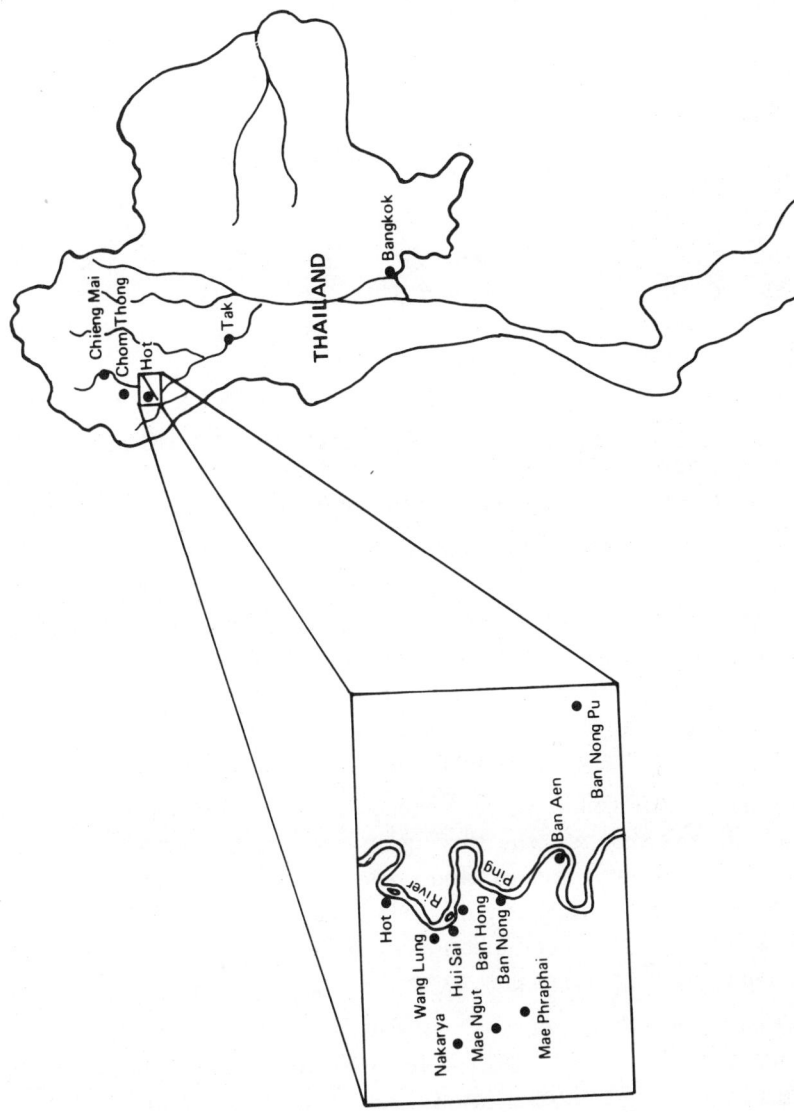

FIGURE 2 Research Area and Village Locations

As the bus moves along, it stops frequently to pick up or let off passengers and goods of various types in small villages and towns along the way. It is possible, therefore, to get a view of

Thai villages to be contrasted later with those of the Karen. There seem to be three general types of Thai village. The "strip village" is the most common. Here, the houses of the village form a "strip" of two rows, usually facing each other, with the road or a canal or river between them. Behind the houses, the paddy fields stretch into the distance. The second type is the "cluster village," usually set back from the main road a short distance and clustered around a few trees, coconut palms, or bamboo thickets. The paddy fields lie all around and a secondary road leads off from the main road to the village. The third type, if it can be called a village at all, is the "dispersed village." This is a rare pattern in which a house or two or three are spotted here and there, the location being determined by the terrain, paddy fields, foothills, and water supply (see also Blanchard 1958:53, and deYoung 1955).

After about three hours and many short stops, the bus reaches a relatively large town that is an important market. This is Chom Thong, the administrative center of *Amphur* Chom Thong. The bus unloads here for about forty-five minutes while people eat and shop in the large open bazaar. Until about the end of World War II, the road ended at Chom Thong.

When the driver is ready, he toots his horn and the passengers pack themselves into the bus again for another two- or three-hour trip to the village of Hod. As the bus leaves Chom Thong it turns south again, traveling between the foothills and the Ping River as the river meanders toward and beyond the destination of the busload of passengers.

Just beside the road as it goes over one hill is an old, crumbling pagoda, a short distance beyond that is a huge painted figure of the Buddha about thirty feet tall, with a wooden frame built over it for protection from the weather. Here, the road turns directly toward the river and Hod village appears among the trees on the river bank. As the bus turns into the main "street" of Hod, the two-story brown wooden-frame buildings of the administrative headquarters can be seen facing the river.

Here is to be found the police contingent, the *Nai Amphur* ("Mr. *Amphur*"), and his assistants. This man is responsible for law, order, tax collecting, and other administrative duties. He is something like a combined sheriff-judge-mayor.[3]

The bus travels down the main street of Hod, stopping every few feet to discharge passengers and goods at the various shops and houses. It is soon through the village with only two miles to Wang Lung, the larger and economically more important market village.

The Ping River makes a sweeping dramatic bend of more than ninety degrees where Wang Lung is located. This village of approximately 300 houses is centered around two perpendicular streets, each of which is parallel to an arm of the river. Wang Lung is the social, economic, and religious center of *Thambon* Hod.

In Wang Lung may be found several shops selling goods from as far away as Hong Kong, Japan, and the United States. Two schools, a rice mill, two temples, two restaurants, a government health clinic and a turpentine factory are also in Wang Lung. There is a government veterinarian, a second class doctor, and a nurse-midwife. People come long distances to Wang Lung to buy and sell goods and to take advantage of the various services available. One of the most important groups coming to Wang Lung to shop is the Karen.

Wang Lung is the end of the regular bus line (buses go irregularly to Ban Aen and to Nakarya to the west and south of Wang Lung), and from here it is necessary to walk to the various outlying villages.

THE PEOPLE OF THE VILLAGE

Physically, the Ban Hong villagers look much like Northern Thai, except for perhaps being a shade darker. They are thin and well-proportioned. The men are about five feet, six inches tall or a little less, and the women are generally shorter (see also Marshall 1922:16). The men seem to have a little more body hair than the Thai, with a few showing a short stubble beard. Body hair, except on the chin, is usually pulled out. (I am not certain about pubic hair, since the Karen are so modest and "clever" that the pubic area is not exposed, even during bathing.)

The most dramatic difference between the Thai and the Pwo Karen is in their dress. The people do not wear the drab "jungle blue" peasant clothes of the Thai farmer, but are very colorfully dressed. The married women wear loosely tailored blouses with a design of large, bright red and yellow diamonds. Their wraparound skirts are multicolored too, with a red, yellow, white, and black design. The dress design signifies the subgroup of Karen to which one belongs. Their hair is long, black, and kept neatly in a bun with a distinctive knot, low on the back of the head.

Unmarried girls wear a one-piece sack dress which is basically white except for a multicolored woven design around the waist and small red and black diamonds embroidered about two inches apart encircling the bottom half of the dress, which reaches nearly to the ankles. Their hair is put up like that of their mothers. Both married and unmarried women wear many necklaces made of small beads, different strings of which are red, black, yellow, and white. Both old and young women and girls also wear bracelets, sometimes reaching nearly to the shoulder. These are made of bronze, silver, and cotton that has been blackened and hardened with a type of pitch; currently bracelets are also being made of buttons strung back to back. All of these bracelets are worn simultaneously, the unmarried girls always wearing more than the married women. All women have their ears pierced and may wear colorful ear decorations of yarn or silver spools. Nearly all women smoke long-stemmed pipes of black wood decorated with silver bands. For footwear, they either use a crude sandal made of discarded tires and bought in the bazaar, or they go barefooted.

The women of the village are seen at various activities. Some may be seen sitting on the ground under their houses weaving on a simple belt loom which has one end attached to a horizontal pole and the other fastened to the woman's waist. Other women may be feeding their pigs and chickens, while still others may be coming into the village carrying firewood in large baskets on their backs, which are attached around their foreheads. Young girls may be seen carrying water to the village by either of two methods. First, water is carried in two buckets, one at each end of a pole across the shoulder, or perhaps the water will be carried in the old way in several bamboo joints about two or three feet long, attached together from a band around the girl's forehead and carried over the back. A couple of women may be carrying rice either to or from the Wang Lung rice mill, each woman carrying two woven baskets, one at each end of the shoulder pole. Another woman may be carrying her rice in a large woven-cloth bag on her back, again with the strap around her forehead. Some women will be tending their children and cooking rice.

Few men are in the village at midday. Most are either off hunting with a crossbow, tending the paddy or the dry-rice field, or hoeing the garden. Some would be gone for a few days either working for wages in the teak forest, selling and buying goods, or making fields for wages for a Thai. One might see a man on his porch, however, making rope or a basket.

There is more variety in the clothing of the men than in that of the women, although the men's clothing is not quite as colorful as the women's. One of the common costumes consists of a knee-length red and black striped tubular skirt that is folded in front and tied at the waist with a piece of rope. With this is worn a buttonless, short, white jacket with a thin red trim and red diamonds down the center of the back. Sleeves reach about halfway between elbow and wrist. One might see another man with long hair wound around his head and forming a knot on one side. Around this is worn a kind of turban. This man might be wearing a sleeveless pullover red blouse with thin white stripes which reaches just below the waist. He may also be wearing a pair of black, loosely tailored, knee- or ankle-length pants, similar to those of Thai and Chinese peasants. These pants are folded, tucked, and tied at the waist. Most men nowadays wear their hair cut short, but a few still wear it long. Hair style does not go with a particular clothing style. Most men, at least of the older generation, are tattooed from just above the waist to just below the knee. There is an elaborate design that entirely covers this part of the body (one may see a single small tattoo near the ankle of some women). Men have the same footwear as women.

If one happens to see some teenage boys, they might be dressed like a Thai peasant in jungle-blue pants and jackets. Or they might be wearing western-style shirts, pairs of pants and sneakers, all bought in the Wang Lung bazaar. As they get older, they will tend to wear more traditional clothing. Very young boys are dressed in a small version of the male sack blouse of red and white mentioned above and nothing else.

All the men have the ubiquitous long-bladed, usually blunt-ended, machete knife. This is carried in a wooden case, stuck in at the waist at the back. The men carry at their side a cloth bag with a shoulder strap. In this bag they carry their pipe, tobacco, and betel supplies.

The general tenor and mannerisms of the Karen are also different from the Thai. As one goes through a Thai village, the people are generally curious, interested, laughing, and friendly. The Karen, however, are not friendly at first. They may show hostility or fear, emotions that should not show in the Thai even when they might exist. The Karen language, beliefs, and value system are different from those of their Thai neighbors.

This, then, is the first superficial impression one might receive on contrasting Karen with Thai.

PHYSICAL DESCRIPTION OF THE VILLAGE

Ban Hong is divided into two parts. The "lower village" of seven houses is snuggled in a bamboo grove on an old river terrace a short distance back from the west bank of the Ping River. This is Ban Hong proper. The "upper village" is located a few yards farther west on higher ground. It encompasses twenty-eight houses, and was formerly called Ban Phae'. The upper and lower villages are now two sections of a single village, but the division with separate names has social and historical import which will be discussed in detail later. For most purposes, "Ban Hong" refers to both sections today (see Figure 3).[4]

The land on which the upper village is located is flat, but it slopes gently toward the river to the east and toward the south. The northern boundary of the upper village abruptly drops off about fifteen feet into a depression that is now paddy land owned by a Thai. This steep slope follows around on the eastern edge of the upper village so that one must go down a steep path to reach the lower village. The southern edge of the upper village gradually slopes into a depression which is a paddy field owned by one of the villagers. The village ends where this field begins. On the west, there is no sharp physiographic demarcation, but the houses end and the short scrub trees take over.

The boundary of the upper village is well defined on three sides, but the lower village is clearly delimited on two sides only. The eastern boundary is the river, and the western boundary is the steep slope which bounds the upper village. On the south, the lower village blends into large trees and bamboo clumps, while, on the north, the village area ends where the path takes a fairly steep incline up and away from the river about one hundred yards from the first house. This large area is now unoccupied, but several mango trees and old house sites indicate that it was once part of the lower village.

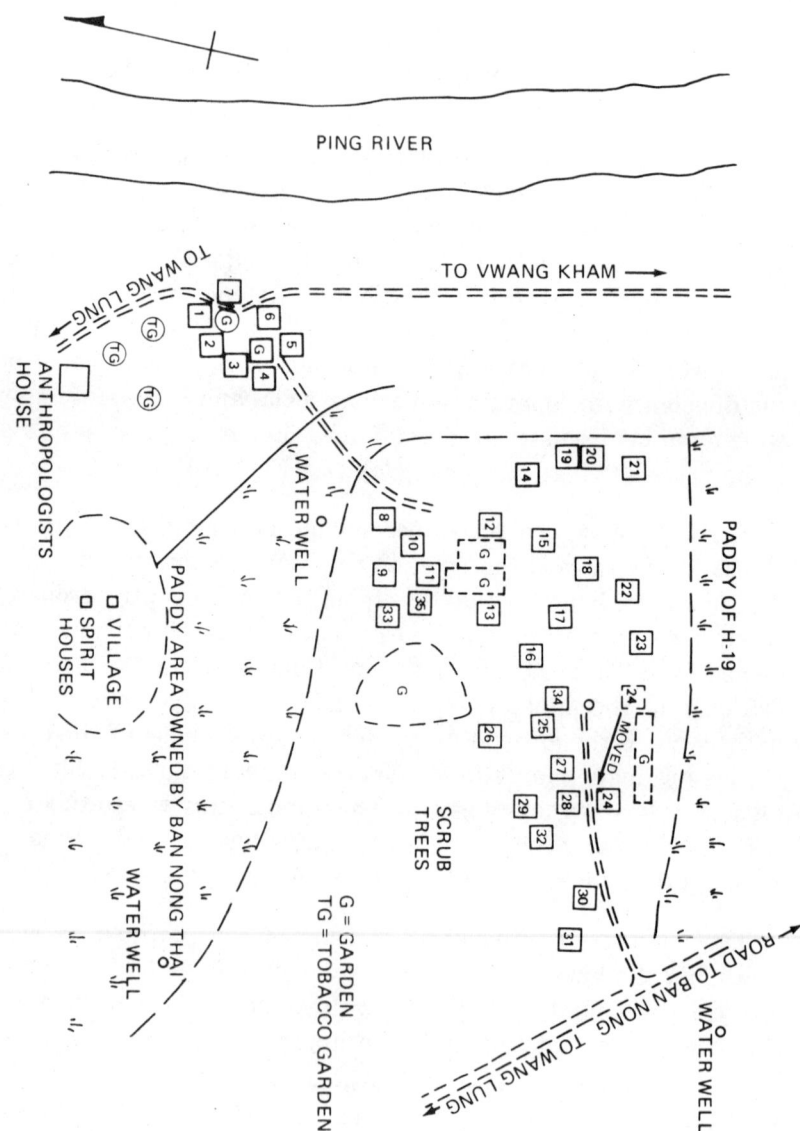

FIGURE 3   Ban Hong Village

The village's two small spirit houses, standing on stilts, are now located on a low, hidden hill to the west of the lower village and to the north of the upper village. The spirits which protect the villagers from danger reside here, and two annual ceremonies, plus other irregular ones, take place at this location.

There are four main access routes to the village. One path leads to the lower village from Wang Lung to the north. Another path, which branches off from the first about a quarter of a mile from the village, leads across a Thai-owned paddy field and enters the upper village from the north. The third path branches off from a dirt cart road leading to the Thai village of Ban Nong and enters the upper village from the western side. A fourth path leads into the lower village from the Karen village of Vwang Kham to the south.

The village water supply comes from three shallow wells and the river. The first well, which is located behind H-8, is too close to the village to be safe for drinking, so the water is used only for household purposes and for baths. The second well is used mostly in the high-water season and is located at the upper end of the Thai paddy, just north of the upper village. The third well is also located in a Thai paddy field to the west of the upper village across the cart road. This one is used mostly by villagers on the western side of the upper village, but in the dry season there is little or no water in it. During the time of the dry season, all villagers carry water from the river. They dig shallow wells in the sandy beaches of the river and get very clear, safe water which is used for all purposes. Baths also are usually taken daily (often several times) in the river; in the wet season, however, the river is too high for sand wells to be dug because the beaches are flooded, and the water is too swift for bathing. At these times the wells are used continuously.

Though there is no street in Ban Hong and no regular alignment of homes, the houses are placed to conform to definite rules. The houses must all face the same direction. If there is a river or stream nearby, the houses must be parallel to it.

Thus, in Ban Hong they all face roughly southward, which is downstream. No two houses should face each other, nor should a new one be built separating the houses of a lineage segment. Three houses should never be arranged like the three stones of a fireplace. It is also improper to have a garden at one end of a house and another garden or animal pen at the opposite end of the house. Disregard of any of these restrictions will cause "unhappiness," "inability to work," or "disease." There is, therefore, organization and reason for the arrangement of the houses in a Karen village, haphazard though they may seem to the outsider.

VILLAGE DEMOGRAPHY

There are 198 people living in the thirty-five households of Ban Hong (in 1961), including 83 males and 115 females (see Figure 4 and see also Table 3 for summary). It is a relatively young population, with approximately half of the group under fifteen years of age. In the first half of the life cycle, ages zero to forty-four, there are thirty-two more females than males, but in the second half of the cycle, ages forty-five to eighty-nine, the number of males and females are equal. The village demography is summarized as follows:

TABLE 3 Summary of Village Demography

Total population	198
Male population	83
Female population	115
Of 43 adult males (some now dead) in 35 households, there were:	
Marriages	49
Divorces	2
Death of spouse	8
Living spouse	39

TABLE 3 Summary of Village Demography—Continued

Of 43 adult females (some now dead) in 35 households, there were:

Marriages	45
Divorces	4
Death of spouse	7
Living spouse	34
Living males who have been married (now in village)	35
Living females who have been married (now in village)	39
Marriages with both partners living (at present)	31
Males never married	51
Females never married	74
Number of households	35
Number of families (mother, father, unmarried children living together)	21

The composition of the households varies considerably, but the norm is for one household (house) to include one nuclear family (see Appendix C for a tabulation of household composition). Of the thirty-five households in the village, there are twenty-one nuclear family households which include only a husband, a wife, and their unmarried children (see Figure 3 for location and relationship of households). There are two households which include only one parent plus unmarried children, and there are two households which include a single adult (the spouse died in both cases). One household includes a couple plus a grandchild who is ill.[5] One household includes one old man and his grandchild, whose parents live next door. There is one household which includes one adult woman plus a married daughter and her husband. One case includes an adult couple, a married daughter, her husband, and their children. There are four cases of households which include an adult couple, unmarried children, and a child who was married but is now divorced or widowed. Of these four cases, one divorced daughter has a child; another of these households also includes a young married couple. There is one household which includes one adult woman, a divorced

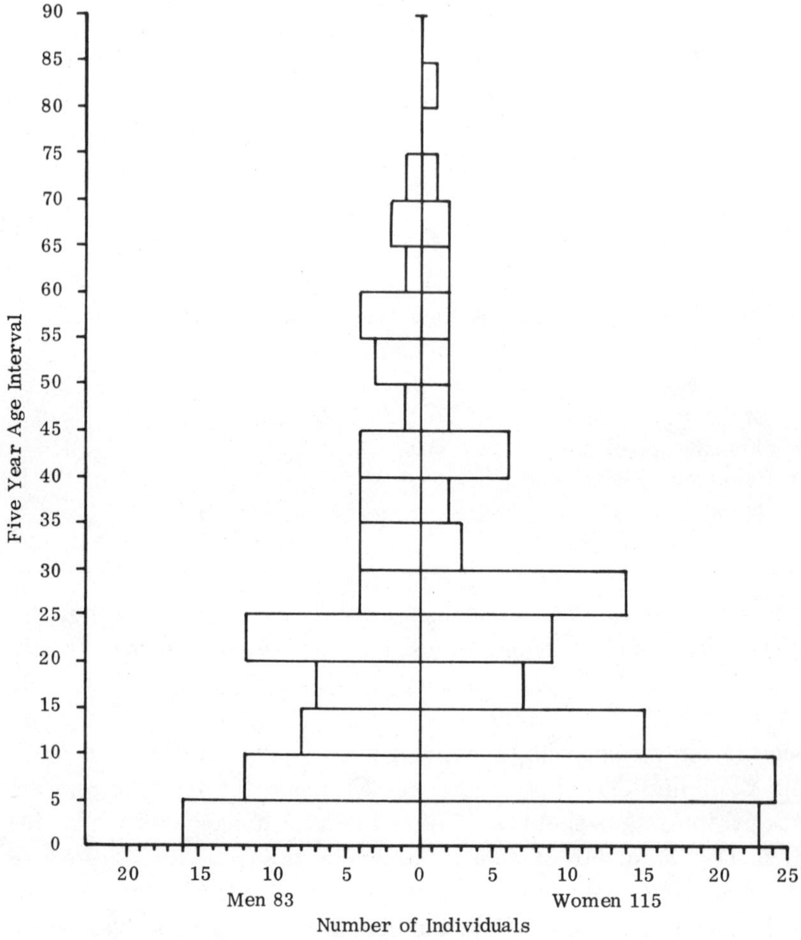

FIGURE 4 Population Distribution in Ban Hong

daughter, and her unmarried children. Finally, one household includes only a young newly married couple.

The ideal and generally realized marital residence pattern is matrilocality; that is, the husband generally goes to live with his wife and her parents. There is no village exogamy, however, so a man may not move very far from his own parents. Nevertheless, there are small clusterings of married daughters around older women. This residence pattern will be discussed in detail below (p. 119), so it now will be left in order to turn to a discussion of marriages in the village (Appendix D). Among forty-three adult married women in the village, there were forty-five marriages (two women had been married twice). Of these, thirty-one marriages are still intact. Of the eleven dissolved marriages, four are due to divorce and seven are due to death of a husband. Among forty-three adult men married in Ban Hong, there were forty-nine marriages (one man had married four times, and three men had been married twice). Of the ten dissolved marriages, two are due to divorce and eight are due to death of a wife. When there is a divorce, unless the wife is clearly at fault (as in the case of adultery, which is rare), all property, except paddy land previously owned by the husband, reverts to the woman. Therefore, if there is a divorce it is more likely that it is the wife who is dissatisfied and demands it.

Children are desired by both men and women; the sex of the child is not too important if there are both boys and girls. The number and sex of children living in each household are summarized in Appendix C under "Persons Never Married." [6] Birth and death statistics for children of all women in Ban Hong forty years old and older are summarized in Appendix E. (The figures under "Number of Pregnancies" and "Miscarriages" are probably not completely accurate, but all other information is accurate.)

The Karen believe there are two coincident causes of pregnancy. They understand that gestation is eight or nine months and that sexual intercourse causes pregnancy, if at the same time a "spirit child" wishes to be born. Since there usually is such a child wishing to be born, intercourse generally causes conception. The fact that it does not always cause conception "proves" the second contention.

There are two general Karen categories of death. First, there are "natural" deaths such as old age and possibly certain diseases such as cholera, dysentery, and fever (usually caused by malaria). Second, there are "violent" deaths which include accidental death, death by magic, spirits attacking humans, death in childbirth, and murder. This second form may result in one of the "diseases" of the first, if, for example, magic is used. Suicide is known but rare; it is considered a violent death.

HISTORICAL SETTING

According to local tradition, the ancestors of the Karen on the plain in *Amphur* Hod came from the mountains in the west toward Burma (see Figures 1 and 2). As they began to move into the area, Mae Ngut at the foot of the western mountains was formed as an early (possibly the first) village of Karen in the Hod area. This was roughly 200 years ago (on the basis of ethnological inference and estimate). Another village known as Mae Phraphai was formed nearby. From these two villages the Karen moved east and spread out. Some went northeast to *Amphur* Ban Hong,[7] and some went southeast to *Amphur* Li. Both of these *Amphur* are on the other side of the eastern mountains which border the Hod plain, in *Changwat* Lampoon. There are major pockets of Karen in both these areas today. In the past, the eastward movement went a little further, both in the north and in the south.

One of the early villages on the Hod plain was Ban Phae', the present upper village of Ban Hong (see Figures A and 3). The settlers, for the most part, probably came from Mae Phraphai. One of the residents of Ban Phae' became the grandfather of the present headman of Ban Hong. During the eastward movement of the Karen, the grandfather went to Mae Thern, an *Amphur* just east of Li in *Changwat* Lampang. He married there, and lived, as is customary, with his wife's family. According to the story, he had three children, two girls and one boy.

As the Karen were moving east, however, the Thai were also moving and expanding. Many Thai began to move into *Amphur* Li and Mae Thern, and the Karen began to retreat west again. The Karen were "afraid to stay," (the way my informant put it) but it is obvious that there was land pressure and the Karen were losing out as the Thai claimed the land. As they moved back toward the west, some Karen stopped on the western side of the eastern mountains and formed the village of Nong Pu while some others came back to Ban Phae'. For thirty or more years no Karen have lived in Mae Thern, according to my informants.

The grandmother of the present headman of Ban Hong died in Mae Thern, so the husband and his three children moved back to the Ban Phae' area. This man remarried, but there were no children from the union. Of his three children, one girl remained childless, one girl had a son who later became a headman in the village of Vwang Kham, and the boy became the father of the present headman, Mang Thi, of Ban Hong.[8]

Mang Thi's grandfather did not move into Ban Phae' when he returned from Mae Thern, but built a house across the river from the village in what is today the large paddy field. It is said that he planted the large mango tree where a small spirit house is located today, and he began clearing paddy land. This man had some claim on a position of authority because his sister was married to the headman of Ban Phae', and after a time he and his family moved across the river to where the present lower village of Ban Hong is located. With two or three households, he formed a new village and became its headman. This became a daughter village of Ban Phae', owing to kinship and spirit connections between them. Ban Hong and Ban Phae' were two distinct but related villages, both had headmen, who were related in a couple of ways, and both had village spirits. The present location of the two village spirit houses, on the hill between the upper and lower villages, was the original spot for the village spirits of Ban Hong, the lower village. The spirit houses of Ban Phae' were farther west, probably beyond H-29.

During the heyday of the two villages, maybe seventy years ago, there were sixty to seventy houses; later, however, the upper village, Ban Phae', was abandoned three times due to illness and death. The disease, *bae thê lawng piu'*, which means vomitting and diarrhea, was probably cholera; within about twelve hours a person would sicken and die. The first time this happened, about sixty years ago, the people left Ban Phae' and formed a new village, Hui Sai, about one mile to the north. A few stragglers returned after a time, but there was another epidemic and they moved south a couple of miles to the Vwang Mô area. This was probably the beginning of the formation of Vwang Kham as a separate village. The third time the disease struck, people from Ban Phae' moved to an area that is now a Thai paddy nearby. Apparently no village formed from this last move, but this was the end of Ban Phae' as a separate village. The area of the present upper village, old Ban Phae', was completely abandoned for a number of years, although Ban Hong, the lower village, was never abandoned from the time of its founding. About twenty to thirty years ago, there was a migration south, apparently partly from the lower village of Ban Hong. The present village of Vwang Kham was formed, with an older brother of Mang Thi becoming headman of that village. The present village of Ban Hong, both lower and upper village, has only a few representative of the old Ban Phae'. The core of old Ban Phae' now forms the village of Hui Sai. The people living today in the old Ban Phae' area are only a population expansion of the old Ban Hong.

To summarize, Mae Ngut is probably the first and oldest village in the area. Mae Phraphai and a couple more villages nearby are daughter villages of Mae Ngut. People moved down into the plain, and Ban Phae' was formed. There was apparently a migration, or perhaps two, further east across the mountains to Ban Hong and Li in *Changwat* Lampoon, and to Mae Thern in

Changwat Lampang (the dialect and clothing are slightly different from those of the Hod plain). A group of returnees from the east, who had originated in the Hod plain, formed Nong Pu or went to Ban Phae'. Ban Hong was formed as a daughter village of Ban Phae'. The people of Ban Phae' moved and formed Hui Sai. A daughter village of Hui Sai split off and became Mang Mêng, located across the river and at the north end of the large paddy. Daughter villages of Ban Hong include Dong Dam, which is across the river near the south end of the paddy field; Vwang Kham, located about a mile south of the parent village; and Vwang Mô, located about a mile south of Vwang Kham. The approximate ages of these villages shown in Table 4.

TABLE 4 Village Ages

Mae Ngut	200 years
Mae Phraphai	200 years
Ban Phae'	150 years
Nong Pu	100 years
Ban Hong	80 years
Hui Sai	70 years
Dong Dam	35 years
Mang Mêng	15 years
Vwang Kham	25 years
Vwang Mô	15 years

SOCIAL SETTING

All the Karen villages analyzed in this study are within *Amphur* Hod, which in 1960 was roughly 1,600 square miles in area (Figure A). Including Thai, Karen, and others, the total population of the *Amphur* in 1960 was 36,089, including roughly 5,000 Karen and 2,000 Lawa. This gives a density of 22.5 persons per square mile.

Muban 4, which is called Hui Sai and is a subdivision of *Tambon* Hod, includes only the Karen villages of Hui Sai, Ban Hong, Mang Mêng, and Dong Dam. It has an official total population of 641, including 300 males and 341 females.[9]

The administrative headquarters of the *Amphur* is Hod village. It is apparently the oldest Thai village in the area of concern to this study, being something over three hundred years old.[10] There is a story that the first *Nai Amphur* was killed by a group of Karen and Thai because of his policy of enforcing taxing and unpaid labor. At that time, according to the story, a prince of Chiengmai was governor of the whole area. One Ban Hong informant says the whole Hod plain area was Karen land when he was a boy, but there were, no doubt, at least a few scattered Thai houses.

The age of the large village of Ban Aen is somewhat in doubt; it is apparently much younger than Hod, however, because the Karen in Ban Hong say there were no Thai there in the early days of Ban Hong. Ban Aen is probably around forty to fifty years old.[11] This administrative unit of around six hundred houses is in a different *Tambon* and is of little import to the present study, however, since the Karen included in this study have very little contact with it. It does, although, give an indication of the concentration of Thai population, compared with that of the Karen; also, some Thai from Ban Aen own part of the large paddy across the river from Ban Hong.

The next oldest Thai village, and the most important one as far as the local Karen are concerned, is the 300-house village of Wang Lung. This village, which is the main market center for both Thai and Karen in *Amphur* Hod, is approximately forty years old. It developed mainly because of the trade contacts with the Lawa and Karen, although currently there has been more and more contact with the Maeo. It has also become an important center for the local Thai. The government built a new market pavilion for the village during my stay in the area.

Ban Nong is south of Ban Hong and about half way between Wang Lung and Ban Aen. This Thai village of perhaps one hundred houses is approximately the same age as Wang Lung, although it might be a little older. There is a Thai curer in the village, and a Thai woman is a local spirit medium. Both of these practitioners are consulted by Karen as well as Thai, and they are important people to the local area.

Ban Hong newlyweds. Wife now wears clothes symbolizing married status.

Ban Hong man dressed in work garb. Note tatooing which extends between knees and stomach. Tatooing is performed in a puberty rite and symbolizes the male's adult status.

Ban Hong midwife and her grandchild.

The final Thai village of importance in the area is Nakarya, located about one and one-half miles west of Wang Lung. This village has possibly two hundred houses, and is approximately thirty years old. Nakarya is of little significance to the Karen, since they generally bypass it to come to Wang Lung to buy and sell. Nakarya and Hod are the only two Thai villages which have no claims on the large paddy area across from Ban Hong.

The road which connects the Hod plain to Chiengmai was completed about 1940. Before that time, it ended at Chom Thong, about twenty-five miles north of Wang Lung. The road between Wang Lung and Ban Aen is three years old, but Nakarya has been connected to Wang Lung for some time longer. There are at present ten buses running between Chiengmai and the Hod area. Five originate in Chiengmai and run daily to Wang Lung; one runs from Nakarya to Chiengmai; two buses

Head elder's wife and her grandson visiting author's house.

originate in Ban Aen, but since these alternate days, only one runs daily to Chiengmai; and three daily buses run to Chiengmai from Wang Lung. All these private, Thai-owned buses carry passengers, but their major importance is in carrying goods to and from Chiengmai.

A young man of Ban Hong on his way to the market in Wang Lung.

Before the road was completed, the local Karen went to Chiengmai by foot or by boat via the Ping River to buy and sell goods, and the round trip took seven days. Now that the buses ply the road daily, nearly all economic activities are carried on in the bazaar of Wang Lung, and the Karen have very little direct contact with the outside world. The local Karen used to go to Chiengmai to buy foodstuffs, salt, betel nut, tobacco, *miang* (a fermented tea chewed with salt), and fish, and to sell cattle, cloth, and other local products. One old man of sixty-seven years in Ban Hong has been to Chiengmai five times in his life. Most men and boys have gone there a few times, but the women almost never make the trip since very few women travel outside the local area. The road has, therefore, brought the outside world to the Karen, at least indirectly and very selectively. For example, the United States Information Service regularly brings movies to Wang Lung, and some Karen attend these. There have also been missionaries from the Overseas Missionary Fellowship in the area for the past eight years, although there are as yet no Karen or Thai converts. These local peoples are being introduced to Western ideas and goods, many of which they do not understand or care about; they are, however, particularly impressed by Western medicine. Now and then Karen listen to a Thai-owned radio, but they do not understand central Thai dialect well and miss much of the discussion. They enjoy Burmese programs.

There are schools in all the large Thai villages, but no Karen still living in their own villages attend them. However, three or four Karen children whose parents have left Hui Sai to live in Wang Lung do attend. There are two Buddhist temples in Wang Lung, and the few Karen who attend important Buddhist holidays go to *Wat* Hui Sai, the temple at the south end of Wang Lung near the Karen village of Hui Sai. There are no local Karen in the priesthood at present, but one from Hui Sai was the head priest at *Wat* Hui Sai until he died a few years ago. One young man living in Ban Hong attended *Wat* school for a year, but his mother is a Thai from Ban Nong who married a Karen.

In Wang Lung, the medical clinic, rice mill, and small turpentine factory all affect the Karen to some extent. The clinic has the threefold purpose of administering general first aid, including the dispensing of medicine and giving injections (B-complex, streptomycin, and penicillin); of providing care for mothers and babies; and of providing veterinary care for domestic, economically important animals. The clinic has been in Wang Lung for around thirty years, but the Mother and Baby Clinic, which is a subdivision of the general clinic including a midwife training program, has existed for only seven years. In this government clinic, there is an *Amphur* medical officer in charge who has been at the clinic for a little over ten years. There is also a nurse-midwife who was trained in Bangkok and has been at the clinic for eighteen years. A government veterinarian who has been in Wang Lung for a little over a year completes the staff. Medicine is generally sold, except that for mothers and babies, which is free. However, there is a donation box for those who wish to gain religious merit, and a charge for delivery levied by the midwife. A fee of 5 *baht* (25¢) is charged for injections. Powdered milk and DDT have been donated by UNICEF. From time to time, the Thai villages in the area are sprayed with DDT, and some Karen have complained that their villages are always skipped. The powdered milk is, in theory, free to all mothers who ask for it, but I am told that, in fact, it is sold. The Karen generally cannot afford it, so it too is usually distributed only to Thai. However, Karen mothers who have had trouble with their own milk supply have purchased some powdered milk from time to time. The veterinarian has not treated Karen animals to my knowledge.

The major volume of clinic work is midwifery, but again the fee is prohibitive to the Karen. My Thai cook had a baby while in Wang Lung, and the midwife fee was 100 *baht* ($5.00). I do not know, however, whether this is the normal charge, because I was unable to get a definite figure from the nurse at the clinic. However, the Karen would not be likely to go to a Thai midwife at any rate. Part of the nurse's duty is to train midwives in a six-week course. She has trained thirty-five in this *Amphur*, and four of these were Karen women. One lives in Hui Sai, one in Mae Phraphai, one in Hui Fang (a daughter village of Mae Phraphai), and one now lives in Wang Lung. The best known and busiest Karen midwife in the local area lives in Ban Hong, but she refused to go through the training course.

The public rice mill in Wang Lung has been in operation for nine years and is the only one in the local area. Some Karen from the surrounding villages take their rice there to be milled. There is a charge of 75 *stang* (a little less than four cents) for a five-gallon can of unmilled rice (one *ma*), which is about fifteen kilo, or nine liter of milled rice (see also Judd 1964:64). The bran, which is kept by the customer, is used for pig or chicken food.

The turpentine factory is a small operation run by four employees, one of whom is the manager [12] for the absentee landlord who lives in Chiengmai. Thai are contracted to bring the raw turpentine from the surrounding hills. These in turn hire Karen to collect the turpentine and deliver it to the factory, using pack animals supplied by the Thai middleman. The factory will not buy directly from the Karen, they must work for a Thai who has been contracted by the factory manager. The Thai are paid 25 *baht* [13] ($1.25) per beep can [14], and they in turn give the Karen 10 *baht* (fifty cents) per beep can. The turpentine is refined in Wang Lung, poured into large, lined, wooden boxes, and shipped to Chiengmai and beyond. This refined product is sold for 300 *baht* per box. It takes about ten beep cans to make a box of refined turpentine. The Thai who are contracted by the mill make a profit, after expenses, of 7 *baht* (thirty-five cents) per can, and the owner of the operation makes 50 *baht* ($2.50) per box. Last year's profit was 100,000 *baht* ($5,000). The total Karen income was $1,000, but this was spread out among many individuals. To my knowledge, none of the Karen in local villages engaged in this activity; therefore, I do not know how much a single individual receives for this work.

There are many small shops in Wang Lung, and the Karen trade in all of them. Items purchased will be discussed a little later (p. 202). There is also a cafe in the village, but only rarely do the Karen buy the prepared food.

The long arm of the law sometimes reaches the Karen too. The son of the headman of Ban Hong was caught with an illegal lottery ticket two years ago and was fined 600 *baht* ($30.00); he was not sent to jail, however, as offenders often are. Karen have been caught smoking opium and sent to jail for a term. The making of illegal rice liquor has sent a few Karen to jail. One man from Dong Dam was caught with contraband liquor and received a two-month term, or 200 *baht* ($10.00) fine. He went to jail and villagers brought him rice twice a day. There have been cases of murder, or attempted murder, which are always investigated by the police who sometimes, but not often, catch the guilty party.[15] Some crimes and their consequences are listed in Table 5.

TABLE 5 Crime and Punishment

Offence	Punishment
Shooting a thief	Short time in jail
Opium smoking	3 months for first offence, more for further offences
Chicken stealing	3 months in jail
Illegal lottery	3 months in jail and a fine
Illegal production or consumption of liquor	3 months in jail and 500 *baht* fine
Buffalo stealing	18 months in jail
Killing a thief	1–3 years in jail
Murder	10–20 years in jail

THE CULTURE IN OUTLINE

The political organization of a Karen village consists of a group of elders, which includes the adult male head of each household, presided over by a traditional headman whose position is usually inherited patrilineally. From time to time, a meeting is called of the elders at the house of the headman. Decisions are made or enunciated here, information is passed along, and disputes are settled (see also Marshall 1922:127, and Young 1962:100). This group also links the village with the outside world through the intermediary of a Thai-appointed Karen headman who may be in charge of several villages. He makes reports to the Thai officials and, in turn, takes orders, directives, and information back to his villages. This man is not usually the traditional headman of even his own village. The role, which is new and not part of traditional Karen culture, is a Thai overlay (see also Young 1962:100).

The social organization of Karen culture is based upon a household, a lineage segment, a lineage, a village, and a village-complex. The nuclear family occupies one household. The house is generally near the wife's mother's house. The next larger social unit is the matrilineage segment, which is a residence unit (a group of households). The nonresidential lineage is presided over by the oldest living female who conducts special lineage ceremonies during illness, from which nonmembers are excluded. One can be a lineage member only by birth.[16]

The largest residential socio-political unit is the village, which is presided over by a male political-religious headman. Besides the political duties mentioned above, he conducts village ceremonies two or three times a year propitiating the village spirits, and presides at special propitiatory ceremonies when there is a crisis or a break in custom that might anger the village spirits. Daughter villages break off from time to time and take as their village spirit a "child" of the community spirit of the parent village. There is, therefore, a tenuous symbolic relationship between parent and daughter villages. This "set" of villages forms a village-complex.

Karen economy is based on rice agriculture, now employing both wet and dry techniques.[17] There is some hunting, gathering, and fishing. There are vegetable, fruit, and tobacco gardens. Pigs and chickens are kept by the women. Some of the groups have elephants (but not the group that I studied), some of those having paddy land own water buffalo, and some people speculate in cattle. There is some production for cash by all groups. Such production includes weaving, the raising of produce (except rice, which is rarely sold), rope-making, basketry, gathering wild foods, and fishing. Labor, in addition, is sold or exchanged.

Religion among the Karen varies, depending upon the kind and degree of contact and acculturation. There are approximately 200,000 Christian Karen in Burma and approximately 3,000 Christian Karen in Thailand, almost exclusively Sgaw (Young 1962:94). Many Karen in both Thailand and Burma can be considered to be Buddhist. Hackett (1953) says all the group of Pa-o that he studied are Buddhist and there are some Pa-o who build Buddhist temples in their villages. Stern (1968) discusses very interesting Buddhist influences among Pwo Karen farther south in Thailand. There are no Christian Karen in the area where I worked although missionaries have been there for eight years. The few Pwo in the area who might be called Buddhist are, for the most part, no longer living as Karen, but have moved into Thai villages. Some Karen villagers, however, are nominal Buddhists who go to Buddhist ceremonies from time to time, though do not attend consistently. The great majority of Karen in all areas are Animists. A local Karen cult has developed around a defrocked Buddhist priest, called the White Priest, however (see Hinton 1969). This is discussed more fully in Chapter 10.

It is believed locally that there are thirty-two (sometimes thirty-three) "spirits" in the human body, the most important one residing in the top of the head. One must have his wrists tied in a special ceremony from time to time so this spirit cannot leave, as this would cause illness or death. There are also lineage ancestral spirits which must be propitiated by the lineage head when there is a serious illness which is not cured by other means. The village spirits can only be propitiated by the headman of the village, and he does this at special occasions each year.

Indeed, there are many spirits which must be avoided or propitiated from time to time which reside in trees, paths, rivers, rice fields, and so on. If one becomes ill, a fortune teller may be consulted who may send the sick person to a curer-magician to be treated. More will be said below about magic, religion, and the supernatural.

NOTES

[1] The term *Muban* refers to a Thai administrative unit meaning "village." This may or may not be an actual social unit. In the area where I worked, it was not a natural social unit as a single *Muban* might include both Thai and Karen villages. The term *Thambon* has been translated as "commune" but "subdistrict" is probably better. It is similar to an American township. *Amphur*, translated as "district" is similar to our county, and *Chiangwat* translated as province is roughly equivalent to an American state. The phrase "Northern Thailand" refers to one of the four geographical cultural divisions of the country, but is not an official administrative unit. The term "Hod" has a conventional spelling, which I have not changed, but it should be pronounced /hôt/ (see Appendix B for the pronunciation and spelling of Thai and Karen words). There is a *Muban* Hod, a *Thambon* Hod and the *Amphur* is named Hod.

[2] The exact location of Ban Hong is 18°5′ north latitude, 98°35′ east longitude. It must be stressed that the ethnographic present for all

but the last two chapters is 1960–61, that is, before completion of the Yanhee Dam and subsequent migration of local people.

³ For further details, see Blanchard 1958:187.

⁴ In what follows, *Ban Hong* will refer to the total village, unless otherwise specified, and *the village* also refers to both sections unless otherwise stated. A letter-number combination, such as H–8, refers to a household (see Figure 3).

⁵ Since my return from the field, this child has died.

⁶ It is possible for a person to reach adult age without ever having been married, but this is rare and there are no cases in Ban Hong. Such a person is considered a child, and women must wear the unmarried girls' dress, no matter what their age, if they have never married. There are a few cases of this situation in some of the other Karen villages on the Hod plain. I know of only one case of a (feebleminded) man, who has reached adult age and has not married. Since there are fewer men of marriageable age than women, this pattern would be expected.

⁷ A Thai *Amphur*, and not the Karen village of this study.

⁸ The village genealogy (see Figure B) does not show all these relationships.

⁹ This Thai administrative unit, *Muban* 4, does not correspond to the Karen conception of the relationships of the villages (see summary of village connections, p. 33). For a complete discussion of the Thai structure and divisions, see Blanchard 1957 and Mosel 1957.

¹⁰ The great-grandfather of a Wang Lung shop-owner was born in Hod village, and the Karen founder of Ban Hong obtained a title to land from the administrative headquarters in Hod. According to Starnstein's maps (1964), Hod is not shown in 1317, but by the year 1590 it appears.

¹¹ The ages of villages are by local estimate and may be far from accurate.

[12] This man is a Mon, another of the ethnic groups living in Southeast Asia.

[13] A Thai monetary unit, equalling approximately five cents per *Baht*. One *baht* is divided into 100 *stang*.

[14] A beep can is the local term for a five-gallon can.

[15] There have been two murders in Ban Hong, in both cases by shooting. One victim was "argumentative" and a trouble-maker, and the other was a thief and opium smoker. The previous headman, the brother of Mang Thi, was shot at but missed. It was believed that he is a black magician. He now lives with his wife, who was wounded by accident, in Nong Pu.

[16] Marshall's description would seem to imply the same organization for the Sgaw in Burma (1922:254). He also mentions that the Sgaw in the hills lived in long-houses which may have represented predominantly one lineage. Marshall calls them clans. Hackett specifically says that the Taungthu do not have lineages (1953:448).

[17] This is apparently true for all major groups of Karen except the Bwe in Thailand (see Marshall 1922:75, 87; Hackett 1953:175; Young 1962:107). Lehman however informs me (personal communication, 1973) that the Kayah of Thailand use both wet and dry techniques.

3

Ecology and Economic Activities in the Yearly Round

INTRODUCTION

This chapter is concerned with the interaction between the Karen and their natural environment in the activities of making a living. After first characterizing the relevant environment, I will discuss the Karen use of this environment. The exploitative activities carried on by the Karen to be discussed below include agriculture, animal husbandry, hunting and gathering, fishing, and various types of domestic endeavors. The selling and buying of goods will be discussed more systematically in Chapters 7 and 8.

CLIMATE, SOILS, AND FLORA

Thailand, having two distinct seasons, falls within the tropical region of the world.

From late March or early April to September, the low-pressure area over Lake Baykal and a similar high-pressure area over the Indian Ocean cause warm moist winds to be drawn from the southwest across the Bay of Bengal and into Thailand, bringing moisture that precipitates over the land mass. In the remaining months of the year (September-March) a high-pressure system over Lake Baykal sends dry continental winds from the northeast toward the lows of the Indian Ocean, and the "dry monsoon" is dominant (Blanchard 1958:45).

The climate in the Hod plain during one year of my stay is summarized in Table 6 (see also Spencer 1962:45–68; Dobby 1958:265–266; Blanchard 1958:44–45). There are times when drought is a problem. There is never enough rain to grow the all-important rice, so irrigation from the Ping River is a necessity. If the river is too low due to lack of rain, the rice may be lost or the yield may be low. Thus, rain is a constant topic of discussion and is quite important to the agricultural cycle. Chiengmai receives 85 percent of its precipitation in the rainy season, from May to September, and the mean annual temperature is 77.8 with a mean range of 14° (Blanchard 1958:45–46). The average yearly rainfall in Chiengmai is forty-eight inches, but the wide variability in annual precipitation is a distinct drawback to the northern rice cultivators (Dobby 1958:266–267).

The soils in Southeast Asia generally, according to one authority, are the pedalfers or aluminum- and iron-bearing soils. There are, of course, local variations and subtypes. These soils are generally acidic in reaction.[1]

> Some crops prefer soils that are definitely basic, among them being wheat, some of the sorghums and millets, most of the oil seeds, cotton, and numerous vegetable crops. Others prefer definitely acid soils, among them being rice, tea, and the oil palm. Maize, some of the millets, tobacco, the coconut palm, coffee, many of the tree fruits, and many vegetables prefer neutral to slightly acid soils (Spencer 1962:76).

Along the river systems of Thailand, the subtype of pedalfer called alluvium is found. In the Hod plain there is little or no problem with annual flooding. The river does, however, change levels quite drastically between the seasons, and alluvial deposits are left along the river banks. Tobacco gardens are planted in these areas. Since the paddy fields are not flooded, large water wheels are used to irrigate from the river and large amounts of alluvial soil, as well as edible aquatic life, find their way into the paddies yearly.

TABLE 6 Summary of Climate during 1960 [a]

	Mean Temp.[b]	Mean Max.	Mean. Min.	Precip.[c]	Rainy Days
Jan.	20.95	29.19	12.72	10.7	2
Feb.	25.06	34.63	15.49	0.0	0
March	27.94	37.33	18.55	39.6	5
April	30.16	37.90	22.43	116.5	8
May	28.58	33.30	23.87	219.2	18
June	27.29	31.25	23.34	83.8	19
July	27.40	31.40	23.40	84.6	19
Aug.	30.41	30.86	22.97	111.8	21
Sept.	27.20	31.50	22.80	88.3	18
Oct.	26.10	30.50	21.70	161.2	15
Nov.	25.92	31.34	20.50	54.5	5
Dec.	21.90	27.90	15.80	13.8	3

[a] This information is from government weather records at *Amphur* Hod.
[b] Temperature is given on the centigrade scale.
[c] Precipitation is measured in millimeters.

Although deciduous teak forest is the major vegetation found in wet monsoon area in the northern region of Thailand (north of about 17° N), rice predominates in the valleys. There are also outcrops of thorn and bamboo thickets here and there. In the Hod area some cactus is found, and some of the soil is quite sandy. Areas forested with tropical evergreens are also found. In all the northern forested area, oils, resins, and stick-lac are collected, and a local economic endeavor is charcoal making (see Blanchard 1958:46–47; Dobby 1958:268–269).

The Karen use only some varieties of the various kinds of trees that grow on their lands. Teak and other hard woods serve for building. Bamboo is very important for all types of structures, basketry, and other items. Various barks, roots, and herbs provide medicines. One plant is used as a fish poison, and another provides a dye. Rope is made from jute that is collected. Stick-lac is gathered from the branches of certain trees. Mushrooms, bamboo shoots, and tender greens are gathered, and other types of flora are also used. There is a large variety of tropical fruit.

Besides the many varieties of rice, there is an abundant array of domesticated coconut, jack fruit, mango, durian, papaya, banana, lichee, longan, cotton, tobacco; there is also a large variety of vegetables such as tomato, melon, cucumber, squash, corn, and others. Of course, not all of these plants were domesticated in Southeast Asia, nor have all of them been in the area for a long period of time.[2] However, all of these plants are important today in Northern Thailand.

FAUNA

The wild life in Northern Thailand is varied, and some of it is important economically. Larger animals are sometimes taken, but not many of these are found on the Hod plain. Tigers and smaller members of the cat family are reported, and one Karen in the hills showed me his scars to attest to their presence. There are still a few wild elephants and pigs in the area. Various types of monkey and gibbon can be destructive to garden crops. Both monkey and gibbon are considered good to eat. These anthropoids are caught and either eaten or, more often, sold from time to time. In general, however, the larger of the wild animal population is not very significant to the Karen in the Hod plain.

Small animal life, on the other hand, is much more important. Squirrels of various types abound and are eaten. The great variety of birds must constantly be chased away from the young rice plants. In slack times, a group of men will hunt birds and squirrels to add variety to the menu. There is a variety of reptiles including snakes and lizards. A very large lizard is hunted for food; a small species is often caught by using a snare and added to the family curry. A few snakes are poisonous, and a few are eaten at times. Honey is considered a delicacy. A large variety of insects, including beetles and ant larvae, are collected and used in curries.

Meat consumption in general is quite low compared to other areas of the world (Spencer 1962:97). The most important items to the Karen are pork and fowl—both domesticated. Aquatic life of various types, therefore, becomes a protein supplement and is an important item in the diet of Southeast Asians. In Northern Thailand, the Karen capture several types of frog at night which are sold and used for food quite often. Fish are caught in a variety of ways and are consumed nearly the year round. Besides frogs and fish, various varieties of fresh water mollusks and crustaceans are caught and eaten.

There are important domestic animals found in the area. These include water buffalo (carabao), zebu cattle, elephants, pigs, chickens, ducks, and dogs. A few people make use of the horse, but the Karen do not.

LAND USE

The Karen are primarily rice agriculturalists, therefore, land for growing rice is of primary importance to them. Generally in the past, and currently in the hills, the technique of cultivation is that of slash-and-burn (see Kunstadter 1964:10). However, wet-rice techniques have been adopted by Karen both in the hills, where possible, and in the valleys and plains (Hinton 1969).

When the Karen had only swidden fields, rainfall was the only significant source of water for agriculture. But as they began to use wet-rice techniques, irrigation also became important and began to effect the settlement pattern and water usage. During about six months there is almost no rain in the area under consideration (see Table 6, p. 51), and during the other six months, it rains on the average of a little more than eighteen days a month. This has an important bearing on the growing period and on the planting and harvesting periods. This is true even for irrigated fields, because there is some dependence on rain to water the wet-rice fields and the water wheels will only operate with a high river. The Ping is a large, major river which always has water and fish. In the dry season, however, it is impossible to irrigate from the river because the water level is too low. Some of the minor streams dry up almost completely.

Since agriculture is the major economic occupation, details of land-use patterns and changes which have occurred will be considered. The opening statement of Chapter 10 by Marshall (1922) characterizes the old land-use pattern of the Karen in the hills of Burma; it points out that due to government interference, land currently does not usually lie fallow long enough to maintain its potential productivity. Marshall (1922:75) says, "At least seven years should intervene before a plot is cleared and planted a second time, and even this period is too short for the production of the best crops." The area of dry-rice cultivation used by the people in Ban Hong is very restricted, and is used far too much for the effort to be worthwhile. The Thai government has recently stipulated that no new swidden fields may be started in the hills by cutting down existing forests. The Thai government enforces this prohibition with a heavy fine or imprisonment. A tax is also charged today for cutting timber to be used for building purposes. There are, of course, some clandestine activities in these areas. Besides these restrictions,

Thai population increase is putting more pressure on the land. The added people are apparently taking over some traditional Karen lands and growing peanuts and other crops. One can take effective legal control of land by registration, and the Karen are only doing this with paddy fields.

At any rate, the land which is available for dry-rice fields is so small and restricted that it is used from one to three years at a time, and then is left fallow for only about three years. There is an attempt to use old techniques of production; that is, cutting, drying, and burning. With this overuse, soil exhaustion is inevitable and, of course, yield is drastically lowered. But the Karen say poor yield is due to insufficient rain.

The other main pattern of land use is to prepare the land for continuous planting year after year. This land is fertilized in the main through the irrigation process. This is the wet-rice or paddy field technique, and among the Karen, two types of irrigation are used. The fields of most people in Ban Hong are across the river from the village. All land in this paddy area is irrigated by the use of large water wheels that raise the water about twenty feet in bamboo tubes attached to the wheel; in the process, much fertile river silt as well as water life is added to the fields. Cow manure is used as fertilizer irregularly and only in a few plots. This method of irrigation is efficient, but the water wheels must be rebuilt each year and rain water must also be depended upon in order to keep the water at the proper level in the fields. Water life caught in the fields is a diet supplement during the rice growing period.

The second method of irrigation is practiced by those away from the Ping River and by those who have fields on the western side of the river. For the most part, the land slopes toward the river and the water wheels cannot be used. In these cases, small streams or natural drainage areas are dammed, and a small reservoir is made at the high side of the field to be irrigated. In all cases that I observed, these reservoirs depend on rain water which is allowed to flow from the reservoir into the paddy for irrigation. These fields must, of necessity, be small. Their location is restricted by land contours and they depend to even a greater extent on sufficient rainfall. Nowhere in the Hod area is there intensive wet-rice agriculture by proper irrigation.

The following statements by Marshall characterize the old settlement pattern and land tenure system used by the Karen in Burma. These comments may partially describe the situation in the early days of the Karen in the hills and foothills of Thailand —according to my informants.

> In the Pegu Hills we find the single-structure village, which seems to have been the characteristic Karen dwelling from early times. It might be described as a bamboo apartment house on stilts, accommodating on the average from twenty to thirty families. It is spread out on one floor, and each family occupies not one "flat" but a room . . . which faces a central corridor running the length of the barrack.
>
> Such a village . . . is usually rebuilt on a new site each year. The new location is sought by the local chief during the hot season, after conference with the elders and after the crops have been brought in. The place selected by the chief is fairly level, adjacent to the area to be cut over the coming year, and near a spring or stream that will not dry up during the hot weather. In the old days it was also necessary to choose a site that would be high and easily defended against raids (1922:-56).

He goes on to say:

> It is characteristic of this [shifting] cultivation that a new field . . . has to be selected, cleared, and burned off each year. The planting of the grain must follow immediately after all seeds and small roots have been destroyed by fire, or no crop can be raised with the primitive implements in use, on account of the rapid resuscitation of the jungle. The ashes from the consumed vegetation act as a fertilizer, without which the crop would scarcely be worth the reaping. At the

present time the Government [of Burma] so limits the areas open to the Karen for cultivation in some districts that a sufficient interval does not elapse between plantings to allow the growth of enough timber for the production of the ashes necessary to fertilize the soil properly. Hence, crop production is declining in all these districts.

When a crop has been harvested, the village chief and elders choose the ground to be cut over the following year. Each village has its well-recognized farming areas, beyond which are the lands of the neighboring village. Each member of the community then picks out his particular plot for cultivating (1922:75-76).

I doubt that the village was moved annually, but Marshall's comments show a contrast to present-day Ban Hong and the Hod plain in general, yet some of his description characterizes current practices on the Hod plain and surrounding foothills and thus indicates that present practices came from just such behavior. Through time and due to various influences, the Karen land-use pattern has changed. Originally in the Hod area, new plots were used each year for dry-rice cultivation. These frequent moves maintained high yield, and they meant that from time to time the village itself had to be moved (probably not yearly, however, as Marshall suggests, since no Ban Hong villager remembers moving for this reason and Hinton (1969:9) says the hill villages are relatively permanent). More recently this technique has been restricted by the Thai government, and so the Karen have begun using wet-rice techniques with more permanent land use. In the face of government restrictions and lowered yield, however, the Karen have attempted to maintain dry-rice fields. They cannot move or travel long distances in order to maintain high-yield swidden fields and at the same time remain permanent and own paddy fields. So a kind of compromise has resulted which has not produced entirely satisfactory consequences in rice yield. A few Karen in Ban Hong have paddy land and no swidden fields, and the swidden plots in use are more or less permanent. There are some Karen who try to maintain both. Since they divide their time in this way, and since they are not able to carry out the old techniques to the maximum extent, their yield and efficiency in general are lowered (for current swidden practices, see pp. 61 ff.).

VILLAGE AGRICULTURAL LANDS AND THEIR HISTORY

The main paddy land owned or worked by local Karen is directly across the river from the lower village, but a couple of fields are on the same side as the village (see Figure A, p. 13). Several tobacco gardens are located on the gentle slope of the river bank south of the village. There are also several tobacco gardens owned by villagers of Ban Hong, as well as other Karen villages, located on the island in the river slightly north of the village.

Directly across the river from Ban Hong there is a steep bank about twenty feet high; here several water wheels raise water to irrigate the paddy fields. Wooden barrages running obliquely across the river direct the water toward the wheels to make them turn faster. These barrages do not dam the water, but merely direct it. In the high-water season they are completely under the surface of the river, but nevertheless direct the undercurrents toward the water wheels. Also, during this time they do not hinder water travel.

There is a large mango tree at the top of the bank just across the river from Ban Hong. At the foot of this tree is a small spirit house on stilts where the spirits of the paddy field are propitiated. Beyond this tree and stretched out in both directions for a total of about a mile and a half or two miles is the large paddy field. It runs roughly north and south parallel to the river, and is about a quarter of a mile wide at the narrow end to the south and about a half mile wide at the wide end to the north. The Ping River forms the northern and western boundaries of the fields. On the east and south the field abruptly ends and the scrub forest begins. There are two Karen villages on the eastern fringe of the paddy field; Mang Mêng is located near the northern end of the field and Dong Dam is located near the southern end. These two villages are located among the trees, and the roofs of a few houses may be seen from the river's edge at the western side of the paddy field. Villagers from these two villages, as well as from Ban Hong and Hui Sai, own or work plots in this large paddy area. There are also a few Thai who own part of the land.

Many vegetable and fruit gardens belonging to Ban Hong villagers are scattered among the bamboo groves of the lower village, around the houses of the village, and sometimes at the fringe of a paddy field or beside a swidden field.[3] The dry-rice swidden fields are scattered over the countryside, but most are concentrated south of Ban Hong, near Vwang Mô (see Figure A). Since these fields are not held in permanent ownership, only the general area of the fields is shown on the map; others are not shown at all.

A major motivation for moving into the plains and valleys in the first place was economic. As the Karen moved down from the hills, they adopted wet-rice techniques, and paddy land became important. Villages were formed near the areas that were suitable for such fields. The present location of most of the Karen villages seems explainable in these terms, because today there is a large paddy area near almost all the villages.

There is a story in Ban Hong that the first paddy in the area was developed by the founder of Ban Hong, the grandfather of Mang Thi the present headman. The founder also invented the water wheel. Before that time people had only swidden fields. This is doubtful, however, since some of the large paddy area is owned by people in Hui Sai, and since the older villages of Mae Ngut and Mae Phraphai are situated beside large paddy areas. Also, it is the rare Karen who can buy paddy land today; thus, the paddy lands were no doubt cleared sometime in the past.[4] The water wheel was probably borrowed from the Thai.

At any rate, the following is apparently what happened: A few hardy individuals cleared land and made fields around present-day Mae Ngut and Mae Phraphai. Some of the people from those two villages moved and founded Ban Phae', but there was no paddy in use around Ban Hong. Many years previously, however, a different ethnic group, the Lawa, had inhabited the Hod plain and had apparently made paddy in the area where the present-day paddy fields are located across the river from Ban Hong (see also Hinton 1969:8 and Kunstadter 1964).

When Mang Thi's grandfather returned from Mae Thern, he planted a garden which included the mango tree mentioned earlier and was located across the river from Ban Hong. He built a house and started to work clearing and reclaiming some or all of this abandoned Lawa paddy. He purportedly invented the water wheel, and thus wet-rice was introduced to the Karen of the central Hod plain. Before this time, the Karen say, the Ban Phae' villagers had only swidden fields. The present paddy land ownership and distribution seems to bear out this somewhat mythological history.

The village founder received a license or title from the Thai administrative headquarters in Hod village. Then he made boundary signs on trees and cleared a small strip around the land, thus staking his claim to more than one hundred *rai* of land.[5] Much of the northern portion was sold to Thai, and other portions were lost to Thai over the generations. Today the land is owned by villagers from Ban Hong, Dong Dam, Hui Sai, and Mang Mêng, and by Thai from several villages. By the time the land was to come to the present generation in Ban Hong, only the father of the present headman had any left in the family. This was inherited by Mang Thi, his three brothers, and five sisters. Of these nine people, only three maintain their portions; four sold their shares to Thai, and two parcels were given to daughters and are maintained by their husbands.

Currently, there are eight households which own paddy land, but only seven which have land in the large field claimed by the founder. Paddy ownership is closely associated with descent from the village founder. Appendix G summarizes the paddy land ownership today.

Paddy land is individually owned and inherited by both males and females, and it may be bought and sold. It must be registered legally with the Thai government, and a small tax must be paid on its use. Paddy land does not readily come into Karen hands, and the trend seems to be for them to lose their land rather than gain more. There are three methods of obtaining paddy land. First, one may receive land through inheritance; this method is by far the most important and prevalent. In every case but two in Ban Hong, the individual inherited his paddy land; also, in every case but one, the paddy owner or worker can trace direct descent from the founder of the village. The second way in which one may gain paddy fields is through clearing the land and making them, although this method is not important today—only one person (H–28) in recent years has gotten paddy land this way, and his crop failed due to lack of water. There is not enough good land near water for this method to work today with the technology available. In the past, however, this second method was the only one used by Karen; and in all but one case, the present land used by Ban Hong villagers was gained originally by clearing of land by Karen. The one exception here brings up the last way to gain paddy land, which will be more important in the future; that is, through buying and selling. H–19 is the only person who bought paddy in Ban Hong because he inherited sufficient money from his father. Other Ban Hong villagers are not able to buy paddy land, however, because they are not able to accumulate enough money to do so at present and there is little available land to buy.

If inheritance is the only way to receive land, the Karen inheritance system is such that eventually everyone will lose his paddy land, since new land can no longer be cleared. The oldest and youngest child in a Karen family receive equal portions of the inheritance, and the middle group of children receive lesser portions. This means that in a very few generations a large paddy area is divided into such small plots that the yield per family is not worth the effort. The inheritance system worked well enough when land was not an inheritable item because marriage would recombine resources, but this system does not work if only a few people own paddy land in the first place. Thus, if the Karen are to remain paddy farmers in the future, a way must be found to buy fields (or to limit population increase).

AGRICULTURE AND HORTICULTURE

Swidden (Dry-Rice)

As pointed out, in the past the basis of the economy was swidden cultivation, and this is still true of the hill Karen (Hinton 1969). In terms of total yield produced, however, this type of cultivation is not very important economically to Ban Hong, but it still holds a central position in the belief system as the basis of the economy.

Within the area of village swidden land, which is near the small village of Vwang Mô, a person chooses a plot which he wishes to work for a year. A person may work one plot from one to three or four seasons at most, then he moves to another plot. The plot left unused is then available to anyone from the village, but it is usually allowed to fallow for three years or more. The Karen in Ban Hong reason that the fields must be allowed to fallow for a time or "the weeds get too thick." [6]

In 1960, only eighteen of thirty-five households in Ban Hong were working swidden fields; most, though not everyone, had their swidden in the Vwang Mô area. In 1961, of a total of twenty households making swidden there were seventeen which had fields at Vwang Mô. There was one case where a man used a plot in 1960, and his brother used it in 1961. In two cases a household used the same land for four years. One man, forty-three years old, made his first swidden field in 1961; previous to that, he had only helped his father in the paddy. Another household had been making swidden across the river for several years, but in 1961 went back to the Vwang Mô area. Households may not make swidden fields every year. The decision coincides with other considerations, for example, limited labor in the household to make either swidden fields or paddy, but not both.

In the past, after the land to be used during the year was chosen by the headman (presumably in consultation with respected elders), the men of the whole village were involved in the initial phase of preparing the land for planting; they cut the foliage, and burned and cleared the land (see Marshall 1922:76ff). Each household then raised the rice on its own chosen plot. At present, the following procedure ensues: it is no longer possible for the headman and elders to decide on a new area for the village swiddens since land use is restricted by the Thai government. Household members go to the village lands and pick a plot to be worked that year. Since available land is restricted and used differentially, some plots are better than others in fertility. The Karen in Ban Hong seem to know this, but cannot state it in this way. At any rate, there is some ranking according to which of the households will use the "best" or larger plots. This is based on the ranking of elders; the most important may choose what seem to be the best plots and this shows up in the yield later. As far as I could determine, there is no specific allocating agent, but apparently tradition and status determine the order of choosing plots.

All plots must be fenced to keep wandering animals from destroying the crops, but not every plot is fenced separately. If there are several contiguous parcels, these will be fenced as one large plot and individual households will work their own parcel within the large fenced area. The land formation may be such that the plots of one or two households are set off from the rest. The households within one area cooperate in the initial work of burning, clearing, and fencing. Those in another area cooperate in like manner. When this cooperative work is finished, the household members finish clearing, hoeing, and weeding the plot.

As the plots become ready, the word is passed that a particular household will plant at a particular time. Some member or members of other households who have swidden help with the planting. This procedure is repeated until all parcels are planted. From this time on, all work is carried out by household members. This includes some transplanting, weeding, protecting the seedlings from animals and birds, and finally harvesting. In the past, the village presumably acted as a unit in the initial work of field preparation. This is no longer the case; households which do not have swidden fields do not cooperate in the work.

Capital requirements for swidden fields are relatively simple and inexpensive. The work requires cutting foliage with a machete. Each household has several machetes which are purchased for about 50 cents and which last several years. Burning a field requires only a means of starting a fire. While a very few people use flint for starting fires, most adult males in Ban Hong have cheap Japanese cigarette lighters fueled with kerosene for this purpose. (In the long run such a lighter is cheaper than matches, which are seldom seen in the village.) Clearing the field and making the fence require only manpower. The fence is made with logs, branches, and the rubble cleared from the field. The field is chopped with a hoe; the head of the hoe is available in the bazaar for 18 *baht* (90 cents), and the handle is made of a strong sapling found freely available. The largest outlay of capital and goods comes during planting since it is then that a small rest house is built to be used during the growing period to watch the young rice seedlings. Proper ceremonies to insure a good yield must be observed, and these involve the use of rice whiskey, rice, two or three chickens, and some vegetables, peppers, and salt. On the day of the planting, several digging sticks with metal tips must be available. The proper amount of rice seed has been saved from the last year's harvest. Food must be supplied for all those who help plant, but each helper usually supplies his own rice which is eaten with the provided curry. After the rice is planted and has grown for a time, some seedlings are transplanted to thin the plot for better yield. This requires a digging stick at most. The plot is weeded by hand or with a hoe until harvest. Requirements for harvest are small knives or sickles, a bamboo rack for threshing the rice, homemade bamboo baskets in which to carry the rice, and large baskets kept inside the house for rice storage. Those with paddy fields have rice granaries. The yield from dry-rice fields is so small that it is pooled and consumed exclusively by the household, except for the amount saved as seed for the following year. The yield is summarized in Appendix M. Consumption figures will be discussed later.

Swidden rice is harvested before the paddy is ripe and is usually eaten by the time the paddy harvest is finished. Therefore, the household is the consumption unit for rice from the swidden fields. This was probably true in the past as well since all households maintained swidden fields.

Paddy (Wet-Rice)

Paddy land, quite unlike swidden land, is individually owned and inherited and so enters differently into social organization. Swidden areas are village lands; they are available to all the villagers and sometimes "belong" to a village-complex. This is not so with paddy land. In the past, one merely cleared land on which he wished to grow paddy; this is still going on to some extent today. Twenty years ago, though, it was required by Thai government regulation that a person go to the local Thai administrative headquarters and report his paddy fields. Also, in the last eight years all irrigated land has been registered at the *Amphur* headquarters. For the last twenty years or so a tax has had to be paid on land of over one *rai* which amounts to about 2.50 *baht* per *rai*. All land in use, whether swidden, paddy, garden, or house area, is supposed to be registered, but the Karen register only their paddy land.

The following is a general description of labor organization in paddy production. The work cycle may be divided into a series of stages during which the managerial household is involved. The term *managerial household* will refer to those households which own paddy or manage it for others.

It will be noted that each work-group stage is preceded by one in which the manager or owner of the field and his household have done the necessary preparation. The "managerial" stages are ones in which the work can easily be handled by a single household because of the nature of the work or because speed is not required beyond that which a single household can handle. Work-group stages are those which require extra cooperative labor or must be done quickly (see Table 7).

TABLE 7   Stages of Work–Group Activities

Stage	Work Done By	Work
1	Manager (and household)	Build barrage across river, assemble materials for water wheel
2	Work-group (includes manager, members of his household and others)	Build water wheel
3	Manager	Water field, repair dikes, plow and harrow seed bed, sow seed bed, plow main fields, harrow main fields, pluck and tie seedlings
4	Work-group	Plant main fields
5	Manager	Maintain water level, weed, keep dikes in repair, prepare threshing floor, make threshing rack
6	Work-group	Cut ripe rice, carry and stack rice, thresh
7	Manager	Measure amount of rice, distribute rice, store rice, tie and store straw

There are two work peaks in the rice cycle, planting and harvesting. During these times, all available laborers in the village are busy whether or not they own paddy fields. If they do not own fields, they are part of a work-group or they work in Thai fields. (The dry-rice field work peak does not coincide with paddy fields—they are planted before the paddy fields and also harvested first.) Since there are peaks with wage labor for Thai and necessary work in the swidden fields which overlap, the work-group composition is variable and does not follow strict kinship lines, except for the manager households. Pay for labor occurs only at the two peaks of planting and harvesting. All other activity is either preparation for planting or maintenance of the field.

The work-groups for building water wheels, which is difficult and time-consuming work, are always groups of young adult men. These are special work-groups composed of the men in managerial households. This is merely reciprocal work exchange; there is neither any idea of pay nor a kinship obligation involved.

The planting work-group is composed of women and girls. It may either consist of the women of the managerial household plus women from several other households, usually the younger ones, or may include any females in the household. It takes several days to plant a field, and the same women work on a plot throughout the planting period. They may not all work every day, however, because of domestic duties. The harvest work-group is similar except that it also includes men and boys.

The possibilities for payment are:

1. Payment in reciprocal work.
2. Payment in rice.
3. Payment in meals during the work day with the laborer providing his own rice (this is in addition to another kind of pay).

4. Payment in money (this is rare between Karen and Karen).

The first kind of payment is rare in planting and harvesting work-group activities because people who form managerial households work on their own plots, although it does occur from time to time. The second type of payment is most common and is the main reason for the formation of the work-group. Payment in money does occur in some cases where the plot, the yield, and the work-group are all small. The third kind of payment, a meal during the workday, is usual for all activities that require a day or more of labor. If a meal is not provided, however, other pay is increased. The rate of pay is as follows: one person for one day of labor may receive 3 *baht* (15 cents) plus a meal, one person without the meal receives 4 *baht* (20 cents) per day, and one person for two days of labor receives 6 *baht* or one *ma* (15 kilo) of unmilled rice at harvest.

Since not all own paddy, it is not possible for all villagers to be involved in the village rice paddy cycle. The village is, therefore, divided into two parts in terms of labor force: those who work on paddy lands, and those who have nothing to do with villagers' paddy fields. The characteristics of this second group include:
1. Households in which there is now no usable paddy land, either owned or managed.
2. Households in which the parents of neither spouse own paddy lands, or in which the parents are not managing their own lands.
3. Persons who are too old for the sustained difficult work required.

The above labor organization of the village reflects kinship linkage as well as land holding, but it is a concomitant and not a cause of the dual labor organization. In other words, all individuals who own or manage paddy lands (except possibly three, H–12M, H–16M, H–28M), can trace descent directly from the village founder. However, all individuals who can trace such descent do not necessarily own or manage paddy; few who can trace descent from the founder received their land in other ways (H–2, H–19). The husband or wife of every household who participates in wet-rice production can trace descent from the village founder. In nearly all cases, of those households which are not involved in paddy production, one member of the household, usually the man, cannot trace descent from the founder.

The material and capital requirements for wet-rice production are more varied and expensive than for dry-rice cultivation, This, coupled with the land problem, is why not all Karen may own paddy fields; the availability of labor is no problem. Capital, material, and production costs will next be discussed in terms of the stages of the rice cycle.

Stages 1 and 2: The material required for barrage production (to increase the current which turns the water wheel) is taken freely from the surrounding forests. One needs only a good machete and a heavy wooden mallet for constructing the barrage across the river, but building a water wheel is more difficult. A large quantity of bamboo is required for its construction, as well as some hardwood for the main frame, axle, and spokes of the wheel. The hardwood is usually taken from the forest by stealth, to avoid government prosecution. However, all local bamboo clumps are individually owned and one must therefore either own bamboo or buy it.

Stage 3: Wooden troughs are needed to transport water from the wheel to the field. They are made of hollowed-out logs and last several years. The water level is maintained by many small dikes around small plots, and these dikes must be repaired often. For this work a hoe is essential, the head of which is bought in the local bazaar. When the ground becomes soft from irrigation, the plowing and harrowing are done first in the small plot for growing seedlings and later in the main fields. One must own or have access to, through kinship obligations, two or three water buffalo for this work. All the equipment for plowing and harrowing, except the small metal tip of the plow, is made in the household. The seedbed must be fenced against animals, and for this task bamboo and a machete are needed. Rest houses are built during this period. As the time arrives for Stage 4, the seedlings are plucked and tied with bamboo withes into small bunches. The bunches are then transported to the main field in baskets of loosely-woven bamboo.

Stages 4 and 5: The planting in Stage 4 requires no capital goods. The seedlings are planted in the water-soaked fields by female labor. The only outlay at this time by the manager is a meal. At Stage 5 a good hoe is necessary for repairing the dikes and weeding, but much weeding is also done by hand. Again, near the end of the growing season this hoe is necessary in preparing the threshing "floor"; a small plot of dry, hard earth that is smoothed and cleared. It is next required that a threshing rack be constructed in the middle of the cleared floor." The rack is made of bamboo and lashed together with bamboo withes. The rice is hit on the rack so that the ripe grain falls through onto the ground, or sometimes onto a large mat constructed for this purpose.

Stage 6: This is the time of harvest. The rice stalks are cut with a small hook-shaped knife and are then tied into small bundles with bamboo withes. The rice is then carried and stacked in a square around the edge of the threshing floor. The only other outlay at this time is food for the workers and for the spirits of land and rice.

Stage 7: The requirements at this stage are fans and trays for winnowing, and carrying-baskets for measuring and transporting the rice. The fans and trays may be homemade but are usually purchased, and the baskets must be bought in the bazaar. The rice is transported across the river by boat. Nearly all managerial households own boats, yet nonmanagerial households do not own them. Rice is stored either in specially constructed rice granaries separate from the house or large baskets inside the house. Finally, the rice straw is bundled and stored, usually on a loft out of reach of animals. The above is a general statement concerning wet-rice production, and there are some detailed differences in each individual case (for more details, see Appendix F and Appendix G).

There is quite a difference between what happens to swidden yield as contrasted with paddy yield. Rice from wet-rice fields, in almost every case, is distributed beyond the household, and in some cases (H–1, H–4, H–17, H–14, H–21) beyond the village. The consumption unit of paddy is the work-group and the owner (who may not be part of the work-group). In fact, the only people who are not generally included in the distribution of wet-rice are those not involved in any way in its production, yet even this is not a strict division because at times those in this latter category may "borrow" rice, and the debt may be repaid in some way other than the return of rice (for a summary of yield and distribution, see Appendix M).

It is impossible to show the specific distribution of rice to the work-groups because the groups are variable both in composition and in terms of number of days worked, but rice distributed to the work-group comes from "net yield" as shown in the Appendices. However, the pay range in rice per person probably ranges from 4 *ma* (paid by H–7) to 15 *ma* (paid by H–16). An additional reason that "pay" for the work-group is difficult to show is that at times individuals are paid in money. Another difficulty is that kinship obligations allow one to ask for or "borrow" more rice than is deserved as pay for labor. The market element of pay for labor with a set value has crept into the thinking of the villagers, but not as yet fully into their behavior.

Gardens and Trees

There are several categories of garden including tobacco, vegetables, fruits, and peppers. There are also trees and bamboo clumps scattered here and there. Tobacco gardens are all individually owned and are found along the river bank next to Ban Hong or on the large island in the river. They are inherited and, therefore, are stable in location. Former villagers living nearby maintain their tobacco gardens as if they were still residing in the village. The gardens on the bank and on the island near Ban Hong are owned by villagers from Ban Hong, Dong Dam, Hui Sai, and Vwang Mô. Not every household in the village maintains a tobacco garden. There are at least two reasons for this; there is not enough land available for all, and those who do a great deal of wage labor do not have the extra time to maintain a tobacco garden.

Vegetable gardens fall into two categories: those that are permanent and have a separate location, and those that are part of the yearly swidden field. The permanent gardens, located in the village or outside it, require constant care and must be fenced to keep wandering animals from destroying the crops. There are sixteen households that have permanent vegetable gardens, and eleven other households grow vegetables in their dry-rice fields.

Suitable land for fruit tree gardens is quite restricted. These gardens require considerable moisture and shade provided by larger trees, and are therefore located only near the river banks. These gardens, all of which have been inherited, are well-established with large trees (see Appendix H).

Bamboo is an all-important and ubiquitous building material; its different types are used for many different purposes. The clumps will only grow where it is moist and cool, and thus are all found in and around the lower village. There are many bamboo clumps, all of them individually owned. The clumps around Ban Hong are owned by people from several villages, including some Thai. Although these bamboo clumps may be inherited, an individual may start his own; thus, many households own bamboo. There are some cases where a garden is owned by one man and the bamboo in it is owned by someone else. In those cases, however, the bamboo was there first and someone claimed the land around it for a garden. In and near the village there are other types of trees similar to bamboo in that they either do not require a garden or grow wild and are claimed.

The labor requirements vary somewhat for the various categories. Tobacco and peppers must be sown in seedbeds, cared for, watered, fenced, and later transplanted. The vegetable gardens must be prepared, planted, and fenced each year. The fruit trees, bamboo, and other trees require little or no care unless they are quite young.

Each household tends its own gardens, trees, and bamboo. For the most part the men of the household do much of the labor required for gardens and trees with the women helping at times with weeding.

The basic capital requirements for tobacco, vegetable, and fruit tree gardens are a digging stick, a machete, and bamboo fencing. A wooden instrument is necessary for holding the rolled tobacco leaves when shredded. The tobacco is then sun-dried on large mats. For bamboo and other trees, nothing is required in production. Baskets of various types are used in transport or storage for much of this production.

There are no recorded figures, but nevertheless some things can be said about yield. Because the tobacco grown is not enough to supply the needs of the households who have tobacco gardens, and because relatives request and receive tobacco, occasionally villagers must buy tobacco. Some tobacco is also allowed to go to seed in order to plant the following year. There are no direct production costs in money. When a new implement is needed for tobacco, it is also used in other kinds of production. There are losses at times, too. In December, 1960, the river rose out of season after the tobacco plants had been set in the permanent beds. At least two gardens on the island were destroyed and had to be replanted, thus requiring new seed and beds, and so forth.

The production procedure for peppers is exactly the same as for tobacco, except that there is no danger of loss by flooding. However, at least one man lost 400 plants in 1961 due to overexposure to the sun and lack of rain. He had to start again and was able to plant only half as many seedlings. The peppers, too, last nearly the whole year for all the village, but a few villagers are forced to buy peppers in the Thai bazaar.

Although fruit trees need not be planted annually, the fruit is seasonal and cannot be stored. Thus, during the fruit season there is an abundance and the whole village is supplied. At this time, those fortunate enough to have a surplus sell it to the Thai at the local bazaar. The yield varies considerably from year to year, so it was not possible to get an estimate of cash income.

The vegetable gardens are like the fruit trees in that the supply does not last until the next harvest. Some vegetables are sold in the market, but many are spread among the villagers through kinship obligations. No one would think of buying seed for his vegetable garden, since seed from one's own plants is simply saved until the next season. For almost eight months there are no available vegetables in the gardens.

The few people in the village who buy bamboo for construction are those who own either small clumps or no clumps at all. There are losses from occasional thievery and from destructive storms. Everyone who owns bamboo clumps sells to both Thai and Karen. There is not enough bamboo for people to be careless with it. In the mountains, however, bamboo is not individually owned; it is plentiful enough that it is a free good. At times, in fact, villagers will go to the hills to cut and bring back bamboo for necessary construction.

The other types of trees (e. g., kapok trees and stick-lac) owned by individuals are usually used as cash crops and their products sold to the Thai. There are no production costs. The distribution is almost wholly to the Thai, and the yield is insufficient for anyone to increase his holdings.

ANIMAL HUSBANDRY

The animals kept by the Karen in Ban Hong and in most other villages are water buffalo, oxen, pigs, chickens, and dogs. There are one or two cats in the village, and from time to time a monkey or gibbon will be found which will be sold eventually.

Water Buffalo

These animals are kept for two very different purposes: for use, and for sale for profit, that is, for speculation. The latter purpose will be dealt with under the next heading, "Oxen," because, although the animal is different, the marketing procedure is exactly the same. The statements in this section, then, apply to the first purpose of using buffalo in rice production.

The ownership of water buffalo is closely associated with paddy land ownership or managership, as Table 8 shows. There are seven people who own buffalo, and thirteen who own or manage paddy lands. However, of all households in the village which do not own paddy land, only two own buffalo and both of these regularly work as paddy managers. There are four owners or managers who do not own buffalo. Two do not work their own land, and the remaining two borrow or rent buffalo for plowing and harrowing.

The labor required for the care of water buffalo can be supplied wholly from the household which owns the animals. During the growing season, someone must be in attendance watching for buffalo all day to keep them out of the fields. For the most part, the buffalo are allowed to wander the land freely in search of food, but their diet is often supplemented. In the evenings, the man of the house will often have to go find his buffalo and drive them home. A fire usually has to be made when the animals bed down to keep the insects away. Some labor is required in building and repairing the corral for the buffalo, and clearing this area of dung. When an animal is sick or giving birth, it requires extra care. Some men become quite attached to their buffalo and spend considerable time caring for them.

The capital requirements for keeping buffalo are not great. But if one must buy an animal, it will cost as much as 1,000 *baht* (about $50.00) for an adult. Beyond this, one needs bamboo for a corral (four households have them), and wood for a hay loft; and, of course, certain tools and implements must be in hand: machete, rope, and bamboo withes. The final requirement is supplementary food, which is never purchased. Since all who own buffalo also own or manage paddy land, rice straw

TABLE 8   Ownership of Buffalo, Land, Corral, and Hayloft

	No. of Buffalo	Paddy-Land Owner	Paddy-Land Manager	Corral	Hayloft
H–1	2		x	x	x
H–2	3	x			x
H–4	0		x		
H–6	4	x		x	x
H–7	2 (and 3 calves)	x		x	x
H–14	0	x			
H–16	4	x			x
H–17	4		x		
H–19	4	x		x	x
H–21	0	x			
H–25	0	x			

is available to buffalo owners, but is never enough. When the rice straw is gone, the children and sometimes the adults in the household cut and collect tall grasses to be stored and used for buffalo food as needed. The only expenditure required is time and energy. Baskets are used to transport the hay, and machetes are used to cut it.

Water buffalo are used exclusively for plowing and harrowing, and therefore have a very short work period during a year. When an animal dies, however, the meat is sold to both Karen and Thai. A man will usually not eat the meat of his own animal.

Oxen

All oxen and some buffalo (as mentioned above) are maintained only for the profit to be realized from their sale. The sale of these animals is almost, if not entirely, to Thai. This is a speculative venture, for it is possible for one to lose money in the transaction.

There are two techniques used in this speculation. The first and least complicated is as follows: a Thai (or sometimes a Karen) buys approximately one to a dozen animals and makes arrangements with a Karen to care for and feed them until they are sold. The owner subtracts his original investment and divides the gross profit equally with the Karen who has cared for the animals. Almost the only cost to the Karen is time and energy. The land, labor, and capital requirements in this arrangement are the same as for water buffalo, as discussed above. One example will suffice: a Thai in Wang Lung bought nine head of young oxen for 800 *baht* and put them in the care of the headman of Ban Hong. Several months later these cattle were sold for 1,500 *baht*. The Thai took his original 800 *baht* and half of the 700 *baht* gross profit, leaving half with the Ban Hong headman who thus received 350 *baht* for his efforts. Since the headman owns buffalo for use in the fields, he was already prepared to care for the animals. This arrangement is always between two individuals, one Karen and another Karen or Thai.

The other technique is a little more complicated. Several Karen borrow a large amount of money from a Thai or several Thai which is exchanged for gold in Chiengmai. The group will then trek across the mountains to the Burma border; there, the gold is exchanged for cattle and other minor items which are brought back and sold in Thailand. This arrangement requires that the Karen pay a tax to the Thai government of 50 *baht*. They reimburse the Thai from whom they borrowed the money at the rate of 5 percent per month per 100 *baht*. This could mount up fairly rapidly, since large sums are borrowed and since it takes a while to make the round trip and sell the animals. Nevertheless, there is considerable buying and selling and the Karen realize at least a small profit.

The Karen tend to be reticent about matters involving large amounts of money, but those who make these trips do not ordinarily go more than once or twice a year. An individual profit is from 500 *baht* to 1,000 *baht* according to one informant, although it is probably closer to the lower figure. This long-distance trading is always a group activity. The individuals involved may be members of a single household, a lineage segment, a friendship group, or a combination of these. People from not more than six households in Ban Hong make these trips, and of these, trading is practiced regularly by only three or four households. Individuals from Dong Dam or Hui Sai are usually in the group, too.

Pigs

The ownership, care, and handling of pigs (except for butchering) are entirely in the hands of women. Table 9 shows how many pigs are owned by the various households. In the past, pigs were kept for use in ceremonies of various sorts including weddings, funerals, and lineage ceremony. They are still used for these purposes, but more often today chicken is substituted for pork; this is because, at present, swine are raised to be sold to the Thai, and the Karen cannot afford to use them in ceremonies as often as they once did.

Pigs are kept in a pen only while they are small or are unaccustomed to their owner. Otherwise, they are allowed to roam

TABLE 9 Pig Population

Household	No. of Pigs	Household	No. of Pigs
H–1	2	H–15	1
H–2	3	H–16	2
H–4	1	H–18	2
H–5	1	H–19	1
H–6	2	H–21	1
H–8	2	H–22	2
H–9	1	H–26	2
H–12	1	H–27	1

and forage for themselves during the daytime. There is no special area set aside for them, only places where they must not go, thus requiring fencing of gardens.

Favorite pig foods are banana tree trunks and unripe papaya. In the evening, the women who own pigs may be seen cooking one or the other of these foods on the ground near the house. When it is thoroughly cooked, the pigs are called if they are not already at hand, and are fed a little at a time in a small wooden dug-out trough. The owner supervises the whole feeding to be sure all pigs get their proper share.

The men of the house construct the pigpen with small hardwood poles obtained from the jungle. If a household does not have enough banana tree stalks for pig food, the men will buy some from time to time for 1 *baht*. Green papaya and various succulent grasses or weeds are collected almost daily by the women and children of the household. Sticks are used to knock down the papaya, and knives are used to cut the weeds. Three large stones hold the five-gallon kerosene cooking can over the fire. The cans are bought in the bazaar for 1 *baht*. It takes about an hour daily to cook the food or gather plants to feed the pigs.

A large fat pig may sell for 150 *baht* ($7.50) or more, and a young piglet may be bought for 50 *baht* or less. The speculation techniques used for oxen are also used for pigs at times. Thus, a Karen from Hui Sai bought a pig for 50 *baht* and took it to the headman in Ban Hong to be raised. When the pig is sold, the buyer will keep his 50 *baht* investment, and he and the headman will split the profit equally.

Some pigs may be lost due to disease. In 1961, a disease swept through Ban Hong and one or two other villages. All the pigs either died or were sold and butchered, but at a considerable loss to the owners. This was a tragedy to the village as it was believed that a custom had been broken. This caused the spirits to punish the village, and thus these village spirits had to be propitiated. It was several months before anyone attempted to start raising pigs again in the village.

Chickens

Chickens are individually owned and are the only fowl kept by Karen. Traditionally, chickens, like pigs, were kept for ceremonial purposes, and today the Karen would not think of eating chicken without having an accompanying ceremony.[7] Although the Karen do not eat eggs (with one rare ceremonial exception adopted from the Thai), the Thai do, and so the sale of eggs is one source of income to all villagers who keep chickens. In addition to eggs, the Ban Hong villagers sell chickens from time to time in the bazaar.

In the daytime, chickens wander freely and eat insects and scraps which they find in and around the village. In the evening, just before dark, they are called and fed a little broken rice or bran by the women who own them. Chickens require no special land since there are no chicken pens or yards, and they require little labor and capital outlay. At night, when the chickens roost, there is physical separation and sorting out; for ideological reasons, chickens must sleep at the household where they belong. Each chicken or each hen and chicks has an individual basket in which to spend the night. These baskets are the shape of overgrown pumpkins and are made by the men of the household with finely woven bamboo. There is a small opening in the top which may be closed with two or three bamboo needles stuck through the basket. These baskets are long-lasting, and the workmanship is fine enough that if a chicken buyer wants the basket too he must pay for it separately.

The women see to it that their chickens are fed and put in their baskets every night. If a hen is setting, she will be kept in the basket and fed there. Karen usually do not buy chicks if they have hens. The chicken population varies from year to year and sometimes from day to day, but at any one time, about half the households in Ban Hong will be raising chickens. In November, 1960, there was an epidemic of chicken cholera, and as a result of the decreased chicken population in Wang Lung and Ban Hong, the price went up 1 or 2 *baht* each.

The price of eggs is rather stable at 2½ cents apiece, and chickens sell for 5 to 10 *baht* (25 to 50 cents) each in the bazaar. There are times when chickens are sold to other Karen for 1 *baht* or perhaps 2 *baht*. This occurs during special occasions when chickens must be used in a ceremony. The chickens are much younger and smaller than those sold in the market. The real point, however, is that in sacrificing a chicken one must use his own chickens. This is important, otherwise the ceremony will not have the desired effect.[8] Therefore, no one asks for chickens, even on "credit." One must either pay for a chicken when he receives it, or he must raise his own.

Dogs

Every household has one or more dogs which are kept for two purposes. The first is to warn the householder or village that strangers are approaching. Occasionally, animals and other items are stolen at night, but thieves must be very stealthy to avoid the numerous village dogs. Dogs thus serve an economic function of an alarm system.

The second reason for keeping dogs is that they are good scavengers and eat discarded food around the house. The pigs and chickens, of course, help them in this task. Dogs (as well as pigs) eat human feces and thereby help keep houses and grounds clean.

A possible third reason for keeping dogs (which no longer exists on the plains to my knowledge) is for food at a wedding feast. The term for wedding in Karen means "eat dog, eat pork." Today, it is considered proper to have a pork curry. Chicken or ox are sometimes substituted, but are considered unorthodox and improper at weddings.

Dogs require and receive very little care. When a puppy is being trained to belong to a household, it is fed a little supplementary food along with the pigs. Beyond that, no labor or capital is expended on dogs, and as they get older they must fend almost entirely for their miserable selves.

HUNTING AND GATHERING

All Karen, young and old, male and female, participate in hunting or gathering. This may be done individually or in groups, depending on the particular activity or upon the inclination of the individual.

Hunting

Northern Thailand still has abundant forest and mountain areas which have game of various sorts. In populated areas, of course, the game decreases, so the hunters must travel long distances. The Karen in the Hod plain still hunt, but it is no longer very important to the diet. In the mountains, however, the Karen depend much more on hunted game, but even there agriculture is still the more important form of subsistence.

Ecology and Economic Activities 83

The Karen in Ban Hong hunt birds, squirrels, lizards of various sorts, and sometimes monkey. No large animals are hunted by the villagers. Only the men and boys go hunting, and they go only when agricultural activities are not pressing. There are no guns of any sort in the village; there is one old rifle in Dong Dam across the river, but it is seldom used. Many of the boys in the village have slingshots made of buffalo horn which are used for hunting birds. There is a bow-sling which shoots stones instead of arrows which most of the villagers have. It is reported that this was once used for hunting birds, but at present it is used only for chasing cattle away from gardens and fields. The cross-bow, which is made in the household, is the only instrument seriously used in the hunt. Ad hoc groups go out from time to time to hunt squirrel or birds. A man and his son sometimes go as a lone pair. Nothing is ever sold from the hunt except baby gibbons and monkeys, and these are rarely caught.

Gathering and Collecting

Gathering is much more important to the Karen of Ban Hong and surrounding villages than is hunting. Collecting provides a supplement to the rice diet when all else is gone. In general, the items collected are roots and leaves of various sorts, bamboo shoots, herbs and bark for medicinal purposes, wild fruit, frogs, small lizards, insects of several varieties, paddy crabs, ant larvae, honey, mushrooms, firewood, weeds for pig food, and even snake at times.

The land requirements for gathering foods are large areas of relatively uninhabited or "undisturbed" jungle and hill. There are no private collecting areas set aside for individuals or villages. If one claims a beehive or ant nest, however, others will respect this claim.

Collecting is done mainly by the women and children of a household for consumption in the household, but there are several notable exceptions. Frogs are always caught at night during the rainy season by parties of whole households or several households. Certain herbs and barks that are used for medicine are collected by men. One type of wild yam is collected by men only, because they must travel a relatively long distance and the yams are heavy.

Capital goods required for the various collecting activities are few. Torches of burning bamboo sticks or small tin kerosene lamps are used in collecting frogs. A metal-tipped digging stick is used for several varieties of tubers and some ground-living insects. An ingenious bamboo trap is used to catch underground lizards. For collecting new leaves from trees, a long bamboo pole with a "v" curve cut in one end is used. A stick found along the way may be used to knock fruit from a tree. The machete is used for nearly all activities in one way or another. Bamboo withes and sticks are used for stringing frogs, insects, mushrooms, and so forth. Baskets of various types or Karen cloth bags are used for transport. Yield varies considerably due to the uncertainty involved. Collecting of some sort goes on throughout the year, and the yield supplements garden items sufficiently so that almost no food other than rice is purchased. Beyond this, some things are collected specifically to be sold, and occasionally some food items are collected in abundance and sold in the bazaar. Generally, however, the unit of distribution and consumption is the household.

FISHING

Fishing techniques are well developed among the Karen, and one sort or another is practiced throughout the year.

There is one technique, pond fishing, that requires area rights. During the dry season when the river level is low, a pond is made in the river by forming sand banks around an area of water. This is done by dredging and piling sand. A small opening is left in one end so that fish may swim into the pond, which may be fifty yards long and ten yards wide. The pond is made ineffective when the water rises due to the rains, and one's area rights end at this point. The next year a pond may be constructed elsewhere. One may stake his claim to an area in the river by marking it with a taboo sign. This consists of a bamboo pole with a star-shaped design on top of it, also made of bamboo, which is about eight inches in diameter. No other type of fishing has water rights.

Other methods of fishing are: short and long pole with line and hook, throw-net, fish trapping, and "surround." The "surround" method consists of using a long rope with long thin leaves attached to scare the fish into one small area. This is used on conjunction with the throw-net. The final method is paddy fishing with baskets.

The organization of labor varies with the technique used. Pole fishing is done by one person, and little time is actually spent in fishing this way. A person takes his pole or poles to a spot where the water is deep near the shore. The poles are stuck in the ground, and the hook, which is allowed to dangle in the water, is occasionally checked for results.

The throw-net, when used alone, is manipulated by one person. Usually, however, a couple of friends go fishing together, each with his own net. When the net is used in conjunction with a "surround," at least three people are required; one for each end of the surround rope, and one with a throw-net. This group may be only a conglomerate group of friends, or it may be a group of brothers-in-law.

Catching fish with traps is the work of the men in one household. Only one person is required to build, set, and check the traps from time to time, but if a boat must be used in deeper water, two people may check the traps for fish caught.

At least two people are required to make a fish pond, due to the method of dredging the sand and making the banks of the pond. The shore of the river provides one side of the pond, and a natural sandbar may provide another. The sand removal is done with an instrument which looks like a bamboo snow shovel. One man pushes on the long handle while another directs and pulls the blade of the instrument by using a rope attached to its bottom. When the place for the wall of the pond is reached, this man pulls up on the rope, which raises the blade, and the sand is deposited, forming a dike. It may take a couple of days or more to make the pond. Fish may be driven in the entrance of the pond by using a "surround." When fish are to be caught in the pond, the entrance of the pond is blocked with a loosely woven bamboo gate. Fish may be caught in the pond by using throw nets, or by using a plant which is poison to fish but harmless to people. One may not use a fish pond without permission of the owner, and a pond may be owned by more than one household.

The final technique is that of paddy fishing. The women and children of households which own paddy fields, or other individuals with permission, use tapered baskets that are completely open at the large end. These baskets are clamped down in the flooded field from place to place. Then one puts his hand through a small hole in the upper end of the basket and catches any fish or crabs that may have been trapped. These are then stored in another basket.[9]

The capital requirements for fishing are as follows. Bamboo fishing poles are made from local material, but lines and hooks are bought in the bazaar. The instrument for making a fish pond is made from local bamboo. Rope used in the "surround" is made of jute collected in the jungle, or from a tree owned by a villager. The leaves for the "surround" are found in the local area. The throw-net is bought in the market, but lead weights are melted and molded by men of the household; old flashlight batteries and other scraps collected from Thai provide the metal. Fish traps are made of bamboo, as are the baskets of various sorts used in fishing or in storing the fish. The plant used for poisoning the fish grows wild and is collected.

Fish is an important element in the Karen diet, but there are times when people catch fish specifically to sell in the bazaar. Small fish, about six inches long, sell for about 1 *baht* for six to eight fish; larger fish sell for more. It must be remembered that the Thai fish also, so there is not much income from the sale of fish. Most of those caught are consumed in the household.

DOMESTIC ACTIVITIES

Weaving

Weaving, which is done only by women, is carried on throughout most of the year, except during the peak periods of planting and harvesting. Weaving is entirely a household matter. Distribution and consumption are a little more complicated, but this will be discussed later. Mother and daughter or two sisters may weave side by side under a house, each using a simple belt loom.

The woven articles include the married women's skirts and blouses, two types of blouses for men, men's skirts, unmarried girl's dresses, blankets, and shoulder bags. Clothing for young boys is merely a smaller version of one type of men's blouse. Traditional Karen clothing and its variations (made specifically for the market) are currently sold in the local bazaars and in Chiengmai.

A few Karen in Ban Hong grow cotton and spin thread for weaving, but most thread is bought in the local Thai bazaar. Often dye is no longer homemade but is also purchased. (Appendix I is a summary of the woven goods, their costs and labor, and the prices asked.) The Karen woven products most desired by the Thai are the shoulder bags, variations of the married women's skirt, and the men's jacket. The "variations" are non-traditional and are not worn by Karen.

The women weave most of the clothing for their own household members, though men often wear clothes bought in the bazaar. Women also weave extensively for the market, however, and they report that they now weave much more than before, thereby supplementing the household income. The sales are always made to Thai, for Karen never buy woven goods from each other. A salesman from the village usually acts as agent for several women; a woman may, however, take her goods to the local bazaar from time to time and sell them directly. Or a Thai may at times contract with a particular women to weave an item. The Thai may supply the yarn and will agree upon the price before the job is undertaken. Because of the absence of kinship obligations, the Thai never pay in advance. Woven goods occasionally find their way to Chiengmai, to Bangkok, and beyond.

Tool Manufacture

Men make most tools and implements including jute rope, basketry of various types, fish traps and weirs of bamboo, plows, harrows, and yokes of hardwood. Looms and wooden spinning equipment are homemade or purchased from other Karen. Various other types of household goods made of wood, bamboo, gourds, coconut shells, and so on, are made in the household.

These items are made for household use, and most require only one person for their manufacture. The raw materials are generally available in the surrounding jungle. The major tool used in all manufacture is the all-important machete. Tool and implement manufacture is done when necessary, but is carried on mainly in the rainy season when there is a lull in field and garden work.

Construction

The major structures made by the Karen are houses, fences, rice granaries, animal corrals and food lofts, and water wheels. All of these except houses and granaries have already been discussed.

When a family decides to build a new house, a great deal of assembling materials and prefabrication go on over several months by close relatives and friends. House posts are picked, cut, notched for crossbeams, and allowed to dry out. Bamboo is secured and split for walls and flooring. The long grass used for thatch is gathered, and the thatch sheets are made for roofing.[10] This thatch roofing may be made by both men and women in their spare time. However, a household may have a thatch-making party on some moonlit night. The word is passed around that thatch is to be made by a household; then all the older unmarried boys and girls who are able will assemble and have a good time chatting and teasing while they work. The boys and girls are not paid for their labor, although the householder may provide tobacco, betel, or fermented tea. Later, the children of the householder will in turn help someone else at the same task. Adults never participate in this work party, but some may assemble on the porch to chat and chew.

When the day comes to put up the house, the word is passed and at least one male from each household comes to help. The house is assembled and built in one day.

Nowadays, it usually requires cash to build a new house because some materials must be bought, food must be supplied, and tobacco, and so on, must be available. If a person does not have enough bamboo of his own, he must buy it from other Karen or Thai. Table 10 shows the costs of a sample of houses in Ban

Hong. The costs listed are approximate and include materials and food:

TABLE 10 House Construction Costs

H–21 cost 200+ *baht*	
H–15 cost 300+ *baht*	
H–24 cost 100+ *baht*	
H–17 cost 400+ *baht*	
H–28 cost 100+ *baht*	
H–35 cost 50+ *baht*	

Construction of a rice granary is basically similar to that of a house. Since it is smaller and less elaborate, it takes less time and is not as costly. A few men who are free help in the prefabrication and construction when that day comes; it is not the occasion for a village work day.

Village Work

Two or three times each year, at least one male member of each household will assemble for two types of cooperative communal work. These include, first, a general village cleanup which includes cutting and clearing underbrush and repairing the two main path entrances to the village. The second task is to repair the village spirit houses and to clear the surrounding area where the all-village ceremonies are held. This latter task is just prior to the ceremony which is normally held twice a year. The only tools required for these jobs are machetes, hoes, and sometimes digging stocks. Of course, bamboo and thatch are needed to rebuild or repair the spirit houses. These materials are supplied by the village headman, but money comes from a general fund kept by the headman and collected from villagers.

Specialist Services

The services performed by the various specialists (to be named and discussed in Chapter 6) are "paid for," at least in part, by greater respect and prestige given to the specialist. Currently these services have also acquired an economic aspect, as the specialist may now receive some goods or money too. Increased respect or prestige may have direct or indirect economic or social effects such as first choice in land for swidden, a larger share of pork at a feast, a favored seat at a ceremony, etc. Although the pay in money or goods is easier to measure, it is not as simple as that, because payment may continue over a long period and it is difficult to tell whether one is paid for past services, or for expected ones in the future. The immediate pay for a service can be stated, of course, if there is such, but this varies from specialist to specialist and is different for various types of services performed. The point is that specialists are generally in a favorable position economically as well as socially.

NOTES

[1] I collected paddy soil samples in 1961 and again in 1969 after the flooding. Neutralizable acidity in 1961 was 4.0. In 1969, it was 7.0. In a swidden soil sample collected in 1961, the acidity was 1.5 (swidden was not retested in 1969 since so very few were making swidden and since the flooding had not affected previous swidden areas). In all cases, the soils were deficient in calcium and potassium for good crops. Soil analyses were conducted by the University of Missouri—Extension Division, Columbia, Missouri.

[2] For a general discussion of plant domestication in the Orient and the general spread of usable plants, see Spencer (1962:88 ff.), and see his bibliography.

[3] Only a few permanent gardens are located on Figure 3.

[4] When I first heard these stories, it was Mang Thi's father who settled and cleared the land. It seems that a generation, or perhaps more, is being lost as time passes. It may even be an older ancestor than the grandfather who founded Ban Hong, however, the retelling of the events by different informants in consistently the same way implies that the sequence is essentially correct, even if the time may be slightly compressed.

[5] One *rai* is equivalent to .4 acre, or, one acre equals 2.5 *rai* (Kingshill 1960:234).

[6] Currently there is some encroachment into Ban Hong swidden land on the part of local Thai to plant peanuts. They apparently do not use it for dry-rice, although some Thai do practice swidden cultivation too.

[7] My wife and I liked the chicken curry, so we asked a Karen family to make some in our presence in order that we could obtain the recipe. The family agreed on the condition that they have a wrist-tying ceremony, since they were going to cook chicken. I was, therefore, able to observe a ceremony in detail as well as obtain the recipe.

[8] When the work season involving water buffalo is finished, a special ceremony is held for the animals in the household of the owners. Part of the ceremony involves the sacrifice of two chickens. When H–7 had his ceremony, I provided the two chickens because the old man had done many things for me. The man appeared reticent to accept but finally agreed. A short time after the ceremony his buffalo became ill, "because he did not use his own chickens." The ceremony had to be done again in order for the buffalo to get well, and fortunately it did. Thereafter, no karen wanted free chickens from us, but they did buy our chickens for ceremonies.

[9] The Karen know about the Thai dip-net, twist-net, and dynamite fishing techniques, but seldom use them.

[10] At times, for temporary repair or for paddy-field houses during peak season, large leaves woven into sheets are used for roofing.

4

The Geometry of Kinship and Descent

INTRODUCTION

This chapter is concerned with the abstract principles on which Karen conceptions of relationship and descent rest, and on which the substantive groups are formed. The principles may be conceived as dealing with "lines," "groups," "sets," "relations," and "affinities"; which explains the use of the term *geometry* in the title. These abstract principles, however, must be derived from concrete data. There will, therefore, be some discussion here of substantive relationships from which the abstract principles are derived. It is true, however, that the structural ideology is not obvious from analysis of the substantive groups and kin terminology. In fact, there is some controversy over whether or not the Pwo Karen ought to be considered matrilineal. Lehman (1971:34–39) does not believe they should be so considered. However, in agreement with my findings, Hinton (1969:14 ff.), discusses the matrilineage among more remote Pwo Karen.

This chapter will conclude that the Pwo Karen have a cognatic or bilateral system of filiation, but that descent is matrilineal.[1] Now, there is a theoretical problem involved in this controversy and that is the issue of the analyst's conception versus that of the native. We might say with Fortes that ". . . filiation originates in the domestic domain, descent in the politico-jural domain . . ." and go on from there in determining descent and filiation in a given society. This bases the determination on structural-functional criteria set up by the analyst. Or, we may use purely linguistic criteria (i. e., terminology) as Lehman does, and say that

> . . . the term *descent* must mathematically be kept as meaning precisely the whole set of ordered rules that generate the culture-specific kin-category system mapping the infinite set of universal geneological kin-terms into the finite culturally specific set of categories. . . . Note that I am talking about the system of descent as coextensive with the entire k[in]-system of labelled k[in]-categories (Lehman, 1973).

It seems to me that both approaches are too rigid and arbitrary and ignore the empirical data of the actual behavioral relationships, ideological conceptions, and substantive groups from which the operating principles must be derived. Looking at the Karen data, Fortes's statement leads one to assume a priori unilineal descent, and Lehman's statement leads one to assume a priori cognatic descent. The actual operating principles need not be entirely "conscious" (as phoanemes, for example, are not), but they must be verifiable if they are to be considered causative. There is, therefore, a methodological problem as well as the theoretical one, and that is the issue of verification from the native informants. I hope this chapter will resolve the issue. It will at least enjoin it. A more detailed discussion of the nature of the substantive residential groups of Pwo Karen society will follow this chapter, and they will add detail to the arguments presented here.

KINSHIP TERMINOLOGY

The kinship terminological network (see Figure 5) is based on the following distinctions: Ego (male or female) distinguishes *Fa* from *FaBr*. He equates *FaBr* and *MoBr*. Ego calls Mo *mu*; he calls *FaSi* and *MoSi mu* plus a number suffix (relative to the birth order of either *Fa* or *Mo*). Ego calls *GrFa* (paternal and maternal) by one term, and he calls *GrMo* (paternal and maternal) by another term. *GrFaBr* and *GrFa* are equated, and *GrMoSi* is equated with *GrMo*. Ego equates *GrFaSi* with *GrMo*, and he equates *GrMoBr* with *GrFa*. A suffix is added to the terms for *GrFa* and *GrMo* to distinguish *GrGrFa* and *GrGrMo*. He equates grandparents' sibling's *So* with *FaBr* (or *MoBr*). He equates grandparents' siblings *Da* with *Mo* (plus the proper suffix).

Ego distinguishes his *Br* and *Si* by birth order only (relative to himself); the terms, therefore, gloss only as "older/younger sibling," but, if pressed, he adds a suffix to distinguish sex. Ego equates all cousins (cross, parallel, maternal, paternal) with one another, but again, if pressed, will add one of two suffixes to distinguish members of his lineage from nonmembers. He does not distinguish sex but can do so. *Br* and *Si* are distinguished from cousins. Ego distinguishes his own *Ch* (adding a suffix for sex) from *BrCh* and *SiCh*. He equates *Ch* of his *Br* and *Si* with *Ch* of his cousins. Ego is able to and may count down three more "generations" with a separate term for each generation, which equates all children in each generation. This is conceived as affiliation, however, not descent. Ego may use the term *li* (own *GrCh*) for all small children.

Birth order is important, but is usually used only in the first ascending and descending generation. A parent always knows and takes account of birth order of his own generation.[2] According to Murdock's terminology, this is a lineal system, and

FIGURE 5 Kinship Terminology

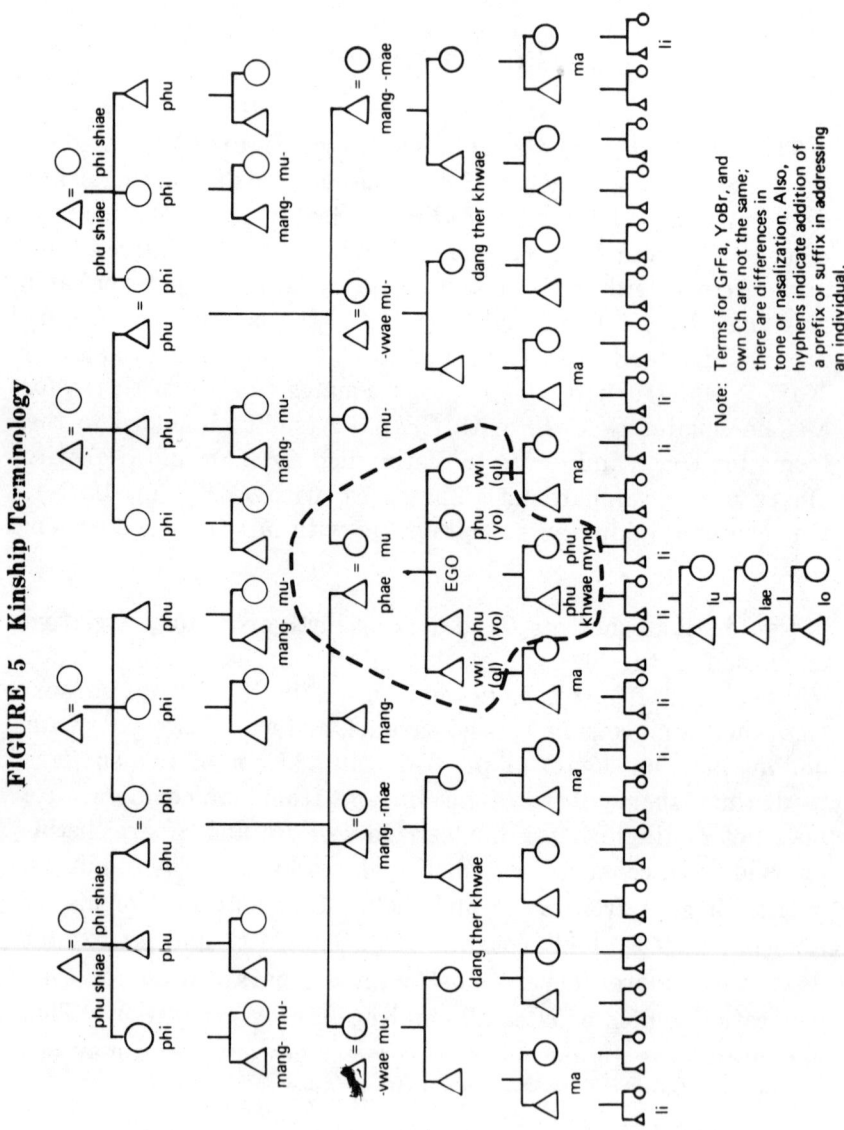

the so-called "kinship structure" is basically normal Nankanese (see Murdock 1949:142, 241).

An obvious and major function of the kinship network is that of linkage. Through the network individuals are able to interact in predetermined, predictable ways, and the kin system is extended to Karen who are nonkin in order to allow interaction.

The network of bilateral kin terms is focused through the recognition of the relationship between a man, a woman, and their children, as well as the surrounding set of relatives of the husband and wife. The bilateral kinship network, even though it contains a genealogical component, does not result in a sociologically significant descent group (unless the nuclear family be considered a "descent group"). It leads rather to a system of filiation, consisting of a set of statuses with correlative behavior patterns for structuring relationships (see "Karenness" below). A marriage unites two matrilineal descent lines (note that I did not say descent "groups"; see "Lineage" below). However, the actual residential groups which are thus united are two lineages segments (see below p. 132), and the offspring of a marriage are affiliated with both, but trace descent only from one.

Scheffler (1966:542–43) in trying to deal with this issue points out that

> Descent-constructs [meaning locally recognized *"genealogical continua* connecting persons with their ancestors"] should not be confused with the simple recognition of several filial steps, which is a more general phenomenon constituting the basis of what we call kinship. . . . A parent . . . may be both a "parent" and an "ancestor" (or either/or), depending upon the context. . . . Likewise, a grandparent may be either the "parent of a parent", linked only by successive filial ties, or an "ancestor," linked by descent. . . . In other words, a parent may be linked to his or her child by descent ties or filial ties, and the former occurs where their position in a genealogical *continuum* is at issue . . ..

In the Pwo Karen case, a person is *affiliated* with his father, and paternal relatives, but is *descended* from his mother, and maternal relatives. The ritual surrounding the substantive groups makes this clear (see p. 138).

DANG RELATIONS

Beside specific kin-pair relationships, which determine and regulate behavior, cooperation, and so on, there is also a set of connections between individuals on the basis of kin category membership. When there is a marriage, a *dang dông* is formed. This means "related lineages," or "related families." The two individuals who married are called *dang mae vwae*, which means "related wife and husband." A person calls his sibling's parents-in-law *mi dông*, and the reciprocal is *law dông*. A group of brothers and sisters is called *dang phu vwi*, which means "related younger and older." Finally, there are two types of cousin sets: one is the *dang thê khwae baw'*, which are lineage-mates (a person may not marry within this group) and the *dang thê khwae jai*, a set of cousins who may intermarry, and are not lineage-mates. Various kinds of behavior are determined by these *dang* relationships.

The grouping and relationship of cousins is important to the Karen. There is a general term for the children of a set of brothers and sisters, which is *dang thê khwae*.[3] If these cousins are children of a brother and sister or of two brothers, they are called *dang thê khwae jai* (the last meaning "far"). If they are children of sisters, they are called *dang thê khwae baw'* (the last term meaning "close"). The *dang thê khwae baw'* group are members of the same lineage. The others are not. Children of *dang thê khwae* are called, or call each other, *khi thê khwae*. Finally, children of *li thê khwae* are called *je thê khwae*. There no other phrases used. The initial term in each of these expressions is a number ("one" is taken for granted) starting with *khi* which means "two"; *öa* means "three"; *li* is the word for "four"; and the number five is denoted by *je*. The phrases, then, count the cousin sets, each group more inclusive than the last.[4] However, in everyday usage the general phrase *dang thê khwae* is used, no matter what the actual *thê khwae* relationship is.

The degree of closeness of cousin relationship therefore, may be stated, or determined, by the nearest *thê khwae* relationship between individuals. Individuals may still be *baw'* or *jai*, no matter what degree of *thê khwae* relationships they may have, because "close" or "distant" is determined by whether or not they are related through males or females. This, of course, states lineage relationships between cousins.

DESCENT

The Karen kinship terminology might lead one to believe that descent is reckoned cognatically because of the bilateral nature of the terminology. However, on the basis of marriage restrictions, and ritual one would assume that descent is matrilineal. A person is descended from his mother and her relatives. If a man and woman are directly related to each other through a pair of sisters and through women on each side, then the couple should not marry because they are members of the same *lê dong* (lineage or "family").[5] However, if only one male "breaks" the descent chain, they may marry.[6]

The apparent dilemma between bilateral terminology and matrilineal descent is resolved if it be admitted that a person may be "related to" or "affiliated with" both father's and mother's relatives, but that he is "descended" only from mother's relatives. A person is affiliated with his father because this man married the person's mother. There is no conflict in these two systems of relationship. They serve complementary functions. A person is a member of a lineage by virtue of descent, or actual genealogical connection. On the other hand, one may be affiliated with a household, a lineage segment, a village, and a village-complex, through marriage, residence and ritual. Children, of course, are connected to a household, aside from residence, via descent from their mother, and women are connected to a lineage segment, besides via residence, through descent. Married men are connected only by filiation to the substantive groups.

THE LINEAGE

In discussing what I have called the "lineage," I may be treading on a transitional area between the principles or ideology of relationship on one hand, and substantive groups on the other. Technically, however, lineages are not "groups" but rather sets of individuals. At any rate, the lineages are not named but the term for "lineage" is lê dong.[7] In trying to discover the meaning of this term, I was given the analogy of a hen and her chicks. When I asked if the rooster, which had fertilized the eggs, was part of the lê dong, the Karen laughed: he belonged to the lê dong of *his* mother. In trying to determine the abstract principle (rule) underlying the terms, I was given a concrete "grouping" in explanation. But this is still abstract, and not equivalent to the lineage segment, because that substantive group does include males-married-in.

The lê dong, then is an exogamous matrilineal descent line, not a "descent group" proper as discussed by Scheffler (1966:543). Membership, which includes males and females, is by birth only. Since it is an exogamous group, and since marital residence is generally matrilocal, the lineage could never be a residence group for both male and female members. As it turns out, it is not a residence unit in any sense, because its members are spread around in different villages. A further characteristic of the social structure which assures that the lineage is nonlocal, even for women, is that a brother or son normally succeeds the village headman, so wives must be brought into the village. Thus several matrilines are represented in any village. However, a village tends to form around one main lineage. In the past this tendency may have been more pronounced. Today, there are economic reasons also for not following the traditional residence pattern and so more reasons why the lineage is nonlocalized. In most, if not all, cases, one can trace his or her actual relationship to others of the lineage, but if one could not he would theoretically still know all other members by whether or not they have the same lineage head.

The traditional rule for lineage head succession is simple and straightforward. The oldest living woman in the oldest generation in a lineage must be the head. She is called the *thê myng xae a 'khu*, or "head of the female spirits". However, there is apparently confusion at times concerning succession. For example, I was told of a case in which a lineage head died. It was believed that she was the last woman in her generation, so a woman in the next generation (presumably her daughter, since it goes through sisters, then daughters) became the new head. However, in a short time she died and her sister became the new head. However, in a short time she died and her sister became head; she, in turn, died shortly thereafter. Lineage members consulted a spirit medium and found a living sister of the first head who had died. This woman became head of the lineage and all was well again.[8]

Lehman, who is not convinced that the Pwo Karen should be considered matrilineal, in commenting on my data, said (personal communication, 1973):

> In fact the "lineages" are clearly successions of (residential) families, and the families are matrilocal on, roughly, the grounds that (a) women are (using a Chin expression) "inside-house" people. Therefore, properly most close to house-spirits; hence (b) one ought to reside near one's own (spirits) inside-house controllers, in the sense that there should be a natural succession of such persons.

Now, first of all, I think that Lehman has confused lineage with what I have called lineage segment. The lineage is *not*, and cannot be, a residence group. It is a set of individuals, related through females having the same spiritual head. One may become a member of this set of individuals *only* by birth. A lineage segment, on the other hand, is a residential manifestation of the lineage, but it includes non-lineage members in the form of husbands and sons-in-law. A "young" lineage segment may consist merely of a single house with a wife, her husband and children. Only the wife and her children are members of the lineage, however. An "older" lineage segment may consist of the house of a woman, and the surrounding houses of her married daughters. Men do not become members of a lineage by marriage (they remain lineage members of their natal matri-group), but they do become members of a residential lineage segment this way.

Secondly, there is only *one house* in the whole lineage, that of the lineage head, that contains the ritual place of propitiation for the lineage spirits, and only the lineage head may perform the ceremonies. There are, of course, house spirits residing in every Karen house, but these must be thought of as the animate force of the house (a house is not an inanimate object as we conceive it), and not lineage spirits. The house spirit may be given an offering of rice liquor by any elder in the *di.lang thê* ceremony for the protection and good fortune of *all* household members. The lineage ceremony, however, excludes nonmembers.

A lineage is nearly always represented by its segments in more than one village, and there may be separate segments of a lineage in a single village. The segment is a cluster of houses; the lineage is a descent line.

LINEAGE FUNCTIONS

The woman who is head of a lineage keeps a small spirit house inside her own house for the *thê myng xae,* or spirits (ancestors) of the lineage. At times of serious illness to a lineage member the lineage head will perform a special ceremony at which a pig is killed and sacrificed. The curry remaining from the feast must be distributed to all lineage members to eat. This means it must be taken to several villages, sometimes at rather long distances, which serves to unite the whole lineage with a feeling of strength and well-being. When a marriage occurs, the lineage head must make a sacrifice to the spirits; this ceremony is performed by the lineage head of the bride, and by the lineage head of the groom. These are separate ceremonies, done at the houses of the two lineage heads, which sanctify the union of the two lineages. It is the lineage ancestral spirits that come to the final feast for the dead at a funeral (Hamilton, in press).

As a unit, the lineage has no specific economic functions, but the relationship of lineage mates allows, and sometimes demands, economic cooperation and aid. This means that any particular individual has many people on whom he can depend, in many villages, if the need arises. The political-legal aspects of the lineage might better be called social control, for the lineage has no specific political functions other than sanctioning or condemning individual behavior. However, since the lineage is not a residence unit, this function is minimal and is usually handled by the lineage segment, which includes nonlineage members, usually men. As mentioned, the lineage does regulate and validate marriage. The marriage union serves the important function of relating lineages to each other, thus allowing many ramifications for political relationships, economic aid, cooperation, ritual connections, and social discourse and control beyond that of even a single lineage.

Since the lineage is never a residential group it always crosscuts several villages and village-complexes, and thus ties together all the residential units through the connections of individuals within them.[9] Not only does the lineage link individuals in several villages through membership, but whole lineages have ties among otherwise unrelated individuals. A marriage is not just between individuals, or even just between households. A marriage links lineages, and special terms denote the relationships. Such links provide broad connections and provide a means of minimizing inter-group conflicts over territorial and other specific economic rights, as well as establishing political connections.

FRIENDSHIPS

A type of interrelationship beyond that of consanguineal, affinal, and residence group relationship is a quasi-kinship network. It is the status position of "friendship." There are at least two types of friendship relations.[10] One is an informal but intimate relationship between two or more males. It is usually a relationship which develops between young men, and between teenage boys, and it may last into old age. It may be a friendship group, and act as a "work-group" at times. It is not so formal that all men have such friends, but many sets of friends are found in Ban Hong. The relationship, although informal, is signaled by the use of a derogatory term between the friends. The word *thue*, which means "dog," is a typical one, and the use of such a term between others might cause a fight. The friends may be of the same or different villages, and they may, at the same time, be cousins of any type, but they need not be related. The content of the relationship has varied aspects. Friends visit back and forth; they go to ceremonies together; they go on trading trips together; they sometimes just go "visiting" (*li cai*), which is a favorite pasttime of Karen (and Thai) during

The Geometry of Kinship and Descent

leisure periods. This is the act of going to other villages, Karen or Thai, far or near, for the sheer pleasure of the trip. An important aspect of friendship relations is economic, however (see p. 135).

The second type of friendship, which may grow out of the first, is formalized by the typical ritual of drinking of each other's blood, and by pledging lifelong, undying loyalty between two men. The older members of Ban Hong know about blood brotherhood, and say that it persists in the hills, but that no one in

Midwife's new house under construction. Tradition requires each household to contribute labor to the building of all houses.

the village has a blood brother. Apparently, a man may develop such a relationship with more than one person. However, a group does not become blood brothers to each other. Person A may have brothers B and C, and Person B may have brothers A and D, or D and E, besides A. The dyadic blood brotherhood is a lifelong relationship, and it is said that the "brothers" cannot get angry with one another, and they completely trust and help each other. When two men decide to become blood brothers, each cuts his finger and lets the blood drip into a cup. The cups are exchanged and each person drinks the blood of the other. As they do this they make a pledge, saying "You will believe my

A village boy digging for edible insects.

The Geometry of Kinship and Descent

heart completely," "I will trust your heart completely," "We will truly and completely trust each other." The men in such a relationship stand up for each other in disputes or accusations. They will defend one another against violence, and protection and succor are supplied when one is in the home of the other. The relationship develops typically between men of distant villages, and the bond is said to be as close as or closer than that between true brothers. Again, the men may call each other by some derogatory term. The content of this relationship is similar to that mentioned above. The difference is that blood broth-

Headman's wife feeding her pigs.

Top: Village girl spinning cotton. *Bottom*: Weaving cotton cloth on Karen belt-loom.

The Geometry of Kinship and Descent

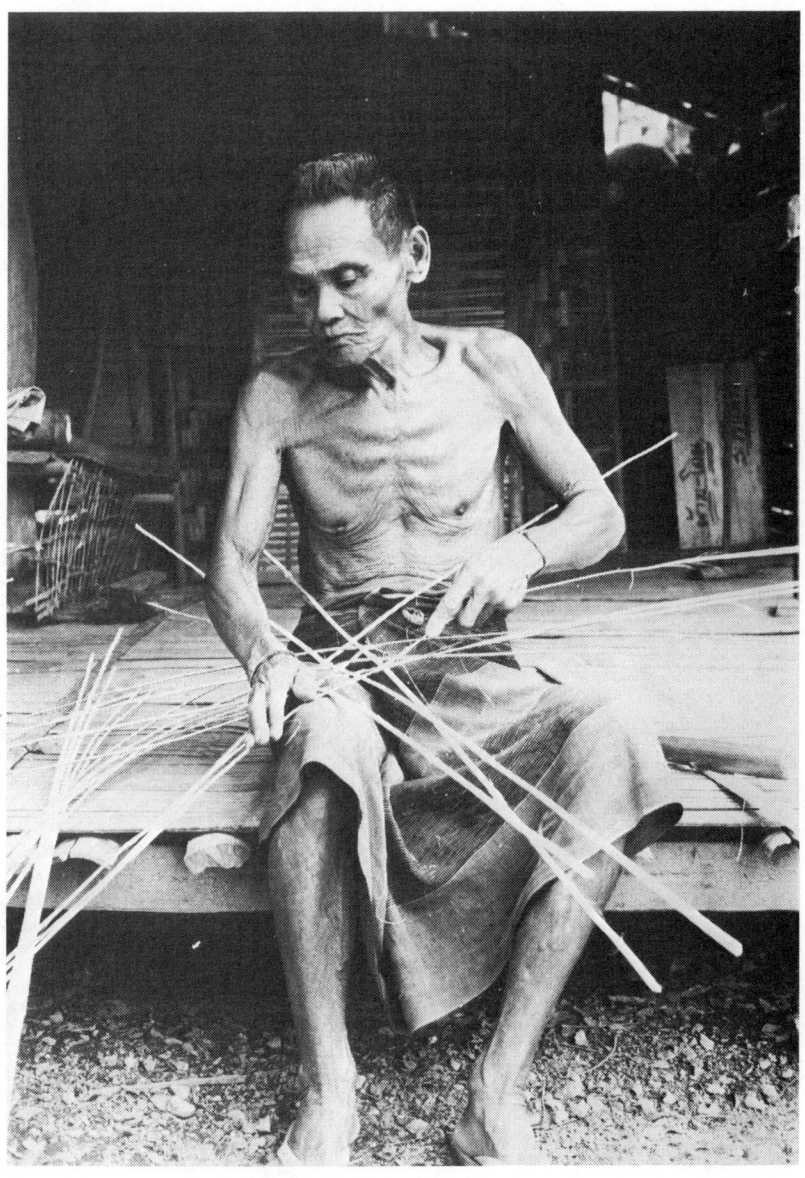

The head elder weaving a chicken basket.

Weaving fish trap. Material is split bamboo.

Weaving fish trap.

Headman displays his new fish trap.

erhood is, apparently, entered into later in life, is more serious, more lasting, and more formal.

The friendship statuses are a special kind of extension of kinship that links individuals for specific activities, usually economic at base, but sociability is involved too. Developing a friendship, or entering a blood brother relationship, are ways of linking two or more individuals, often living long distances apart, for mutual interdependence that could not be done any other way, given Karen culture.

New fish traps made by village headman to be used in the Ping River.

Villager on his way to tend garden. Mango trees and bamboo clumps are in the background.

"KARENNESS"

Another type of relationship I have named "Karenness." The tribal units are tribe, subtribe, and local subgroup, and in addition to providing the formal characteristics of the Karen group, also serve as status positions for individuals. Karenness is understood possibly at all three levels, but at least at the level of "*all-Karen*" (the tribe), and at the level of "all-Karen-most-like-me" (the local subgroup). Karenness is expressed or manifest in terms of custom, dress, kinship, and language similarities or differences. When two individuals meet on a path in the mountains they know immediately how to refer to one another, and this signals how they should behave toward one another. If one is a Karen and one is not, they will mistrust each other, and act in a rather formal manner.

If they are Karen of different groups, they may still mistrust each other, but will "feel" a kinship and will attempt to establish a relationship. The kin terminology is a characteristic of Karenness, and it serves the function of relating any Karen to any other Karen. By use or extension of kin terms, a Karen can interact with any other Karen in predictable ways. This is true whether or not actual relationship is known between them. Any person of Ego's grandparent generation is called by the term for grandparents.[11] A person of parent's generation is called by the term for *MoBr-FaBr*. A person of own generation is called by a neutral term for male (*khwae cô*), or female (*nang myng*). Finally, any person of Ego's child's generation is called *phu khwae* (little boy), or *phu myng* (little girl), terms which may be used in addressing his own child. Four terms, then, plus their correlatives and one or two for sex distinctions, are all that are needed to structure a relationship with an unknown Karen. Once the status relationship is set, on the basis of group identity, age, and sex, a pair of terms is picked and the two individuals can interact in many situations and ways known to both.[12] Karenness, then, is important as a distinction from such groups as Thai, Burmese, Lawa, and others, as well as making finer distinctions within the tribe and on the basis of age and sex. In short, Karenness enhances group solidarity, and is thought of as a status distinction.

The total Karen group includes perhaps two million individuals and it does not have a political superstructure. In one sense the total group is not held together at all, but in another it may be held together quite efficiently. Karenness has the socio-cultural function of distinguishing Karen from non-Karen; it serves to define a boundary. All within the boundary are Karen and are linked together in various ways and in various degrees. The whole group is, therefore, linked together via the defining characteristics of Karenness. Within this, finer distinctions and connections may be made.

NOTES

[1] Fortes says, for example, that "since the great majority of societies give jural recognition to the parenthood of both parents, filiation is normally bilateral, or as we might even say, equilateral" (Fortes, 1959:-206).

[2] The terms used to "count" children are used as names, or terms of reference, for the children, and other relative, to distinguish birth order, and are as follows (sex is not distinguished except in the case of first born): first born (male) is called *cô*. First born (female) is called *nang* (usually *nang myng*, which means "first born female"). Second child is called *pai'*. The third child is called *klae'*; the fourth is *long*; the fifth is *di'*; number six is called *no'*; the seventh is called *na'*; the last child (determined by the mother reaching menopause) is called *ö daê*. Children between the seventh and last are given irregular names. The terms are not numbers, but they do give birth order. Birth order is important to the Karen because there are status differences between older and younger people. The older must be respected, and so on, and the younger must be cared for, and so forth.

The first and last born are set apart because of special relationships to the parents. These two inherit more than the middle group of children. Even in the case of twins, one is older than the other. The twin who is born first is considered younger because this one must have entered the womb last in order to be born first.

³ The term *dang thê khwae* literally means "related thing male." However, the term *thê*, besides meaning "thing," is used as a prefix to form nouns (see also Jones 1961:25), so the term *thê khwae* is translated "cousin," and the whole term means "related cousins," including females. The term *dang myng dang khwae* is also used to mean the same thing, and is literally translated "related female related male." The term *dang thê khwae* is probably a shortening of the longer phrase.

⁴ Persons who are, for example, *khi thê khwae* in relation to a pair of siblings two generations above, may also be *dang thê khwae* if they are children of siblings of one ascending generation. However, two individuals who call each other *khi thê khwae* are not *dang thê khwae* also if their parents were not siblings.

⁵ Such marriages have occurred from time to time, as discussed on p. 126, but they are rare, and apparently considered incestuous, and the individuals must propitiate the spirits and live outside the village until a child is born.

⁶ A male does not really "break" a line of descent. It merely stops with him; his children trace descent through his wife, their mother. A man may not participate in the lineage ceremony of his wife and children; they may eat part of the lineage feast at home while the husband prepares his own meal.

⁷ The term *lê dong* here translated as "family" or "lineage" does not refer to a residence group, but to the group of persons related directly through women, wherever they may be residing.

⁸ It seems doubtful that this woman was a real sister of the previous head. This was probably a way of rationalizing the picking of a new head for the lineage. I suspect that this is the way in which new lineages form. The Karen do move around and lose connections, and I would guess that at a death it would be possible for two lineages to

result for distant groups of individuals. Confusion may also result if the daugther of a lineage head is younger than the daughter of a sister of the lineage head. However, this would probably be a "problem" only if there was a great discrepancy in age, since the Karen do not know their actual chronological ages. I also know of a case in Ban Hong in which a lineage ceased to exist when the head died with no living female relatives.

[9] The fact of nonlocal lineage relationships allows much greater flexibility for adaptation to stress, crisis, and threats of various sorts. When I arrived in Ban Hong there was only one lineage head in the village, with very few lineage members. This woman died during my stay, which left no lineage head in the village. During times of lineage ceremonies, for any lineage, every person in Ban Hong now has to go to some other village. The contacts and affiliations thus maintained are obvious. A Karen, a group of Karen, or a village, always has many more people to turn to for aid and sustenance than the local group implies.

[10] See also Marshall (1922:136–138) for a discussion of the possibility of a third such relationship, which he disputes, however.

[11] The oldest man in Ban Hong (H–33) is there only because he has no other place to go. His only living relative is a young man who is his ex-son-in-law. The old man moved to Ban Hong after his daughter died and his son-in-law remarried a girl of Ban Hong. Everyone calls this man by the term for grandfather.

[12] Once I was accepted into Ban Hong, by adhering to and practicing local customs, and by being informally adopted by the head elder, I was referred to as *mang cô* (uncle number one), or *phu öê dae* (youngest brother), or *naai* (a Thai term of respect) depending upon who was talking to me.

5

Household, Lineage Segment and Work Group

THE HOUSEHOLD

The household is the smallest residential unit of Ban Hong society. It is the minimum unit for economic production and consumption. The household is the smallest unit that must be represented politically; it is also the smallest unit of the village that must be represented ritually in every all-village ceremony, which occurs twice a year. It is a unit which produces, nurtures, and trains new members of Karen society. The household, in other words, performs some basic economic, political, ritual, and social functions necessary to maintain the society. The structural features and economic activities of the Ban Hong household, however, are the major concerns of this discussion. Ritual activities are deferred to the end of the chapter.

RESIDENCE

The household group lives in a separate house and ordinarily consists of wife, husband, and unmarried children. However, a new household does not usually form until a married couple has a child or two. Therefore some households include (besides parents and perhaps some unmarried children) a married daughter, her husband, and their children. There are other possible combinations which were noted and discussed in Chapter 2.

The composition of the household has an important relationship to the general rules and pattern of residence. The basic rule of post-marital residence is matrilocal, but some qualification is necessary in order to understand the Karen residence pattern. Of forty-one married women in Ban Hong on whom I have residence data, there are thirty-six whose mothers also live (or lived) in the village (see Appendix C). There are five whose mothers did not live in or come from Ban Hong. Of the forty-one men in these marriages, the mothers of twenty-two also live in or were from the village. Nineteen men have mothers from other villages. Endogamy and exogamy do not apply to the village as a whole. There are only twenty males in Ban Hong who moved from a different village when they married. There are twenty-one men who did not change village residence on marriage. Matrilocal residence, therefore, means about half of the time, that men merely change location within their own village. There are five families who have made permanent residence near the husband's parents. Of forty-two married couples, thirty-nine couples lived near the parents of the wife, but seventeen of these families also lived with the husband's parents for at least a while (see Appendix C).

The following generalizations can be made concerning marital residence: (1) immediately after marriage, a young couple may live with either set of parents for a time; (2) they never, at this point, set up residence away from both sets of parents-in-law, unless an illicit union has been made; (3) they are most likely to live with the wife's parents first; (4) they may go to live with the husband's parents for a short time later; (5) the woman most always stays in the village with her mother; (6) about half the time the man stays in the village of his birth; (7) almost always the couple makes permanent residence near the

Household, Lineage Segment and Work Group 121

wife's parents; (8) a group of sisters, their husbands, married daughters, and unmarried children, tend to form a residence cluster (group of households); (9) when both parents of this group of sisters have died, the sisters tend to disperse somewhat, each forming a nucleus for her own children and grandchildren; (10) sometimes, particularly in the household of the headman, a son or sons will be part of the extended family cluster or lineage segment.

In order to present a picture of the residence pattern over time, I will describe two case histories. First, the parents of the present headman of Ban Hong had nine children, four boys and five girls, all born in Ban Hong. All except one girl are living today. The oldest son married a girl from Hui Sai, made his home in Ban Hong, and became headman of Ban Hong when his father died.[1] Thus, this son did not follow the matrilocal residence pattern. The oldest girl died some years before I arrived in the village, but her surviving daughter is marred to the brother of the headman of Dong Dam, and she lives across the river in that village. The next oldest son (H–22) married a girl who came from the mountains with her mother, sister, and brother to Ban Hong to live with an "uncle." The couple lived near his parents for a time, and therefore this marriage also did not follow the expected pattern.[2] The next daughter (H–7) married a man who had ancestors in the original Ban Phae' village. They lived with her parents for a time, and then went to live with her husband's parents in Hui Sai for about a year. Then they came back and built a house which they occupy today near the site of her parent's original home. The next daughter married and brought her husband to live with her parents. Later this man became the headman of Vwang Mô, so he and his wife no longer live in Ban Hong. Another daughter (H–8) married a man from the mountains and settled near her parents. Later they moved to Vwang Kham, but then returned to the upper village after about a year where she still is at this time. The next daughter (H–25) married a man from Mae Phraphai and settled near her parents. Later they lived with his parents, then returned to the upper village of Ban Hong. The next son, the present headman (H-1), entered a forbidden union (see page 126), and he and his wife lived in the paddy area across the river for two years. He and his wife returned to the village after a child was born, and it was necessary for him to become headman. They moved into his mother's house, but by this time both of his parents had died. The youngest and last son (H-6) married a Thai girl from Ban Nong and moved in with her parents for about a year. Then they moved to his paddy field across the river from Ban Hong for a few years. Finally, they moved into Ban Hong and built a house near his brother, the headman.

In this family of nine children, all the sons broke the normal residence pattern and all the daughters followed it, at least for a time. This case is unusual, however, because of the agnatic succession of headmen, but I use it to show what further happens: six of these families are still in Ban Hong, and they all have children of their own now. These six are scattered throughout the upper and lower villages (see Fig. 3), and are no longer clustered around the site of the parents' home. However, each of them is now forming the nucleus of new clusterings: the headman (H-1) has no married children yet; H-6 has one married daughter nearby; H-7 has a married daughter nearby; H-8 has three married daughters clustered around her house and one married son nearby (his wife's parents are no longer living); H-11, one of the daughters of H-8, has a married daughter (H-35) nearby; the second son and his wife (H-22) have two married daughters and a granddaughter nearby (H-22a, H-26, H-34) and another woman (H-25) has a son, two daughters, and a granddaughter who are married and living nearby (H-34, H-29, H-25a, H-32). The oldest son is not one of the six nuclei counted here because he moved to Nong Pu (see Footnote 1) but he has a daughter and a granddaughter who are married and living side-by-side in Ban Hong (H-16, H-17). This group then, some of the sons and daughters of the headman one generation ago and their married children and grandchildren, account for fully one-half of all the families in the village today.

The sons of the headman of one generation ago did not follow the customary matrilocal residence pattern, although his daughters did follow it. However, nearly all the children of these individuals, the grandchildren of the past generation's headman (and in one case, a great grandchild of his), reinstituted the matrilocal pattern.

One more case will complete the picture of the residence pattern through time. A woman of one generation ago (H–3 on the village map, and the same generation as the present headman) married the brother of the present headman's mother. This couple lived with the wife's parents for a time in Mae Ngut, and then made their permanent residence in Ban Hong. Five sons were born to this couple. The husband died, but the wife stayed in Ban Hong with her sons. All five boys are now married, and all went to live with their wives. There are three still in Ban Hong (H–2, H–14, H–21), and they are living near the site of their mothers-in-law. Two went to other villages to live with their wives. One of the males (H–21) still in Ban Hong has three married children—two daughters and a son. The two married daughters are living near their parents (H–21a, H–18), and the son (H–35), after living with his parents for a short time, built a house and moved near his wife's mother's house.[3] In this case, the original marriage (H–3) did not follow the customary pattern (the wife came to Ban Hong) but all her children and grandchildren are following it.

These two cases, then illustrate an important point about the residence pattern: the norm will be disrupted and verilocal residence may be followed if there is an important relationship to the village headman. Economic contingencies may cause verilocal residence also nowadays (discussed later).

MARRIAGE

The most important day-to-day residential group for an individual includes his immediate family, his parents, siblings, and later that of his wife and children. Before marriage and because of the residence pattern, he is most likely to be living near his mother's female relatives. He is barred from taking a spouse from this set of relatives, so he goes to descendants of his father's siblings or of his mother's male siblings to find a mate. There are distinctive terms for father, mother, siblings, wife,[4] and his own children. The only other individuals to whom Ego might apply these terms are people who have married these relatives; for example, older sibling's spouse is called "older sibling," and child's wife is called "child."

Turning to marriage regulations, if a Karen is asked whom he can and cannot marry, he will answer that he can marry any girl not closely related to him; that is, he may marry any female whom he calls *Myng Nang* (except sisters, first cousins, and lineage mates), which is the general term for "unmarried girls." He will further say that the grandchildren of two brothers, or of a brother and sister can marry. However, the grandchildren (whose parents were female cousins) of two sisters cannot marry each other. Patrilateral, parallel second cousins and any second cross-cousins may marry, but matrilateral, parallel cousins (of any degree) cannot. This is because the latter are *lê dong bi öê öu'* (of the same lineage) or because they are *thê myng xae bi öê öu'* (of the same female "spirit"). The Karen informant might answer in another way saying that *dang thê khwae jai* (distant cousins) can marry each other, but *dang thê khwae baw'* (close cousins) cannot get married. Only people who are related through women to a pair of sisters are *baw'*, or "close." Out of forty-five marriages in Ban Hong on which I have data, there are no cases of first cousin marriage (see Appendix J). There are twenty-six cases in which the genealogical relationship is unknown, which means that the relationship, if any, is distant. Of these twenty-six (A, B in Table 11), there are eleven marriages with probably no connecting relationship between the partners. There are nineteen cases of known genealogical relationship between marriage partners. Of these there are ten cases of connection through parallel ancestors: that is, through two sisters, seven cases (F); through two brothers, three cases (G); there are nine cases of connection through a brother and sister (C, D, and E). Table 11 describes the forty-five marriages.

TABLE 11 Relationship Between Marriage Partners

A	Unknown relationship (if any)		15
B	No relationship		11
C	Second cousin marriage	6	
D	Third cousin marriage	2	9
E	Fourth cousin marriage	1	
F	Marriage of male to female cousin's child		7
G	Marriage of female to male cousin's child		3

There seems to be nothing significant about whom one may marry (however, marriages are usually contracted *within* the village-complex). With about equal frequency, marriages are contracted between people who are not related (eleven cases), between distant cousins (nine cases), or intergenerationally (ten cases). If the fifteen cases of unknown (therefore distant or no) relation are counted, there is a clear bias away from marrying a recognizable kinsman.

It is significant, however, whom one cannot marry. In my sample of marriages, there are some cases of proscribed or "bad" unions by unanimous opinion of the villagers. The four illicit marriages in Ban Hong illustrate prohibitions, explain why a Karen will say grandchildren of two sisters should not marry, and make an important point about Karen social organization.

In three of the four forbidden unions, the connecting link between the marriage partners is two sisters. In one case it is two generations ago, and in another case it was back three generations for the female and two for the male (this is an intergenerational marriage). In the third case, the connecting sisters were three generations above both partners. There are matrilineal marriage proscriptions. The impropriety of marriages described above cannot be due to intergenerational union because there are ten other cases which are accepted as normal. It cannot even be due to this particular intergenerational marriage, because there are two other cases of a man marrying his second cousin's child which are considered normal. The illicit nature cannot be due to marriage between second or third cousins (which is what two of the unions are) because there are six other cases where one or the other of these types of marriage occur. Finally, the illicit marriages cannot be due to the fact that the connecting links are sisters, because there are four normal marriages with just such a connecting link between the partners. There is only one alternative that makes these marriages illicit; that is that *all* of the links that lead to the marriage partners are through females. There are no other cases which are similar. The rule then, that explains why these three marriages are wrong is: one cannot marry any person who is directly related to him entirely through women (why this is so, and how the relationship is remembered is discussed below). A person in any other relationship is a proper marriage partner, except that first cousins of any type never intermarry.[5]

The fourth "bad" marriage in Ban Hong, though not considered quite as bad as the first three, illustrates how the Karen try to keep open the relationship between different social groups by contracting alliances between as many as possible. This marriage is between second cousins, and the connecting link between them is a brother and sister. There is nothing wrong with the marriage itself; what is wrong is that there was already a marriage between the two families involved. The situation is illustrated in the following diagram of an actual case:

FIGURE 6   Proscribed Marriage

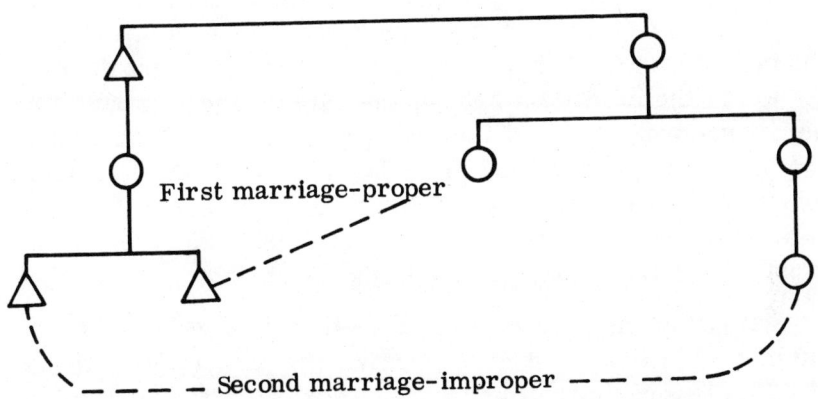

This is not an isolated case. There is another such case of two marriages between two families in a nearby village. The couple of the second marriage, as in the case of Ban Hong, had to elope and live outside their village for a time before the marriage was an accepted fact; this was later finalized by pregnancy. A second marriage rule is, then, that one can marry any person (within the limits of the matrilineal rule above) who is not already related to his lineage segment by marriage; that is, two substantive lineage segments may be related by only one marriage between them [6] (see also Hinton 1969:19).

INHERITANCE

The following rules regulate inheritance aand division of property. The children of a Karen family are divided into three groups: the oldest child is referred to as *a' vwi shiae* ("the old oldest"), the middle group of children are referred to as *a' öa 'klae* ("the hearts in the middle") and the last child is referred to as *a' öê dae* (the "last and youngest").

Expected behavior and inheritance of property follow this threefold division. The oldest and youngest children get an equal share of property, but receive more than each of those in the middle group. This is rationalized by the fact that the oldest works the hardest in helping the parents and in caring for his younger siblings, and the youngest ideally stays and cares for the parents in their old age. The Karen say that mother's milk is not yet sweet, is sour, for the oldest child, and that it is weak and in short supply for the last child. For the middle group of children, presumably, the milk is just right.

Ideally, the inheritance takes place before the death of the parents. When the last child marries, the property is divided. For this reason, Karen like to have a girl as last child (due to residence pattern); it is also important for the children to get married in the proper birth order—oldest first and youngest last. If a child marries before an older sibling, he must make an offering of a pig to the older brother or sister. At the property division, all children (both sexes) get one share, the oldest getting a larger share. The parents keep an equally large share which will go to the youngest on their death, but which, in fact, the youngest controls from this time. The house and all remaining property fall to the last child. The total *"property"* includes rights to swidden lands, permanent gardens, bamboo clumps, fruit trees, other trees which have economic value (e. g. sticklac, dye, etc.), implements, personal property of parents (which is divided according to sex), animals, money, and nowadays paddy fields may be included. It is important that the division take place before the death of the parents to avoid argument and dispute, and also because there is fear of bad luck being attached to the property, particularly personal property, of a dead person. The personal property held by an individual at the time of his death is either destroyed or put into the funeral pyre. These items are taken into the afterworld to be used there by the spirit of the dead person.

DIVORCE AND PROPERTY

In cases of divorce, the division of property is as follows. If the normal matrilocal residence pattern has been followed, the house normally belongs to the wife. She may or may not keep the house, but the children always stay with her no matter in whose group she is living (again indicating the importance of the matriline). The rest of the property is divided between husband and wife, except for that paddy land previously owned by the marriage partners; that land owned by the husband reverts to him and that owned by the wife reverts to her. In one divorce case in Ban Hong, the husband was an opium smoker. Each partner returned to their parents' houses (both in Ban Hong), the wife taking the children and her personal property. The husband sold the house material and kept his personal property. No garden or swidden land was involved. In two other cases, the women kept the children and their personal possessions; there was no joint property to divide since they were both living with parents. Divorce, if it is to occur, usually comes while the couple is young, the children are small and not involved in the property division, and there is generally not yet an accumulation of joint property in lands, trees, gardens, and so forth.

DIVISION OF LABOR

The general division of work on the basis of sex may be characterized as follows. All the heavy agricultural work is done by men; this includes cutting trees, burning the fields, hoeing, plowing, harrowing, irrigating, and so on. The lighter work of planting, weeding, and caring for rice may be done by women, but it is not exclusively women's work. Only women, however, transplant rice in the flooded wet-rice fields. No adult men were observed doing this task, but men do pull the seedlings and tie them into bundles in preparation for transplanting. In general, men do the hunting and women the gathering, but men may collect frogs at night with women and children. Only men gather honey high in the trees, collect larvae from ant nests in trees, carry on the various types of fishing, and cut sticklac. Women carry firewood and water, and do weaving. A man will carry water only if his wife has just given birth, and he will always do it then. As a rule, women cook the daily meals, although men help in preparation. Nearly all ceremonial cooking is done by men, however, and they are very adept at this task. Women, therefore, almost never cook meat (pork or chicken); I have observed women, however, helping the elders with a wedding feast at which chicken was the major element in the curry. Housebuilding is a man's work, but women help to make the thatch for roofing. Only men are involved in long-distance trading. One young man in Ban Hong has been to Yunnan, another has reached Bangkok, and many have been to Burma. Almost no women of Ban Hong have been outside the Hod Plain, and none have gone further than Chiengmai. However, women often go the local bazaar in Wang Lung to buy and sell local goods. Gardening is carried on by both sexes. Pigs and chickens are cared for by women, but men make the pigpens, feed troughs, and chicken baskets in which the fowl are kept. Caring for cattle is the domain of males, generally, but women have been observed making a fire beside the bedded animals at night to keep the insects at a safe distance. All tools, implements, and paraphernalia are constructed by men. Wage labor for money is a relatively new activity to the Karen in which both men and women participate; men are involved more often than women, however, particularly if it requires sleeping away from the village.

Children's work is less defined, but as the child gets older he more and more takes on the economic activities of that parent of the same sex; thus by the time a child has reached puberty he is doing only those jobs appropriate for his sex. Both young boys and girls carry water and collect firewood as well as care for younger siblings. Boys and girls both transplant rice in paddy fields, although boys are seen doing this less often than girls. Karen children begin helping with the work of getting a living as soon as they are able, according to their strength and abilities. At present, a major and important occupation of boys in their teens and of young adult males in general is wage labor. They often supplement the family income in this way, and do not participate in the more traditional activities of the Karen. This, in fact, is beginning to cause some conflicts in Karen society. There is a basic distinction, as far as the Karen are concerned, between work and labor. Labor is the new activity in which the Karen engage for pay, while work consists of all the traditional tasks of production and distribution of goods and services for which there is no market value or payment in money. This distinction, which the Karen make linguistically, and understand very well, is a manifestation of the difference between the two economic sectors in which the Karen are involved. The Karen term for "work" is *mae thê* which in this form is a verb. The noun which means "work" ("livelihood,") is *thê mae*. The term they use for "labor" is their pronunciation of the Thai word, *ha cang*. To a Karen, labor is something done for a Thai and for which a payment is received. The amount of pay is determined before the job is begun, and bargaining is the usual means of setting the price. There is one exception, when the Karen labor boss hires other Karen and pays them with money or rice for labor in the paddy fields which he is managing. However, the distinction between work and labor is clear-cut and important for understanding the Karen economy. Work is traditional, nonmoney or nonmarket oriented, and is an activity carried on by one of the social units of Karen society. On the other hand, labor always involves payment of some sort, is usually carried on outside Karen society, and is much more individualistic in nature. However, groups of Karen sometimes do wage labor together, and part of the income flows back into

Karen society. The introduction of wage labor is tending to break down traditional authority and social structure.

To this point, the discussion has concentrated on distinctions in work on the basis of sex and age, or in terms of the duties of *individuals*. The differences between traditional work patterns and modern labor practices have also been characterized. Now I shall mention *household* economic activities in terms of the organization of work or labor (other social units do different types of work). The production units in Karen economy vary with each particular type of productive activity, or with different phases in the activity. In a great many instances, however, the household is the basic productive unit as well as the unit of consumption. There is general cooperation between household members in many activities, as in much of the swidden work, paddy production, gardens, animal care, some types of fishing, and in all domestic activities. The household never acts as a unit in wage labor activities, but at least some of the income received by the household members is added to the general household larder.

THE LINEAGE SEGMENT

The lineage segment is a residential, affiliated kin-group, and not strictly a unilineal descent group. It consists of a cluster of households, and its structure is based on a rule of descent (matrilineal) and a rule of residence (matrilocal); ideally, women and unmarried children are members on the basis of descent, and adult men are members on the basis of marriage and residence. In ideal (and as far as I know, actual) pattern, the lineage segment is an exogamous unit, and therefore it relates itself to other such units through marriage.[7] The lineage segment might be called a matrilocal extended family; it consists of separate households, however, and even though it is a type of compromise kin group, it is nevertheless the residential manifestation of the lineage. I prefer, therefore, to call it a lineage segment.

Each lineage segment has a nucleus and a set of satellites. The nucleus of a segment consists of a woman and her husband, and the satellites consist of married daughters, their husbands, and the unmarried children. At times a married granddaughter and her family may be part of a single lineage segment.[8] The segments are not named. One village may have several segments of one lineage or segments of different lineages. The lineage segments are interrelated by marriage or descent (e. g., when the nuclei of two segments are sisters), or both.

When the nucleus disappears, either through death or change of residence, the satellites tend to drift apart and become nuclei themselves. In Ban Hong, there are fifteen lineage segments—that is, nuclei of segments (see Table 12). These represent, generally, actual physical clusterings of households around an older woman, and they account for all thirty-five households in the village. The women in these fifteen segments represent ten lineages (see Table 12, Fig. B, and Fig. 3).

TABLE 12 Lineage Connections of Segment Nuclei

Lineage 1	H–7, H–8, H–25, H–1—(Sgmts. V, VI, VII, II)
Lineage 2	H–22, H–26—(Sgmts. IX, X)
Lineage 3	H–24, H–31—(Sgmts. XI, XII)
Lineage 4	H–3—(Sgmt. I)
Lineage 5	H–6—(Sgmt. III)[9]
Lineage 6	H–13—(Sgmt. IV)
Lineage 7	H–16—(Sgmt. VIII)
Lineage 8	H–14—(Sgmt. XIV)
Lineage 9	H–30—(Sgmt. XIII)
Lineage 10	H–21—(Sgmt. XV)

Four segments belong to one lineage, two lineages are represented by two segments each, and the seven remaining segments represent a separate lineage (when men are taken into the count, there is at least one representative of twenty-nine lineages). These lineage segments have economic, political, and ritual functions.

LINEAGE SEGMENT FUNCTIONS

The composition of the lineage segment makes it ideal for group activities which require reciprocal cooperative endeavor. The lineage segment operates as a unit for economic cooperation and mutual aid in activities beyond the abilities of a single household (but see "Work-group" below). The segment has the political function of being responsible for and controlling behavior of individual members. It is responsible for actions of its members and is liable for their crimes; thus, it exerts pressure on members to conform. In cases where a person has broken some custom and must propitiate the village spirits, members of the whole segment are called upon to help provide the necessary liquor, rice and pork, or chicken, and to participate in the ceremony. The segment has no other specific ritual functions.

THE WORK-GROUP

The household is not an autonomous unit. There are some types of production which the household cannot do alone, and some jobs which are done more efficiently if a larger unit works as a team. It seems probable that in the past when basic economy was organized around swidden agriculture, the lineage segment nearly entirely provided the larger organization necessary for such tasks. Due to changes in the culture, however, the members of the lineage segment were not always available when a job had to be done. There are times, therefore, when ad hoc work groups form for some particular activity. That is, "friends" (see p. 104) may join to help their "friend" at a task, and thus reap some of the results of the endeavor. Or members of small lineage segments may join the activities of larger ones to increase the yield for the households in their own segment. The work-group is probably not entirely new to Karen society, and its composition is not entirely due to Thai contact; paddy ownership, for example, certainly has had an influence on the formation of special interest groups.

Several types of activity are carried out by a work-group, the basis of which is usually the lineage segment. Such activities include some types of fishing and hunting, some phases of swidden work, and certain aspects of wet-rice agriculture.[10] The introduction of paddy rice, however, has changed the character of the work-group. In the past, and for traditional activities today, the work-group consists of the men in a lineage segment and sometimes a few others as mentioned above. This partially ad hoc group works, as the need arises, beyond the abilities of individual households carrying out specific aspects of certain jobs; then the individual households finish the productive activity. In the case of paddy work, however, a "special interest" work-group forms, consisting of those individuals who own or manage paddy, which is not based on the lineage segment. There are two types of paddy work-groups. The first consists of the owners or managers who work together in building water wheels and other initial phases of paddy preparation. The second type usually includes, beyond household members, some hired labor to help with planting. This work-group involves an obvious boss-employee relationship which is unique to Karen behavior. The Karen who become employees are those who do not own paddy and who do not have any close paddy-owning relatives; they are the poorer villagers. It seems to be the case that an incipient economic class division is developing based on paddy ownership. Since not everyone has or is able to have paddy land, those who do have it tend to become an exclusive group which sometimes includes paddy owners from villages other than Ban Hong. I do not wish to over emphasize this grouping, however, since it is not yet divisive to traditional social structure even though it is recognized by Karen villagers.

There is yet another type of work group which carries on two kinds of activities. A group of men and boys form a group to go on long distance trading trips, nowadays usually to Burma. The individuals may be from one village, or they may be men from several villages. The important thing is that one or more of them have a friend at the end of the trip on whom the group can depend for helping with the transaction and for caring for the group for a few days while they finish their businesses. It is also important, of course, that the individuals have the time and money or goods to be used in the trading or buying and selling activities. These trips occur at irregular intervals and throughout the year, but usually not at the peak agricultural season. The composition of the group is quite variable, although it is usually based on kin or friendship relations. Ordinarily, goods or money is taken to Burma and exchanged for cattle and buffalo, which in turn are brought back and sold in Thailand. Minor items such as smoking pipes, beads, and local medicines are also brought back on the return trip.

The same kind of ad hoc group forms to engage in various sorts of wage labor for Thai that requires several people working together. Such jobs include short term labor in teak logging, initial preparation of rice and peanut fields, helping with the rice harvest, digging wells, making fences, and building or repairing houses. The groups engaged in wage labor for Thai are quite variable, however, sometimes including Thai laborers as well. Some Karen spend nearly all their time in wage labor, going from job to job and group to group, and thus spending almost no time in traditional activities. The few people in this group may be forming a third socio-economic class; that of the poor, itinerant laborer. The men in Ban Hong who spend most of their time in wage labor are often out of the village during ceremonies and at times of group decision-making, and thus are out of the main stream of village life. These men, for the most part, have few relatives in the village, and at least four of them are opium smokers. These men are never away during the all-village ceremony, however, and the younger men who have not yet formed a household cannot be considered in this third class. It is somewhat difficult to divide the village into three classes, because there is some overlap between the first and second and between the second and third; roughly, however, the top class includes twelve households (Table 13). I believe these incipient classes are an indication of Karen culture change toward Thai peasantry and further incorporation within the Thai state. The

TABLE 13 Socio-economic Classes

Paddy Owners or Managers	Traditional Livelihood	Mostly Wage Labor
H–1	H–3	H–9
H–2	H–5	H–11[a]
H–4	H–8	H–12[a]
H–6	H–10	H–28
H–7	H–15	H–29[a]
H–13	H–18	H–30[a]
H–14	H–20	H–33
H–16	H–22	
H–17	H–23	
H–19	H–24	
H–21	H–26	
H–25	H–27	
	H–31	
	H–32	
	H–34	
	H–35	

[a] Opium smoker

structure of these "classes" is dictated by previously existing Karen social structure; however, it is moderated by contact conditions.

RITUAL AND SOCIAL STRUCTURE

The intent of this section is merely to discuss ritual as it relates to the principles outlined in Chapter 4. I hope to show that ritual activities may be used as evidence for the assertion of matrilineal descent, cognatic affiliation, and the complementary distinction from village-wide ritual. A more complete and detailed discussion of Pwo Karen ritual and belief will be undertaken at a later time. Discussion of ritual concerning the village and village-complex is deferred to these sections below.

Household

There are a series of rituals surrounding the house and household members. When a new house is built a ritual is carried out in the construction process which involves an offering made to the house spirits in the house-post holes. When the house is finished and before the occupants move in, there is a feast and wrist-tying ceremony for the new occupants. A similar ceremony is held when a family changes residence from one village to another. Important village elders officiate at these ceremonies which signify social recognition of a new household in the village as well as protection for the occupants. From time to time after this, ceremonies may be conducted for all or some household members to prevent or cure illness in the household. One such is the *di lang thê* ceremony during which a few village elders each pour out a cup of liquor on several main house posts as an offering to the house spirits with the expectation that the spirits will keep illness away and insure that the household will prosper. Several bottles of liquor are usually consumed by the men on such an occasion and there may be singing and storytelling late into the night.

The wrist-tying, or *khaj chung*, ceremony is also conducted for all household members from time to time to prevent or cure illness or to recall a wandering personal *lae* (or "soul") of some household member. At this ceremony each family member in turn holds a small piece of chicken meat and rice in one hand at a time while a non-household elder calls the person's *lae* into his body. The elder then ties a piece of cotton thread around the wrist to be left in place until it eventually breaks and drops off some weeks or months later. After this ceremony there is a household feast of curry and rice and the elder or elders who officiated are invited to share the food and sometimes liquor.

Family

The above ceremonies focus on the house and entire household group. There is, however, a very important and significant ritual that focuses on a married couple plus one ascending and descending generation. This ceremony is called *bae xe*, and is distinct from the lineage ceremony conducted at marriage (see page 103).

Shortly after marriage a young couple performs this three-day ceremony in concert with the parents of the bride. A short time later the couple goes to the house of the groom's parents and repeats the entire ritual. The ritual consists of a ceremonial feast of a chicken and rooster on the first evening, a ceremonial feast of a small pig on the second evening, and finally a fish feast on the third evening. During the feasting the parents eat first, then the newlyweds, then the younger siblings of bride or groom (older siblings do not participate) depending on which parents home the ceremony is being conducted. This ceremony is a "thank you" and a "beg pardon" to the parents of the bride and groom.

However, the ceremony does much more than that. It serves to establish a relationship between the *lae* of three generations: parental, grandparental, and grandchildren (even though the latter may be as yet unborn). When small children become ill, the parents may be told by a fortune teller to *bae xe* at the home of one set of grandparents of the sick child. The parents and children go to that grandparental household and all participate in a one-evening feast of either chicken, pork, or fish. The object is to request the *lae* of the grandparents to cure or help cure the sick child. If, however, the grandparents have died, the parents of the sick child hold the ceremony calling upon the *lae* of the appropriate set of deceased grandparents to cure the child. When the child becomes an adult and gets married, he goes with his wife to his, and later to her, parents to start the process again. The newlyweds then drop their grandparents from this ceremonial sequence. It, therefore, is only three generations deep.

There is yet another function of this ceremony which concerns the situation where a person finds himself without a matrilineage or matrilineage head to perform important ceremonies. One case in Ban Hong may serve to illustrate the situation: The oldest woman in Ban Hong was head of a small lineage and the last of her line since all her sisters had died previously. She had five sons and no daughters. When she died, therefore, during my period of research, her sons had no lineage head to perform ceremonies when illness occurred. The office does not descend to the son's daughter. One of the sons, a widower, became ill and it was appropriate for him to have a lineage ceremony performed to effect a cure, but that was not possible. He therefore decided to *mae xe*, which involved a chicken feast and the calling upon the *lae* of his mother and father to cure him. In this ceremony, his mother was conceived as mother and not "lineage head," that is, as "parent" and not "ancestor" (Scheffler, 1966:543). The unmarried children of this man participated in the ceremony, but his married children were barred. The ceremony is conceived as a situation where the mother and father (or their *lae*), as parents, eat the feast together with their offspring and their unmarried grandchildren. Married grandchildren have already dropped the grandparents in their own *xe* ceremony. The oldest generation is honored in the ceremony and is asked to "bless" and care for the individuals in the two descending generations.

Lineage

The term *thê myng xae* refers to the spirits which protect the male and female members of a matriline. The term *thêmyng xae a khu* refers to the "head" (*a khu*) of the matriline who performs rituals for members of the descent line.

When a person becomes ill he may be told by a fortune teller (*ang khae du'thê*) that he must *bae thê myng xae*, this is, make an offering to his lineage spirits so that he may be made well again. This ceremony may involve the sacrifice of one or two pigs, and that will determine whether the ceremony lasts two or three days (two, if one pig; or three, if two pigs). The person acquires the pigs and takes them to the house of the lineage head which may be in a distant village. She performs the ceremony on his behalf. The ceremony includes only lineage members and thus excludes spouses and children of male members. The ritual involves a feast for those present of only rice on the first evening. The next morning the lineage head performs a "laying on of hands" ritual with the pigs during which she prays to the *thê myng xae* and asks them to cure the sick person. The pigs are then sacrificed to the lineage spirits and a pork curry feast is held in the evening. The next day the pig heads comprise the feast. On the third day the feast consists of the *ble* or "left overs." However, it is expected that all lineage-mates should be involved in the feasting. Therefore the curry is taken to those who did not attend the ceremony at the house of the lineage head. On each of three mornings after the three-day ceremony the lineage head makes a small offering of rice and pork to the *thê myng xae daw'pha* ("spirits inside the house") at the house-posts inside the house. This is, however, a separate ritual from that of the lineage ceremony previously conducted.

NOTES

[1] This man was nearly shot, and now lives in Nong Pu.

[2] This son, H–22, became the headman of Vwang Kham for a time, but is now back in Ban Hong with his wife.

[3] In describing the foregoing residence patterns, I have also described the makeup of a Karen village in another way than that given in the next chapter. When there is fission and a daughter village splits off, it will be one or more of these family clusters that leaves and forms the new village.

[4] The term of address for "wife" is best considered one of endearment. It is a separate and distinctive term of reference, but one usually uses the technique of teknonomy in talking about his wife.

[5] The evidence against first cousin marriage is only negative. There is only the Karen statement that it is not good. There are no examples to prove the rule.

[6] There is one further restriction: one should not marry a non-Karen. This does happen from time to time, and is tolerated, but it is not considered proper. Having a Karen mother is essential for gaining membership in a lineage, and therefore intermarriage between Karen and non-Karen is kept to a minimum. Nowadays, however, it

does sometimes occur. The children of such unions will be considered Karen or not, depending on how and where they are raised. For example, there are individuals born to a Karen mother living in Thai villages and raised as Thai. These are considered to be Thai and not Karen. On the other hand, a Thai woman married a Ban Hong Karen. She is taking on many Karen traits, and her children are being raised as Karen and are considered to be Karen, even though they do not have membership in a lineage. The children of her sons will have lineage membership if the sons marry Karen girls. If her daughters have sons who marry Karen girls, her great grandchildren will have membership in a Karen lineage. However, the females of this line can never gain such membership, since lineage affiliation is traced through women only.

[7] There are times, however, due to economic contingencies, that a son will bring in his wife to live in the lineage segment of his birth. Therefore, not all women in a segment, at least currently, are related via descent. This is a rare pattern and is the exception. This breaking of the expected pattern led, in one case in Ban Hong, to violent arguments between a new bride, who had moved to her husband's natal lineage segment, and the rest of the women in the group. The couple finally moved to her segment, where they should have gone in the first place. There is also the situation where a headman must bring in his bride. However, this is usually, but not always, the formation of a new nucleus for a lineage segment of the wife of the headman.

[8] I did not observe more than three generations in a lineage segment.

[9] Actually this is not a lineage representative since the wife is Thai. The children do not have a lineage head to go to in times of crisis. However, the husband does belong to the lineage of his mother. This unit is still called a *"segment"* since it functions as such in the village.

[10] Concerning the Pa-o, Hackett (1953:182) points out that in harvesting swidden fields, "usually there are mutual help groups that work together, and the planting and the harvesting times are spread out over a period of time . . . . All the fields owned by members of the mutual aid group are reaped in succession."

6

Village and Village–Complex

VILLAGE STRUCTURE

The village consists of a group of lineage segments which are related either by marriage or descent; it is situated in a well-defined area, territorially distinct from other villages. It is, in other words, a discrete residential unit of Karen society and is the largest political unit of Karen society. At political meetings which are held irregularly at the headman's house, each household of the village is represented (unless there are no men), although each nuclear family may not be represented. The headman presides at these meetings, and his opinion or judgment at the end of such a meeting represents the view and consensus of the village.

Ceremonially, the village is given validation as a unit twice a year. In December–January and again in June–July there is an all-village ceremony, during which time the village spirits are propitiated with a feast.[1] The headman officiates and asks the spirits to protect the village and its inhabitants. Each household provides labor to clear the grounds and repair the spirit houses of the village; then each household supplies a bottle of rice liquor, chicken, and rice as a sacrifice to the village spirits. After the headman makes the offering and the spirits have had the essence of the offering, a large feast is enjoyed by the villagers around the spirit houses. A family may not be living in the village for some reason, but the members are affiliated as villagers if they participate in this ceremony.[2] At the time of the ceremony, taboo signs are placed on the paths leading into the village, and nonvillagers do not enter.[3] Economic functions of the village as a unit are minimal. There is, however, an economic aspect to the village unit in that swidden lands and some property necessary for village ceremonies (e. g., large cooking pots) are considered village property. For certain jobs, also, the village acts as a productive unit. There are two types of activity in which the village is significant as a unit. First, the villagers may complete part of an activity, such as house building and swidden planting. When someone is ready to plant his swidden field, as many households as possible, regardless of kin-ties, will supply labor. Currently, however, usually only those households which have swidden fields cooperate in this endeavor. The job is finished in one day, the next day another field is planted, and so on (in both housebuilding and swidden work, the work-group and household are involved in certain phases of the activity too). The second type of activity in which the village acts as a unit is on occasions where the villagers do the *entire* job. For example, once or twice a year, each household supplies labor to clean the village and the entrance to it and on another day the village spirit houses are repaired or rebuilt. The village, then, is a unit that can be defined structurally, politically, ritually, and economically.

VILLAGE HEADMAN

There are two quite different kinds of "headman" that must be discussed under this general heading, and their jurisdictions are different. The most important is the traditional Karen position.

The second, which I will discuss first, is a Thai appointed headman (phujaiban) who is an articulation point between Thai officials and Karen society.

The nation of Thailand is divided into a series of "Provinces" (*Chiangwat*), each with a provincial governor, and are somewhat equivalent to American states. The provinces are subdivided into a set of *Amphur* (district), each with its political head, and are similar to American counties. Each *Amphur* is divided into *Thambon* (subdistrict), sometimes called "communes," and possibly similar to "townships"; each *Thambon* has a headman. The *Thambon* are finally divided into a series of *Muban* or villages, each having a headman in charge who may report to the *Thambon* headman or directly to the *Amphur* head. These are purely administrative divisions and may or may not coincide with "natural" social divisions. The divisions are geographical as well as administrative ones and are applied universally to the nation irrespective of ethnic grouping.

Amphur Hod consists of fifty-eight administrative villages or *Muban*. These are clustered into eight *Thambon*. The *Thambon* relevant here, also named Hod, includes four *Muban*. One of these, *Muban* Hui Sai, consists of four "natural" Karen villages which are Hui Sai, Ban Hong, Dong Dam, and Mang Mêng (see map Fig. 4). A *Muban,* being an administrative unit (rather than a natural one), may, however, consist of a mixture of both Thai and Karen villages, and it may not coincide with the village-cluster of Karen social organization. For example, Ban Hong and Dong Dam belong to one village cluster; and Hui Sai and Mang Mêng belong to another. There is, therefore, the distinct possibility of a power conflict built into the political system.

Like all others, *Muban* Hui Sai has a single *phujaiban* or headman appointed by the Thai for an unspecified period of time. He is thus responsible for and in charge of all four Karen villages which make up the *Muban*. During the period of research, the headman was a Karen from the natural village of Hui Sai.

Since this "political headman" is a Thai appointee, his initial status and authority derive entirely from the Thai administrative structure. Within the Karen village of his jurisdiction, he commands no more authority or respect than any elder of the village, and outside his own village he may have no status at all, except that which derives from Karen criteria such as kinship or other specialist activities such as curer. Indeed, there may be a conflict of interest between him and the traditional headman.

Karen culture and social relations have powerful means of social control, however, which the political headman is subject to and must abide by if he is to remain within the social system at all. His position thus becomes a difficult one: he must remain a "good Karen" if he is to survive, and if he is to be "obeyed" as the political headman. At the same time, however, he must satisfy the Thai authorities in his responsibilities in the administrative system. He must, in other words, operate and be effective in two cultures.

The duties of the headman include the reporting of marriages, births, deaths, residential moves, and infractions of the (Thai) law to the *Nai Amphur* (*Amphur* head) at a monthly meeting. If someone has a complaint or wants to report a crime, he should do so through the headman. The headman is expected to see that people report and register their land holdings for tax purposes. He insures that a proper corvee labor force is assembled for communal jobs such as road building or repair. When there are directives from the government, the headman may call a village assembly of household heads or at least some representatives of the villages in his jurisdiction, and transmits the information. Sometimes, however, the political headman informs the traditional headmen of his villages and they in turn report to the people of their respective villages.

In the living memory of local Karen, they have always had this Thai appointee distinct from the traditional headman. The eldest man in Ban Hong, the head elder, remembers five such political headmen all coming from the village of Hui Sai. The current political headman is the younger brother of H–19M in Ban Hong, and has held the position for about four years. The previous headman was the older brother of H–7M, the head elder of Ban Hong. He had been the political headman for more than thirty years. About four years ago the traditional headman of Hui Sai died. The village elders consulted a spirit medium, and it was determined via the medium from the Karen spirits that the political headman should become the traditional headman (since he had the proper kinship prerequisites). The man, therefore, resigned the Thai position and became the traditional headman of the natural village of Hui Sai. His excuse for resigning as political head was his advanced years. However, I am told that no one has ever held both positions simultaneously.

At the request of Thai authorities, three men from natural Hui Sai were chosen by the villagers to run for the vacated office, and the current political head of administrative Hui Sai was chosen by secret ballot, the election being administered by Thai authorities. The man chosen was acceptable to *Amphur* officials and was therefore appointed to the position.

The traditional village headman has both political and religious functions. These are not viewed by the Karen as separate duties, however. He is usually called the *Dang Khaw* but may also be called *Mang öa' shiae* ("uncle old heart"). His authority does not extend beyond the boundary of the natural Karen village as does that of the Thai-appointed position discussed above. But he is a much more powerful person among the Karen, by virtue of supernatural sanction.

The political functions of the *Dang Khaw* are to arbitrate disputes within the village (backed by the community and the spirits), to maintain order, and to act as spokesman for the villages. He acts as a go-between for the various social units of the village, and thus represents the village as a social and political unit. His religious function serves as a powerful sanction for his political role. He is the only person who has the privilege of communicating directly with and propitiating the village spirits. He thus relates the village to the supernatural, and from the supernatural he receives his power to act as headman for the village.

Since the village is the largest political unit in Karen society, the authority of the headman is restricted to his own village. His decisions are made in conjunction with the village elders. This informal body of elders consists of the oldest adult male member of each household.

The rules of succession for village headman are somewhat flexible. Normally, a headman's younger brother succeeds him, although other possibilities occur. If there are no brothers available, a son may succeed to the position. Failing this, any male relative of the headman may become the new headman. An affinal relative of the headman may succeed him, if this person had a kinsman who was a headman. Headman succession obviously does not follow strict lineage descent, and so it may pass among the lineages. In addition, one can become headman only with consent of the village elders. Succession generally is "omnilateral" following Bohannon (1963:127), but with an agnatic bias. The headman may be deposed if the villagers are not satisfied with his behavior, or if it is believed he is in ill favor with the village spirits; this is known by crop failures or such disasters as sickness or death of people or animals befalling the village.

The current *Dang Khaw* of Ban Hong is H–1M. The first *Dang Khaw*, at least according to tradition, was the paternal grandfather of the present one. Next in the line was the father of H–1M, and then his eldest son became *Dang Khaw*. There was some difficulty in the village during that period and the *Dang Khaw* was accused of using black magic. Someone shot at him during the night, wounding his wife. They very shortly thereafter moved to a distant Karen village and H–1M became *Dang Khaw*.[4]

The figure below shows relationships between the *Dang Khaw* of various local villages.

FIGURE 7 Headman Relationships

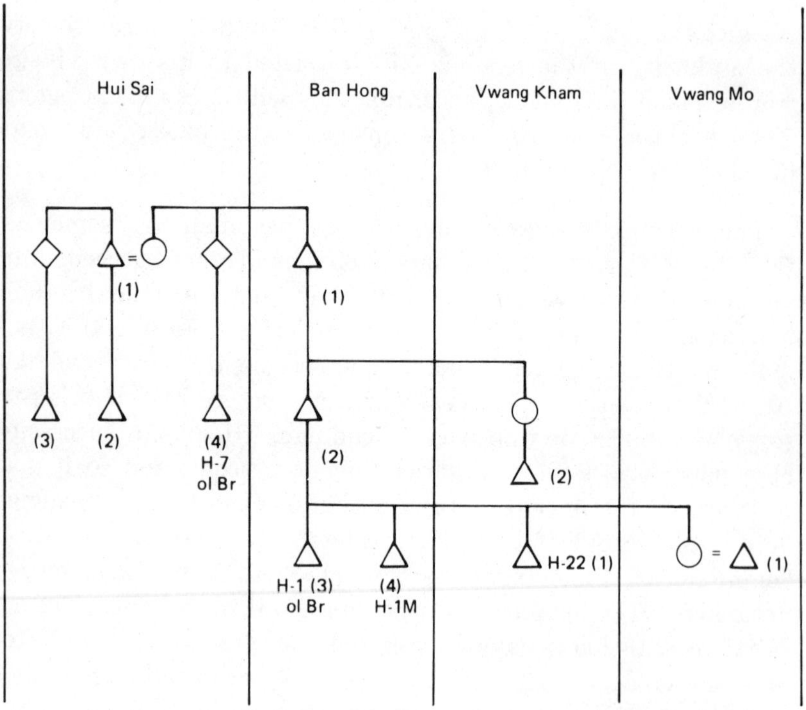

Note: Headmen are numbered in historical order for each village

From time to time, the *Dang Khaw* will call a meeting at his house in the evening around 7–7:30. This is a time when everyone may be expected to have returned to the village from their various daily activities. To notify the villagers, the headman beats on a section of bamboo for a minute or two. The echo quality of the bamboo section insures that no one misses the call. When the men of the households assemble on the headman's porch, he announces the various topics to be discussed. These are debated in turn by the men, and a consensus emerges which the headman summarizes at the end.

At one such meeting, the topic concerned whether or not a New Year's ceremony was to be held this year. After some discussion it was enunciated by each man in turn that it would cost too much, and that it should not be held in Ban Hong. It was to be held in some surrounding villages and Ban Hong villagers could attend.

At another meeting the following topics were discussed: (a) innoculations were to be given at the school in the Thai village of Wang Lung, but no one knew what the innoculations were for; (b) a temple (*wat*) was to be built in a nearby Thai village and donations were being solicited; discussion concerned how much, if any, should be donated by each household; the figures of one *baht* or one-half *baht* were mentioned, but no decision was reached at the meeting; (c) a directive from the *Amphur* headquarters required everyone to cut the weeds around their houses and to make the village generally presentable; this directive came to the *Dang Khaw* via the political headman in Hui Sai; (d) another Thai directive pointed out that it was illegal to drink liquor (at ceremonies) brewed locally and to smoke opium; offenders would be prosecuted; this was mentioned, ascented to, and discussed no further; it was obvious that it would be ignored.

At a third meeting, the people were notified by the headman that each household was expected to contribute three bamboo poles to construct a recruiting office for the army at the Wang Lang school.

It must be pointed out that even though these meetings impart unpopular information or requests the *Dang Khaw* is not held responsible. The meetings are eagerly attended because they serve as a time for catching up on the news and having a sociable conversation for a while.

The *Dang Khaw* has no absolute power or authority in the village. He serves at the pleasure of the elders and the spirits. As long as he fulfills his job well, people will follow his direction. In the past it was he who decided when and where to move the village when that became necessary. The villages are more permanent now and this seldom occurs (but see Chapter 10). His control of behavior is sanctioned by moral restraint and supernatural sanction. During one occasion that I observed, a ritualized free-for-all fight between the young men of Ban Hong and another village got out of hand. The *Dang Khaw* tried to reason with the participants and requested they stop. He was ignored. His next and traditional technique for controlling the situation was very effective: he walked a short distance away from the combatants and in a loud voice invoked tradition by haranguing the sky, kicking up dust, and saying these men would anger the spirits; they were bad Karen; they were breaking custom by showing their real anger. In a very few minutes, all was quiet and the men sulked away to their village and homes.

In his purely religious role, the headman officiates at the all-village ceremony twice a year by offering liquor and food to the village spirits. He also asks their blessing and protection for the people and their crops. During this ceremony, he is honored and feasted by the villagers. At other times, he is consulted by villagers on matters of custom, offerings to spirits, and curing.

There is a third role that may or may not be fulfilled by the *Dang Khaw*. This is what I have called the "custodian of tradition" or "head elder." In Ban Hong, this role is filled by a separate person, H–7M. But in Hui Sai the head elder and headman position are held by one man, the elder brother of H–7M (for a description of the head elder, see below).

OTHER SPECIALISTS

The village headman (*Dang Khaw*) who is always a male and the female lineage head (*the myng xae a khu*) previously discussed, are both involved with the spirits and group welfare. They are, however, concerned with different spirits and groups and their functions are therefore complementary. The lineage head is concerned with spirits vis a vis a set of "people," whereas the headman is concerned with spirits vis a vis "nature" as it affects human welfare. There are also a number of other specialists in Karen society that serve yet different functions. These are the positions of midwife, curer, fortune teller, black magician or sorcerer, salesman, trader, labor boss and head elder. These positions may be filled by anyone with the requisite personal skills and qualifications, but all require some training. In addition, one must be the proper sex: only women may be a midwife; men more often than women are curers or magicians and only a man may become a fortune teller, salesman, trader, labor boss, or the head elder. There are no specific rules of succession for any of these status positions, but there is a tendency for the head elder to pass his knowledge on to one of his sons.

The major function of each of the specialist positions is summarized in the name for each. Beyond these primary special functions, the specialists serve the secondary function of linking the social units. They always serve the individuals and villages in a village complex, and nearly always beyond as well; thus, contact and interdependence among the units is greatly increased and lines of communication are maintained.

A midwife is called in at every birth to direct and help with the delivery. This is an important role in Karen society, and a good midwife is much in demand. The midwife in Ban Hong sometimes travels quite far to aid in a birth. The midwife not only knows the proper techniques to make a birth successful, but she is something of a magician-curer-masseuse who eases birth and any complications which may arise before, during and after the delivery. The midwife maintains contact with many families and villages and is an important communication link between them.

If a person becomes ill, the relatives may go to a fortune teller to determine the cause and the cure. The cure may be through a skilled practitioner of "white magic." This curer may use various herbs as medicine; he may use "magic water" (water that has a special plant floating in it and has had magic words said over it) and a special implement, often a tiger tooth, to rub down the body of the sick person; or he may merely massage the afflicted area, blow on it, and say magic spells over it.

There are various types of fortune tellers; that is, they specialize in different techniques of determining the answers to different types of questions or problems. Curers are "graded," some being more skilled and famous than others. No one village has all the various specialists, so individuals are constantly and regularly travelling from one village to another to enlist the services of one or another of the various specialists.

There is another type of magician, but information about him and his activites is very difficult to gather. No one admits being this type of magician, and no one admits enlisting his aid. This is the black magician, whose purpose is to inflict pain or death. The threat of black magic is a powerful force for social control and conformity. There is an attempt to keep good interpersonal and intergroup relations because of the possibility of the use of black magic.

There are three economic specialists—salesman, trader, and labor boss (Hamilton 1963a). The salesman takes village products, such as woven goods and rope, and sells them for the owner in bazaars near and far. He may be gone several days on one of these trips. Traders deal in nonvillage goods and travel great distances into the mountains or to Burma where there is an exchange of goods. The trader then returns and resells the items brought back to both Karen and Thai. The labor boss supervises the wet-rice agricultural activities for Karen and Thai. He hires or supplies from his family the labor, supervises the work for the owner, and is paid in rice or money. The activities of these economic specialists not only crosscut Karen social units but often articulate them to the world outside.

The final specialist role to be considered is that of head elder. This person is a kind of Karen encyclopedia and trouble-shooter. He is a repository of knowledge, tradition, and custom, who connects the present to the past with his stories. These stories often have built into them injunctions concerning proper Karen behavior, and what happens to both "good" and "bad" people. The head elder knows the proper procedure for all ceremonies; he, in fact, conducts or supervises many ceremonies. This man may have to train the headman (if he himself is not the headman), or he may merely assist the headman. He is, at least, mentor to the headman as well as all other villagers. He is often sought out for advice or approval for some act. This person is a living example of "proper" behavior. He often acts as go-between in marriages, conducts funeral rites, and arbitrates many disputes. His is one of the most important roles for keeping Karen society running smoothly. All villagers seek and respect his wisdom (see also Marshall 1922:143ff). The position of head elder is, however, an informal one; there is no title or specific linguistic designation, and any man from the group of elders who has the requisite knowledge, skill, and popularity, may succeed to the position. He is the most respected and sought after of the male elders.

This, then, is the full complement of Karen specialists; not all these, however, are found in any one village. The head elder of Ban Hong, for example, is sought after by people from other villages to lend the weight of ancient custom to their actions, decisions, or ceremonies. Of all the speciality roles discussed, the following are in Ban Hong: there is one headman (see Table

14) indeed, the definition of "village" includes a headman, and there can be only one headman at a time.[5]

TABLE 14 Village Specialists in Ban Hong

Headman	H–1M
Lineage head	H–3F (now dead)
Midwife	H–24F
Curer	H–22M, H–24F, H–7M, H–30M
Fortune teller	H–26M
Black magician	H–30M, H–30F
Salesman	H–26M, H–16M
Trader	H–6M, H–16 son, H–18M
Labor boss	H–17M
Head elder	H–7

There was one lineage head in Ban Hong when we arrived although she died during the course of field research. At present there are none, but the next in line for one lineage is a woman in Ban Hong (H–7F). The one midwife in Ban Hong (H–24F) travels regularly throughout the area and is much in demand in several villages. There are four curers in Ban Hong, and one of them (H–22) is famous all over the Hod plain, both among the Thai and the Karen. People come to him from quite long distances at times. The one minor fortune teller in Ban Hong is not as important as the most famous one in the local area, who is a former resident of Ban Hong and now lives across the river in Dong Dam. It is reported that one man and his wife are both black magicians in Ban Hong. I do not doubt that the man, at least, is generally considered a dangerous magician because of what was said about him and the way people acted toward him. Ban Hong has only one main salesman, but another man and a couple of boys engage in selling for villagers from time to time. Several men in Ban Hong go on trading trips occasionally, but there are three people who do it regularly. There is one labor boss in Ban Hong, and since this is a new role for Karen, there are very few others in the surrounding villages. The village has one head elder, distinct from the headman. There is a similar situation in Dong Dam, although the one in Ban Hong is more famous. In Hui Sai the headman (*Dang Khaw*) and head elder are the same individual—the brother of the head elder of Ban Hong.

These ten roles are not mutually exclusive categories. Some individuals perform more than one kind of specialty. Thus, one woman is both midwife and curer, one man is head elder and curer, another man is magician and curer, and one man is a salesman and a fortune teller.

THE VILLAGE–COMPLEX

The village-complex is a group of villages that are loosely affiliated. It consists of a parent village and its satellites—one or more daughter villages which have split away from the parent at various times in the past.

When a village becomes large and unwieldly or too large to function as one unit it will split apart. One or more lineage segments will separate from the parent and form a daughter village some distance away, although not so far that all connection is lost. There are still structural relations between the villages; for example, there are several village-complexes in the Hod plain.[6] The headman of the parent village, in collaboration with the elders, picks a person to be headman of the new village. This new headman may be a younger brother or a son of the headman of the parent village. The headman of the parent village, however, has no political power in or over daughter villages.

The village-complex never operates as a political unit.[7] This is due, in part at least, to the fact that the connections between villages in a complex are somewhat tenuous. With time, growth, splitting, and movement, the original connection between parent and daughter villages may be forgotten or lost or may become nonfunctional due to distance. It is also true, of course, that any parent village is, or was, a daughter village itself.

Villages in a complex are linked together in various ways. There are kinship connections between them, which is assured by the way in which the daughter villages form, the lineage segments of parent and daughter villages are related, and the headman of a daughter village has validation through his kin ties to the headman of the parent village. This connection, however, may be only through the wife of one of the headman.

There are also ritual and religious reasons for calling the complex a unit. A daughter village receives its village spirit from

Unmarried boys and girls march and sing around the corpse at a Dong Dam village funeral.

Final rite at cremation of a Ban Hong lineage head. While the body burns, the men in foreground are preparing to invite the dead woman's lineage spirits to come for her.

Top: Funeral ceremony for Headman's mother-in-law. *Bottom*: Night view of bachelors marching and singing around corpse while village elders look on.

Top: Preparing to take corpse to cremation site. *Bottom*: Final death rite conducted by Buddhist priests before cremation of corpse.

A possessed spirit medium fans herself prior to consultation with village elders.

A village elder offering rice and chicken to the spirits of the land.

A village elder makes an offering of chicken, rice, and rice whiskey to the paddy spirit.

An offering to the spirit of the rice field.

Head elder conducting wrist-tieing ceremony for village headman.

the spirit of the parent village. Thus at least for a time a symbolic connection is maintained.[8] The village spirits of Dong Dam, Vwang Kham, and Vwang Mô are "children" of the village spirits of Ban Hong. In addition to these spirit connections, there is an annual New Year's ceremony in each of the villages, with attendance from other villages in a complex. The relationship among the villages in a complex may be observed in the courtship function of a funeral, where the marriageable boys and girls of a village-complex convene to sing and to meet one another (Hamilton in press). This is a situation out of which marriage alliances emerge, and the young people have been heard to say that it is about time for somebody to die.[9]

Economic cooperation between individuals in the various villages in a complex is based on the kin ties between village-com-

The author undergoing wrist-tieing ceremony conducted by village headman.

plex members, and not on any larger economic or political organization. The economic potential of people is enhanced and enlarged due to the loose village complex organization since there is a general cooperation among members of the villages.

The village-complex never acts as a unit in productive activity, but there are important occasions during which individuals from the several villages do cooperate in an activity such as cases where the work group is composed of individuals from the related villages. The connections between villages in a complex, therefore, are all based on kinship, be it real, fictional, or spiritual.

Headman and village elders preparing curry for all-village ceremony.

SUMMARY OF KAREN SOCIAL ORGANIZATION

The residential units of Karen society are the household, the lineage segment, the village, and the village-complex. The composition of the household is based on the nuclear family, but it may include a little more or a little less. Given Karen residence rules and practices, several households are linked together through matrilineal descent and matrilocal residence to form a lineage segment. The village structure is based on a group of lineage segments which are linked either by marriage or descent, or by both. As in the case of Ban Hong, the village usually forms around one main lineage. When the village becomes very large, fission or splitting will occur and one or more segments will separate to become a daughter village, thus a village-complex is formed which is held together through kin and spirit connections. With time and change, a daughter village may become a new independent parent village.[10] A local area embracing several village complexes which are more or less related constitutes a local subgroup. There are several nonresidential matrilineages which crosscut the whole area. Lineage mates generally do not forget their connections, but will maintain their relationships through the many villages in which they are residing. A group of these local subgroups, which may not be contiguous, makes up one of the major branches of Karen (Pwo, Sgaw, Bwe, etc). Altogether the branches represent the group or tribe called Karen in Southeast Asia.[11]

There are two kinds of linkage relationships that crosscut some or all of these units that tend to tie them together in various ways. One might be called mechanical linkage (using Durkheim's distinctions, 1964:Chapters 2 and 3; see also Lévi-Strauss 1969:484) and is characterized by the linkage functions of the status positions and the nonresidential lineage. *Karenness*, based on origin, custom, dress, and language, provides general group solidarity. The kinship network provides a set of statuses with predetermined behavior patterns and allows predictable intercourse between any two individuals. Lineage connections link the various units through descent and marriage relations of individuals. Friendship relations make it easy for individuals to travel from one area to another and receive aid to succor. Also, the specialists link various units into interdependent relationships in the carrying out of their duties.

The other type of linkage might best be called "organic." The social units, besides being defined structurally, may be defined on the basis of their political, economic, social, and ritual functions. Or it may be said that each performs ritual, political, economic, or social activities. However, the specific activities of each of the units are different from the others. Therefore, the social units are in organic interdependence. For example, the household performs certain types of ritual activities, the lineage segment performs different ones, the lineage performs another, and the village yet others. There is specialization of ritual activity for each of the units, and thus organic interdependence is achieved. This is also true of political, economic, and social activities.

In terms of the organization of work of all types, the social units of Karen society are not independent of each other. To a considerable extent, each unit relies on other units. There are, nevertheless, specific jobs which are carried out by the various elements of Karen social structure.[12] It is doubtful, however, that the lineage ever acted as a productive unit because it is not a residential unit on the Hod plain, and could not, therefore, act as a unit in any sustained activity.

NOTES

[1] The Karen follow a lunar calendar. This ceremony may, therefore, fall in either December or January of our calendar, but it is the same month each time in their calendar.

[2] My wife and I were counted as villagers after I participated in one of these ceremonies, even though we had not yet moved into the village. Also, two Karen families who had moved from the village came back to participate in the ceremony because they were still, for a time, considered villagers.

[3] The local Thai as well as Karen respect these signs and do not enter the village. After I became a villager I could come and go at will, but one should not leave the village once the ceremony has begun.

[4] The brother (H-22M) of the current headman was the headman of Vwang Kham for a time, but there was an epidemic of some sort and he was deposed to return to Ban Hong and become a curer.

[5] However, near the Thai village of Hod a "composite" village of Karen is forming which has no headman. It is composed of unrelated individuals from different Karen areas (and different Karen subgroups) in the hills who are moving to the plain for one reason or another. This is not a true village, even to the local Karen. It is really a group of "displaced" persons.

[6] In all my wanderings through the length of western Thailand, I never found just a single Pwo Karen village, but always clusters of them forming village complexes.

[7] The organization of the village complex seems to parallel that of the lineage, the individual villages being "segments."

[8] The village spirit of Ban Hong is apparently a "child" of the spirit of the original Ban Phae', but people are not sure now. Also, the spirit of Ban Phae' was probably a child of that in Mae Ngut or Mae Phraphai, but again people are not now certain.

⁹ Nowadays, at least, the teenagers from more than a single village complex come to a funeral.

¹⁰ This was the case when the old Ban Phae', which was the parent village of the old Ban Hong, moved and formed Hui Sai. In this case, the connections between the two villages withered, and Ban Hong became a parent village to its daughter villages, losing a close relation to the new village of Hui Sai.

¹¹ For a definition of "tribe," see Service (1962); Sahlins (1961) and Sahlins (1968). It is no doubt true that to say *all Karen* form a tribe today is at least misleading. It is more accurate to say, some Karen groups are still at the tribal level of socio-cultural integration, and some are not. I believe it is also accurate to say that the Pwo Karen on the Hod plain and surrounding areas are in the process of moving from the tribal stage of organization into one of peasantry.

¹² There are also ad hoc groups in the social structure with special purposes, and incipient socio-economic classes are developing as discussed earlier.

7

The Ban Hong Economy

INTRODUCTION

The concern of this chapter is the organization of production, distribution, and consumption. The details, activities and fruits of production were discussed in Chapter 3, and will not be repeated or summarized here. The present concern is, first, with the "management" aspects of production, that is, given Karen social structure as discussed above, how is productive "labor" organized and accomplished. Next, I consider the various means of distributing goods and services. Finally, I consider the patterns of consumption behavior in Ban Hong and surrounding villages. Most of the issues concerning money and its effect on the economy are brought together in the following chapter.

Before continuing, however, I would like to distinguish *social structure* from *economic structure* and *organization*. These distinctions are particularly important when dealing with nonwestern or nonmarket economies, as I will try to show in analyzing Ban Hong economy.

When one speaks of "social structure," he is ordinarily referring to substantive groups and statuses and their interrelations for a particular human group. The question is, how is the human group partitioned so that the various activities required for survival are carried out. There is also usually some concern with the "rules" of partitioning. *Social structure* is so used in this work. However, we sometimes use the term *economic (or political or religious) structure* and such use may not only be confusing but also of a different sort, that is, with a different referent than social structure. Economy is not a social structure. It is, rather, concerned with the activities of various elements of the social structure engaged in the process of provisioning society with goods and services. *Economy* refers to a functional category of human behavior. I prefer, therefore, to use the term *economic organization* to indicate the difference. If one uses the term *economic structure*, it must be remembered that it refers to subdivisions of the abstract functional category of economy such as *production, distribution, management, consumption*, and so on.

A society may, of course, include specialized groups and statuses as part of the social structure such as the firm, the bank, a foreman, a manager, and so forth, that exist for economic activities only. There is, therefore, ambiguity at times. However, even if a society does not contain such *special structures*, it still has an *economic organization* in the sense that production and distribution activities are carried out either by all-purpose or many-purpose groups and statuses. The term *economic structure*, therefore, has little direct correspondence to substantive social structure. We may assume that all societies have an economic organization (i. e., the social structure carries out economic activities). We need not assume that all societies have specialized structures for doing so. Indeed, the ethnographic evidence contradicts the idea. We may also assume, however, that as society becomes more complex and differentiated, more specialized structures for economic purposes will develop. There is thus the possibility of an economic continuum organized around unspecialized groups and statuses to fully specialized ones. The Pwo Karen of Ban Hong fall near the unspecialized end of the continuum (I will return to this idea in the next chapter).

MANAGEMENT OF WORK IN KAREN SOCIETY

In all production and in some aspects of distribution and consumption, there must be some authority and control in the organization of work. There must be some agent with responsibility to see that activities get done in the proper order of events. The work force in Karen society includes all the individuals as they are organized into the several social units as previously discussed. Management is that part of the work force which coordinates the factors of production. Management, in the case of Karen culture, is the economic aspect of the various specialists or other status positions, insofar as they control or structure behavior, or manipulate land, labor, and capital. This automatically includes the control aspect of the heads of the various social units; each household has an elder at its head; each lineage segment has a senior male at its head and each village has its headman. The various other specialists have more or less economic importance depending on the particular speciality or dominance of personality. Tradition also plays an important role; everyone knows his job and usually does it.

Management is often quite informal, and for traditional activities, at least, it is subtle; that is, there are no permanent distinctions or differences in group orientation between management and labor. In Karen society, when the household is operating as a unit carrying on the household activities as outlined earlier, the male head functions as the person of authority who directs and is responsible for work coordination. In household domestic activities, it is the woman who directs the operations.

There are situations where the production unit is nearly synonymous with the lineage segment. In these cases, the male head of the lineage segment directs the work (this man is the husband of the woman around whom daughter households form). He directs the traditional jobs done by the lineage segment, such as some swidden and garden work, and some types of fishing. If the male head of the household or lineage segment is missing due to death or divorce, the senior female, alone or in conjunction with her senior son-in-law, takes this role. As mentioned above, there are times when the work-group includes more people than those of a lineage segment. In all such situations, the man with the most knowledge or force of personality stands out and becomes the directing agent. This person is usually an older member of the village with experience, but often the work-group does not include the older men of the village. In such cases, the man who has the most forceful character and who is respected and trusted by others, will take charge merely by suggesting how to carry out the operation, or by beginning it himself. No Karen bullies or commands another to do anything for fear of magical retaliation or physical violence.

The village headman is the person with economic authority when the village is functioning as a single unit. However, where individuals from the village-complex are present, or in work-group situations where the village is not functioning as a unit, the headman is just another elder. Activities in these instances are usually directed by the elder or elders with the greatest prestige and knowledge of the situation. This may or may not include the village headman. In the case of Ban Hong, the headman was always in the background in these situations, but the head elder and one knowledgeable young man in his thirties (H-17, a labor boss) were always in the forefront helping to direct activities.

The labor boss is a new role in Karen economy, and his function is precisely one of economic authority. His job is to direct and coordinate activities in the paddy work. It is usually the case that he commands authority in other activities too, but not by virtue of his position as labor boss. In Ban Hong, the labor boss happens to be a forceful and wise young man.

As there have been changes in the relationship to nature, and in capital and wealth, so too have there been changes in the organization of work and management patterns. In the past, work was organized around the traditional social units carrying out their productive functions, and management was coordinated through traditional status positions with consent and consensus of the managed. Along with changes in land-use patterns, wage labor has entered the economic system, and this has had its effect on the traditional management system and on the social organization of work. Labor for pay has allowed the individual to break out of the traditional system of work control and coordination.

THE ORGANIZATION OF DISTRIBUTION

The present concern is to describe the organization and mode of distribution, and some of the mechanisms and agents which facilitate it. The Karen social units do not produce all that is consumed, and they do not consume all that they produce. Some system of distribution is needed. The one used by the Karen has the additional noneconomic feature of promoting interdependence and solidarity between the various social units. The distribution system determines how goods should and will be divided. By "system of distribution," I mean, the mode of integration for all transfer of goods and services provisioning a society [for a discussion of the "economic controversy" in anthropology see Polanyi (1957), Burling (1962), Dalton (1961), LeClair (1962), and Sahlins (1963 and 1972)]. I shall deal with the organization of distribution by distinguishing four general types of "patterns of integration" [three of which are mentioned by Polanyi (1957:250)]. These types, which will in turn be defined, are pooling, reciprocity, redistribution, and exchange.

Pooling: Whatever is produced by individuals in the household, when they are not operating as part of a larger social unit, or that produced by the household when it is acting as a unit is deposited in the household coffers and all members of the household can and do draw on this fund as needed. In other words, there is a general cooperation, sharing, and work for each other in the household. This is true in spite of the fact that there are demands on one's productive endeavor outside the household. The fact that goods flow into the household does, however, have a centripetal effect on the composition of the household. There is a strong sense of solidarity and cooperation in the household. When a daughter marries, her husband is brought into the household to join this cooperative group. If there are already several married children in the household, the first married daughter and her husband and child build a house nearby and set up a new household, although this is not a new independent unit. The husband still helps his father-in-law in the fields and gardens, and the wife still shares running the household with her mother. The pooling is continued but becomes more complex and begins to differentiate.

As the lineage segment is forming and growing, it is usual that each household begins to accumulate a swidden field, a garden, animals, bamboo clumps, and so forth, and thus individual pooling units are formed. But in many endeavors there is still pooling of resources at the higher lineage segment level (the particular activities and resources are mentioned elsewhere). As the lineage segment gets even larger, and particularly when the original nucleus disappears, the system of pooling turns to one of reciprocity between the households as they form separate lineage segments. An exception is the special instance of the ad hoc work-groups which are formed for specific tasks, usually of short term, such as a group fishing expedition or a group hunt. As mentioned earlier, the composition of the work-group is variable, depending to some extent on the activity performed. It often consists of men from a lineage segment, although it may also be made up of either cousins, which crosscut several lineage segments, or of a group of friends. At any rate, the fruits of the communal endeavor are pooled and there is equal sharing. The catch, if small, may be consumed on the spot, or each individual may return home and share his portion with members of his household who were not members of the productive group.

Reciprocity: In pooling behavior, debts and credits are not reckoned; reciprocity, however, is characterized by debt and credit, that is, by some sort of repayment for goods given or services rendered. Theoretically, reciprocal relations might range from a pure gift to a one-for-one exchange, or even further, to stealing (if you steal from me, I will steal from you). The range of reciprocity types might be characterized by the phrase, "to beg, borrow, or steal." Most Karen relationships fall just short of these two extremes, but even these two sometimes occur.[1]

In Ban Hong, there is a kind of gift-work exchange. For example, when a household needs new thatch, the youngsters of the village are informed, come together on one night, make the thatch, and have a good time together. They are not paid for the work. However, when at some time in the future the household of one of them needs thatch made, another group assembles and does the work. A similar sort of reciprocal relationship is involved in house building when all the households send someone to help build a new house. This is gift-work, but reciprocity is expected if at some time in the future the same or a similar job is undertaken by another household. This same principle applies to several other tasks which are also sporadic or cyclical in performance, such as the distirbution of labor for making swidden fields and water wheels. If a person or household habitually does not help at these times, nothing is said; when that person or household has a job to do, however, no one comes to help.[2]

A good deal of borrowing goes on within a Karen village; sometimes it occurs between villages as well. At times it is phrased as a request for a gift; that is, it is begging for something that is desired. Almost anything may be asked for, particularly if the owner has a surplus (e. g., more than one) of whatever is desired. The request is almost always granted, especially so if it is a kinsman who asked for the item. Indeed, it is almost mandatory that a request from a kinsman be granted. It is expected or hoped, however, that reciprocity of some sort will occur at some time in the future, and of course in theory the kin obligations work both ways. There was a case, though, of a Karen from Hui Sai who started a small shop just outside the village on the road between Wang Lung and Ban Aen. His relatives and friends, instead of buying his goods, requested them as gifts. The shop went out of business within a year.[3]

Traditionally, the response to the various specialist activities included only honor, prestige, privilege, awe, or fear. Sometimes nowadays, however, a token amount of money is paid for services rendered, although this is not considered full payment which ends the transaction. There are constant reciprocal relations between specialist and client. Much of the material reward to the specialist comes through his special privileges. The village headman receives an extra portion of meat at ceremonies, which may be eaten later by members of his household. He is also given extra liquor after a ceremony which is considered payment or a kind of "bribe" for insuring that the village spirits protect the people and crops. The head elder receives some of the curry used in any ceremony at which he officiates, which is relatively often. These two, as well as the other specialists, receive additional gifts of food from time to time.

Reciprocal economic relationships may be seen in several ceremonies. One of these is a ceremony to honor the important village elders. On this occasion some member or members of each household go to the house of the highest ranking elder in the village. Each household gives a small gift of rice, possibly a little money, some tobacco, and betel supplies. These gifts are placed in a large basin or tray, sometimes several, in front of the elder who is sitting on his porch. When each household has presented its gift and all are assembled on and around the porch, the elder either touches or holds up part of the gifts and pronounces a blessing on the assembled group, wishing them happiness, long life, good crops, and so on. After this is finished, the elder and his wife are asked to squat on the outer porch while each person pours special water over their heads and bodies in a beg-pardon ceremony. As the water is poured, the person asks the elder's forgiveness for this liberty, and the elder gives him and his family a blessing. When this is done, the group leaves and repeats the ceremony for the next lower-ranking elder, who may have participated in the ceremony just given. The higher-ranking elders do not "honor" their junior-ranking colleagues, because it is considered improper. This ceremony is not performed for the head of each household, but only for those elders who are also specialists of some kind or are very old and respected. In one way or another, these elder specialists do things for the villages throughout the year and thus during the ceremony they are being both repaid and honored.

There are two ways which indicate the rank and degree of prestige of the elders during this ceremony. The first is the order of presentation, and thus as fewer individuals participate as they move from house to house, the quantity of gifts decreases.

The reciprocity relations are obvious: if curing, magic, traditional knowledge, and propitiating the spirits are viewed as pseudo-technology, then these individuals so honored do much throughout the year to see that life goes on properly and that there is health and abundance for the villagers. The elders are given gifts for their services at the ceremony and in turn they give blessing to the villagers. It is expected that in the coming year the elders will perform their services as they have in the past.

There are several other ceremonies in which varying shades of reciprocity may be seen, but the principle is the same. A striking feature about all ceremonial reciprocity is that the material economic element is of minor importance and is subordinate to the reinforcement of social solidarity. The Karen do conceive an element of "paying for services received," or a "retainer" for services expected, however, and the ceremony does show the effect of rank on reciprocal relationships.

Redistribution: There are a few social situations in Karen culture where the mode of distribution may be called redistribution. These are all ceremonial situations and include the funeral, the wedding, and the lineage ceremony. None of them is primarily "economic" in nature, but all ceremonials everywhere have their economic elements. One significant feature of these redistributive situations is the fact that individuals beyond the village are always included.

The economic details differ between the funeral and wedding ceremony, but the basic features are similar. Goods and services flow into the central point of the ceremony, either the household which has had a death or the household of the bribe, from a limited number of households, based on kin and friendship connections. During the usual three days of the ceremony, these goods are consumed or flow out again to a great many households. Although these flow mostly to members of the village-complex, they always extend beyond it to other more distant villages.

The lineage ceremony is also a three-day affair. An important aspect of the redistribution in this ceremony is that it reinforces kinship obligations and restrictions. The ceremony is held at irregular intervals, at the present at least, usually occurring when someone is very ill or has been ill for a long time and every other effort has failed to effect a cure.

The ceremony is held at the home of the female lineage head. Not all lineage members are required to be present, and non-members may not participate. One or two pigs, which have been presented by the persons desiring the ceremony, are sacrificed by the lineage head to the spirits of the lineage, and a feast is held. A considerable amount of time, goods, and services are involved in this ceremony, and all lineage members must receive and eat some of the food from the feast; the curry is carried to them wherever they may be located. In this way, the food is spread through many villages. As mentioned earlier, nonmembers may not eat this food, and since a father is not of the same lineage as his wife and children, he may not participate in the feast with them.

Exchange: The modes of distribution which were discussed above are all concerned with the nonmarket, internal and subsistence economy. I will turn now to the external sector of the economy which is characterized by market-like relationships.

Exchange is really another type of reciprocity, but it seems wise to separate the internal and external sectors of the reciprocity system because they are organized differently. One is based on some type of kinship relation, and goods or services are always exchanged "directly" even though there may be a long or short period of time before a transaction is completed. On the other hand, the external exchange nearly always has an intervening "medium of exchange," there is usually a very short period of time involved in completing a transaction,[4] and generally no kinship relations are involved. A more important distinction between the two is the fact that *reciprocity* implies a continuing relationship, while *exchange* is organized so as to terminate each individual transaction.

In some situations or societies there is a stage between these two in which some sort of "kinship" or social relation beyond the immediate transaction plays a part in the exchange, the medium of exchange may not be used or it is altered in value due to other considerations, and time may not be specified due to mutual trust or obligations. Where these factors in concert or singly apply in a market system, there has been inadequate analysis (see Mintz 1959:24). I do little better here, partly because the situation seldom occurs in Karen transactions.[5] At any rate, I shall use the term *exchange* to mean those transfer events that occur outside the subsistence economy, within the market economy, and which are unambiguously terminated.

The medium of exchange used by the Karen is the Thai *baht* the exchange value of which during my period of field work fluctuated around 20.60 to 20.80 *baht* for one U.S. dollar. Therefore, all figures in this work assume one *baht* to be equivalent to five cents. The Karen have no money of their own, and the *baht* is the basis of figuring all value for market exchanges.[6]

Most exchanges of goods take place in the bazaar in Wang Lung. There is a daily foodstuffs bazaar in the morning, and there are shops which sell many varieties of goods. The Karen come both to sell and to buy. The Wang Lung bazaar widens the Karen economy considerably because it extends outside the local area and supplies them with many things from the world market. They are able to buy nearly everything from rice to aspirin and from socks to suits to bicycles and radios, if they can pay for them. There are, of course, many items in the bazaar which the Karen cannot yet buy, or for which they have no need or desire (for a list of items ordinarily bought in the market, see Table 15).

Not everything, however, is sold in the Wang Lung bazaar. Capital goods such as oxen and buffalo, labor, and land are not sold in the open bazaar. The buying and selling of these factors of production are nearly always an agreement between individual buyer and seller. It is a much more personal relationship than the buying and selling of consumer goods in the bazaar, and it comes close to the middle stage mentioned above.

Karen participate in the market either as individual householders acting as their own agent, through one or another of three types of middleman, or through the development of wage labor.

Almost every adult Karen who wishes to buy and many who wish to sell in the bazaar act for themselves. For the most part, however, local buying and selling is an activity of women and girls. A group goes to Wang Lung from time to time to sell, for example, woven products and vegetables or fish, and returns bringing rice and yarn. A few young men also go the bazaar to sell small banana trees, rope, and jungle products. The men who do so with regularity are those who do not have paddy fields, and often do not have swidden either.

Karen men who act as salesmen to the Thai are the first form of middlemen. Weaving for women and rope-making for men, as examples, are not new occupations, but selling these for someone else, and for a money profit rather than merely exchange is relatively new. Most individuals do not have the time or inclination to sell all their own products. Thus, the role of salesman has become an important distributive mechanism, as well as a significant source of contact and income. Three or four men and boys in Ban Hong do this selling from time to time, but one man is almost a full-time specialist in it. He is also a fortune teller and has some personal magical power which aids his selling ability. This man is thought to be very clever and is a good bargainer. He nearly always sells all the goods consigned to him by the various women in the village, and makes a little profit for himself as well.

Traders, long established among Karen and others in Southeast Asia, compose the second type of middleman. Several young men go on a two-or-three-month trip to the mountains or more likely to Burma, and carry on trade in gold, cattle, opium, beads, knives, smoking pipes, and other items. Today they seem to make the best profit by borrowing money with interest from a Thai, using it to buy cattle in Burma, and then selling them in Thailand and repaying their creditors. The Karen act as middlemen for a cash profit only. One young man in Ban Hong (H–18M) is nearly a full-time trader specialist who spends very little time in the village.[7]

The third type of middleman is a labor boss. This is probably the newest of the middleman roles and is not very widespread yet. This role, like the others, grew out of the adaptation of traditional economic behavior to the exchange system. The boss is the manager of paddy lands either for other Karen, for some more wealthy Thai, or possibly for himself. He hires labor and sees to it that the cycle of preparing, planting, cutting, threshing, and distribution gets done. Some labor is paid in cash and some in rice. His pay, for this work as foreman in Ban Hong, is in rice. Some Karen are able to maintain swidden fields while also owing paddy land by employing a boss to manage the paddy fields. Whether one is able to do this or not depends on available household labor and other resources.

The labor boss is a middleman in the sense that he stands between paddy owner and laborer. Kin behavior may exist between him and laborers, who are always Karen, and nonkin behavior may exist between him and the owner, when the owner is a Thai. But here again the middle stage of exchange relations prevails due to the extra-economic relationship that develops between the labor boss and the paddy owner. They must trust and respect and depend upon each other, and thus the relationship cannot be analyzed in purely economic terms.[8]

The three types of middleman are, therefore, sales man, trader, and labor boss. The salesman oprates in the local bazaars selling village products. Because he spends nearly full time at this job (rather than working at agricultural pursuits), he is able to travel to several bazaars beyond Wang Lung. The trader deals almost entirely in nonlocal goods and travels great distances, sometimes being gone several months. The boss is a middleman not in the matter of handling goods, but in supplying a service in a new developing market relationship. These men all act as agents for distribution. There is, however, yet another type of economic behavior which is a mechanism to facilitate exchange and in which nearly all can participate. This is the role of laborer. Generally, of course, a laborer is a producer not a distributor. Ordinarily, however, Karen laborers do not produce for Karen economy but for the Thai economy. However, they are distributors for Karen economy in the sense that the item "money" is distributed into Karen economy via the wage laborer.

Most families in the village do not own paddy land. Of thirty-seven full nuclear families [9] eight own some paddy land, seven characteristically manage paddy for someone (usually a close relative), and twenty-two families do little or no paddy work. However, rice must be purchased by all households in the village. Of all these families, the majority cannot subsist on what they produce for use or for sale to acquire additional income (e. g., woven goods, rope, fish, fruits and vegetables, and jungle products). Therefore, the husband, the wife, or if possible, the unmarried sons, from time to time go to the Thai and sell their labor for cash doing various short-term jobs. Or they may work for a labor boss, although he does not have nearly enough work for all. When there is enough money, labor will not be sold. At any rate, wage labor provides a specific mechanism for bringing money into the economy, and nearly all households, although not all individuals participate. Thus, a means is provided to supplement subsistence.

THE ORGANIZATION AND PATTERNS OF CONSUMPTION

The units of consumption in Karen society are the social units as described earlier; each of them consumes as a unit at least some time during a year. There are implications for the causal relationship between social structure and economic organization in this fact: however that will not be discussed at this point. The patterns of consumption for the various social units will now be merely outlined.

The household is the basic day-today consumption unit in the society as well as being the major production unit. Here, for the most part, food, shelter, and clothing are produced, distributed, and consumed. This unit of the social structure is solidly held together by its economic functions, and those are reinforced daily as the group which makes up the household eats, sleeps, and shares as a unit.

The lineage segment or work-group often consumes as a unit when it produces as a unit; that is, when production requires it to act as a unit. When the work-group catches fish, goes hunting, prepares a swidden field, or plants a paddy field, there is at least some consumption by the group. However, the group does not produce as a unit in order to consume together as does the household. The work-group produces as a unit due to productive necessity (i. e., due to the nature of the task), and in order that each member may contribute to his own household so that it may consume more.

The work-group also usually does not consume the basic product of its labors. Generally, it does not consume all the fish caught or all the game of the hunt; as a group it does not consume the rice from swidden or paddy. The group does however, consume the food necessary to sustain it during the productive process. The group may consume the entire product before returning to the village if the fruits were not large. During the work in a swidden field, for example, the work-group divides into household groups as the members eat during the meal time. The owners of the swidden provide a curry for the whole group, but individual households for the most part supply their own rice. When the meal is eaten, household groupings are discernible around the numerous bowls of curry. Nevertheless, in spite of the secondary nature of consumption by the work-group, its behavior is important for understanding the general pattern of consumption. If someone is a member of a work-group where few or no members of his household are present, he or his small household group is invited to eat curry and share the rice with any one of the household groupings because he is a member of the work-group. Normally in the village he might not be invited to eat, or a more strict reciprocity might be expected.

It is true that the work-group is not a primary unit of consumption, but the fact that it consumes as a unit is important for maintaining social solidarity in the group. Those individuals who do not often join the lineage segment work-groups are excluded both from consuming with it and from receiving some of the fruits of its productive labors, and this has an important bearing on the household economy of such individuals. Several men in Ban Hong did not share in the productive activities of their lineage segment work-group as they were expected to do, and not only were they excluded from consuming with it, but they had difficulty in receiving any type of aid when they wanted and needed it. One young Thai married a girl in Ban Hong and moved into the village to live with his mother-in-law. He was finally forced to leave the village with his wife, however, because he never helped in lineage segment work activities.[10]

The lineage, in spite of the fact that it is not a residence unit, is nonetheless a consumption unit at times, even though this important group consumption activity occurs sporadically and not even cyclically today. That it is a social unit activity is indicated by the fact that nonmembers are excluded from consumption and by the ritual aspect of the activity.

The Karen lineage illustrates the fact that it is not merely the production units that are the consumption units. Consumption by a social unit is not necessarily the counterpart of production by that same unit. As far as I can determine, the lineage was never a production unit in Karen society, but consumption by this group is an important aspect of the total pattern that provides group cohesiveness and solidarity. The whole lineage does not assemble for any purpose, and so consumption by the unit is symbolic. The lineage mates neither eat together nor eat simultaneously. However, lineage solidarity is strengthened and reinforced even though all the members do not work together and do not and may not eat together.

The village, unlike the lineage, is a productive unit at times, but like the lineage it consumes as a unit only on ceremonial occasions. Village production is almost never for itself; it never produces in order to consume. The village operates to hlep smaller units in such tasks as in housebuilding or swidden planting. So again there is not a one-to-one relation between the production by a unit and consumption by that unit. The all-village ceremony, which occurs twice a year, is the most prominent occasion at which the village acts as a unit of consumption. During this ceremony which takes one whole day, there is complete cooperation and solidarity among all villagers. Taboo signs are erected at the entrance paths to the village, and no outsider may enter. The acme of the ceremony is reached in the evening with the village feast to which all have contributed and at which all villagers eat together at one place, near the village spirit houses. This ceremony is rather expensive as Karen economics go. Each household contributes one chicken, one bottle of rice liquor (or more) and rice, as well as contributing to the cost of a large pig which is sacrificed and eaten. After the main ceremony, much liquor is consumed by the men far into the night as they sit and sing and tell stories.

The final social unit to be considered as a consumption group is the village-complex. Today, the total village-complex does not function as a consumption unit. Rather, individuals from the various villages in a complex come together to represent the villages on various ceremonial occasions such as wrist-tying for household members, the Karen New Year's ceremony, weddings, and funerals. The village-complex on these occasions, like the lineage segment work-group, is not as exclusive as the other social units. At a funeral, for example, individuals from all the villages in a complex will be present as well as individuals from other villages not in the complex. This is because the dead person or some member of his household will undoubtedly have lineage mates in villages other than those in the complex. Therefore, though the village-complex is the main focus at such events, individuals beyond it may be present. At any rate, there are special ceremonial occasions when members of the village-complex meet together and share in consuming. And on occasion, a ceremony will be delayed until some expected village-complex-mates arrive. Consumption at these times includes or implies no specific reciprocity, since it is consumption by a social unit of Karen society, just as consumption in the household is sharing without expected return for what is taken.

Types of consumption, as distinct from consumption by social units, include three main patterns and a fourth minor one. These are, first, consumption for livelihood, which includes the daily activities of consuming food, shelter, and clothing. The second pattern is ceremonial consumption, which is also very important for livelihood since this is the time when chicken, pork, or beef are eaten. Individual livelihood, however, is secondary to the main purposes of ceremonial activity during which goods are consumed. The third pattern of consumption is that carried out in the acts of production. For example, individuals who help plant a field are given a meal, and bamboo is consumed in building a fence or water wheel. (In a discussion of the particular productive activity, these might be better considered as "production costs" or "investment," but they are nevertheless acts of consumption from the general point of view of the economic system.) A fourth pattern of consumption, leisure consumption, is becoming more prevalent today with Thai contact and culture change. In the past, this use of leisure would have been considered part of ceremonial consumption, but today it is new, separate, and secularized. Karen spend money and time at Thai movies, on prostitutes (always Thai), on candies and other types of dessert foods while away from the village, and on gambling.

All four of these patterns of consumption are tied to the bazaar or market in some way. In livelihood consumption, all Karen in Ban Hong must buy salt, rice, and sometimes peppers. Other food items are bought because money is available, usually not because they are necessary for survival. Yarn and thread are purchased in the bazaar in order to weave clothing; and certain tools and materials must be purchased for use in house construction. Ceremonial consumption nearly always requires liquor which is now purchased, usualy from Thai but sometimes from other Karen. Certain other items are bought also, such as pigs, chickens, and sweets, which are used in ceremonial consumption. Consumption during productive activities requires mainly capital goods, such as buffalo, hoes, plow shares, and metal tips for digging sticks, all of which are purchased. Of course, some items in this category are produced by the Karen, such as bamboo, lumber, hoe handles, wooden plows and yokes. Finally, leisure consumption nearly always requires money and is done at essentially Thai activities outside the Karen village.

NOTES

[1] In actuality it is doubtful that the "pure gift" relationship occurs. Among the Karen of Ban Hong there are times when gifts are given with no expected return, as in the case of giving things to children or in the case of giving rice to poorer families, usually those with an opium smoker in the household. But if a person or household is constantly receiving and never reciprocates in any way, the gifts stop, and when the reciprocity does not reach expected standards, the frequency of giving rice, for example, diminishes. On the other hand, the Karen do steal from each other, and more frequently from Thai, but this is antisocial behavior and usually not done in one's own village. The punishment for a habitual thief, again usually an opium smoker, is to kill him some night.

[2] This discussion of gift-work is of course, not concerned with the distribution of a good, and it could have been discussed under production or the organization of work above. The discussion is, however, concerned with the distribution of a service—that of neighborly cooperation, which is quite important in a society living close to nature—and it illustrates an aspect of reciprocal distribution on a level not usually discussed.

3 My wife and I soon learned to keep the second of anything out of sight until we needed it—we were besieged with requests for everything, and it was only proper that we comply if we had two of any kind.

4 Ordinarily if the time gets stretched out, in the Karen case, uneasiness and anxiety set in, because Karen do not have kinship rights and duties with Thai.

5 In field-work among the Bakuria of East Africa, in 1968, I did note such an in-between economic relation, but have not yet analyzed it in detail.

6 However, there is a monetary system used in "paying" the spirits at times, which is probably based on an old Burmese system. This is never used in the bazaar, and the Thai do not know of this Karen system at all.

7 The trader might be considered both a producer and a distributor. He produces for the economy in general by bringing money in, and he distributes by taking goods to Burma and bringing back other goods.

8 F. K. Lehman in commenting on this relationship, pointed out (personal communication) that it may be best analyzed such that the *exchange* transaction is embedded in a *reciprocity* relationship so that person A has developed a continuing reciprocal relation with person B, and at the same time, pays a fee for each individual transaction within the continuing relation. This does seem to be a very satisfactory way of explaining the situation.

9 By "full nuclear family," husband, wife, and unmarried children living together is meant. This may or may not be a complete household.

10 I think neither he nor the Karen quite understood what the trouble was. There was lack of communication and cooperation due to a cultural conflict between Thai and Karen work habits.

8

Money and the Economy: Kinship, Bazaar, Market

INTRODUCTION

This chapter is concerned basically with the infusion of Thai money into the Karen economy and the effects it has had on economic organization. But, before going into the details, I wish to return to a theme mentioned at the beginning of the last chapter and implicit throughout, that of an economic continuum. Boeke (1953) was the first, I believe, to use the term *"dual economy"* to characterize some of the economies in Southeast Asia that had come into contact with Western market relationships. The term *dual economy* is somewhat unfortunate, however, since it seems to imply two unrelated economies operating side by side. This binary opposition is no doubt misleading. It is more realistic to think in terms of a continuum of economic organization which is the implication meant in the title of this chapter. However, as a heuristic device, the idea of two extreme types of organization may be useful.

The social structural organization of economic activities in Ban Hong may be thought of as having two poles. These are the *"subsistence economy"* and the *"market economy"*. These correspond roughly with *"internal"* and *"external"* economic relations. This is not necessarily or always the case, however, particularly today as money becomes more important, and as some exchange-like or market-like relations develop even between Karen, such as the case of the labor boss hiring Karen workers. To characterize the poles, *"subsistence"* and *"internal"* are often interchangeable for one pole. I will generally call this the *"kinship economy"*. For the opposite pole, *"market"* and *"external"* are usually translatable into each other. I will generally call this the *"market economy"*. However, these are merely two aspects—extremes—of the continuum of economic organization. There are mixtures of relations and rules between the extremes. Exchange relations between Karen, and bazaar activities involving exchange between Karen and Thai, are two such points somewhere along the continuum.

The Ban Hong Karen have a dual economy (note that it is a single economy, not two) only in the sense that its two extremes are very differently organized, both in terms of rules of behavior, and in social structure. The kinship economy is based upon cooperation, reciprocity, mutual aid, and sharing within and between Karen social units. Individuals cooperate in fishing endeavors; they help each other in preparing, planting, caring for, and harvesting crops; they go hunting together, and they cooperate in other ways as well. People may or may not share crops equally, but if one family is in need it may borrow from another family, and return the favor at some later time; in some cases, however, there may be no return at all. This subsistence economy has behavior patterns based on kin, lineage, friendship, and village relations. There is a discernible structure, with rules, in these economic interrelations.

The *external (market) economy* is qualitatively different. The principles of organization are quite divergent from the *internal (kinship) economy*, and the external is—or at least was—quantitatively less important than the internal economy in the sense that it seldom dealt with items necessary to maintain life.

It ordinarily involved economic transactions with nonrelatives or non-Karen. Therefore, the first principle is "to get the most for the least." These interrelations are in barter or sale, generally using a medium of exchange, and bargaining is the proper technique of arriving at an exchange value. The items exchanged, at least in the past, are usually of a luxury nature; exceptions are salt and knives. Given the proper impetus, this external economy could become the dominant form with major or entire reliance on market-type relations based on supply and demand. This is beginning to happen to the Karen on the Hod plain.

It should be explained that by *market* is meant a set of economic relations involving supply and demand concerning labor, natural resources, and capital—these serving as items with a price; it is also concerned with products of the use of these factors of production, serving as commodities in a supply and demand situation. If the factors of production and the products therefrom are not commodities (i. e., items with a price), then there is no market. All individuals in Karen society are involved in the market. The fact that the culture is involved in and affected by the Thai market is a crucial factor for change. Due to the local contact situation, in all its ramifications, an organizational rearrangement is occurring in the Karen economic system which is causing structural changes in all of Karen society. There is a shift occurring whereby the nonmarket, internal economy is being replaced by the market, external economy, as the primary form. However, both forms did and do exist.

The yield from traditional Karen economic endeavors is no longer able to support the society, and therefore, the Karen are more and more forced to enter into economic relations with the Thai. This new economic relationship has a momentum that brings the Karen into even greater dependence on the Thai market, and this whole process has caused drastic changes in the rest of the culture.[1]

Money and the Economy: Kinship, Bazaar, Market 197

This chapter will attempt to document the above assertions and will try to show how the process is working with evidence that production does not meet the consumption requirement, that entrance into the Thai economy does meet the deficiencies, and there are certain consequences to this contact and dependence and that the ultimate result is culture change toward Thai peasant status. A picture of this economic situation will be presented through a discussion of yield (production) and consumption figures, such as they are, and then some time will be spent showing what the Karen are doing about it. This is a somewhat difficult task because the Karen are not entirely within a money market economy, and thus quantitative figures must at times be based on estimates.

The major business of an economy is to provision society, or any appropriate social group, with such things as food, shelter, clothing, and capital goods. This discussion will, therefore, be concerned with production and consumption of these items. The questions of concern to this chapter are the following: What is the evidence for the statement that the Karen need money? How do the Karen use money? How do they acquire money?

THE NEED FOR MONEY

The food items in the Karen diet were mentioned previously. Here, the concern is to show that in general the yield from Karen productive activity is not sufficient for consumption needs. Food will be the first item discussed. The major portion of the animal food in the Karen diet is produced without dependence on money, but there are some instances in which money is required. There is neither consistent nor sufficient pork production for Karen consumption. There is an ideological injunction against killing female pigs. Male pigs are purchased and raised for sale or use, but litters are not produced in the village. Therefore, most pork that is consumed in the village must be bought.[2] Beef, like pork, is consumed only on ceremonial occasions, and beef is not raised for food consumption by the Karen. If a person's animal dies, however, it will be sold or eaten. Chickens are raised solely for ceremonial purposes, and are sold in the bazaar only when a person is in need of money for some purpose. Fowl are not raised specifically for the market. A Karen will buy a chicken for a ceremony only if the "proper" kind is not in his own flock; "proper" being determined by auspicious signs and stated in terms of color. Other types of meat food are more common in the diet and include fish, crabs, varieties of insects, frogs, ant larvae, squirrels, birds, snakes, and lizards. These foods are never bought by the Karen, but some of them may be sold for cash in the bazaar.

Jungle plant products collected by the Karen are not sold to other Karen. Usually enough is collected for consumption needs, and sometimes there is a small surplus to sell in the bazaar. Fruit and vegetables grown in the gardens are seasonal so there is never enough to last the year round, although sometimes they are sold in the bazaar. Although tobacco is grown by many households in Ban Hong, most households buy some annually. A considerable amount of rice liquor is consumed by the Karen and although everyone in Ban Hong buys it from time to time, few make it. Salt is an important item in the diet and every household buys it regularly. Several spices and herbs are used constantly by the Karen, but to my knowledge these are never purchased, only collected from the jungle. In general, then, the plant, animal, spice, and herb food items produced by the Karen are sufficient for consumption needs, with a few important exceptions, and there is a slight surplus of some items which are never sold. However, the staple that characterizes Karen diet is rice. There is not enough rice produced for subsistence needs, and Karen cannot survive on the amount of other food items in

Money and the Economy: Kinship, Bazaar, Market 199

the diet. Appendix M represents both dry and wet rice yields in Ban Hong during my stay. The total yield for the village in 1960 was 1,139 *ma*, or 10,251 liter. The total rice consumed in a year by the village, however, is 50,370 liter of glutinous rice or 36,865 liter of nonglutinous rice (both types are grown and eaten). This is dramatic evidence that not enough rice is produced to sustain the village. Roughly from three to five times the amount produced is needed to feed the village. The villagers must buy what they do not produce. It is not merely that they do not produce enough, they *cannot* produce enough given current land use patterns and size of plots. This alone is ample evidence that today the Karen in Ban Hong must have money to sustain themselves.

Turning now to clothing, the Karen weave most of their own and some cotton is grown for this purpose. Apparently the available agricultural land is too scarce to be used for growing cotton sufficient for clothing needs. It is also possible that due to other economic contingencies, the labor supply is not sufficient to divert to this activity away from more urgent subsistence cultivation. At any rate, to my knowledge, there is not enough home-grown cotton for weaving purposes for even a single household in Ban Hong or in any of the other local villages. Every family buys cotton in the Wang Lung bazaar. It is true that the women of every household spend much of their time weaving, probably more today than in the past due to the availability of the market. It is also true that many of the items made on the loom are not for village consumption; even so, only one or two households grow cotton today. Clothing needs cannot be met without dependence on the bazaar for yarn and cotton thread; besides this, all the men use some items of clothing that are only available in the bazaar.

The major tools used today are the digging stick, hoe, machete, plow, and a small knife, although a small axe is coming into more use and a saw may be found in a few households. Nearly every tool and implement used by the Karen today has some part that must be obtained, or can be obtained with less expenditure of time and energy, in the bazaar. Wooden handles, rope, poles, and the like are produced with local material, but all metal parts, fish hooks and line, nails (when used) must be obtained in the bazaar. It might be argued that the Karen buy these metal parts because they have money and not because they "need" them. However, I have tried to show elsewhere (Hamilton 1963) that the Karen must buy these items in an attempt to maintain or increase production levels on overused or insufficient land. The Ban Hong villagers are not able to produce all the tools and implements necessary to support the society today. They must, therefore, buy these things in the Thai bazaar in Wang Lung.

The various structures built by the Karen include houses, rice granaries, fences, pigpens, hay lofts, and water wheels. Much of the material necessary is available for the taking from the surrounding area. However, bamboo, a basic building material is becoming more scarce, and one usually has to buy some for a major construction job. The construction of the various structures, however, may indeed be a case where money is spent because it is available and thereby the level of living is raised. Nevertheless, the production and maintenance of all capital goods does involve the Karen in the bazaar, even if in some cases it is due to a desired standard of living rather than a necessity.

There are several leisure activities in which the Karen obviously indulge because they have money; these activities include such things as gambling with Thai peasants, going to movies, enjoying various kinds of sweets, candies, and factory-made cigarettes while in Wang Lung or Chiengmai, buying lottery tickets, and so on. I am not specifically concerned with these at the present time, howver, even though they are an indication of how money is used. Under production and consumption for leisure is included ceremonial activities that are involved in the maintenance of the culture from the Karen viewpoint; that is, for present purposes the concern is with "necessary" leisure. The ceremonies, believed by the Karen to be necessary for the maintenance of the culture, include life crisis rites for the individual, household ceremonies, lineage feasts, all-village ceremonies, village-complex activities, and nowadays participation in Buddhist ceremonies and the use of spirit-medium services. The particular requirements vary from ceremony to ceremony, but each requires either food or liquor or a gift, or all three. Ceremonial food usually includes fowl,[3] pork, or sometimes beef. As already pointed out, the Karen today usually do not make their own liquor and so must buy it. The gift used in ceremonies usually comes from the bazaar, but it may be something woven at home. Money is also often given as at least part of the gift.

The rice used in a ceremony nearly always comes from the household supply, but it has already been shown that not enough is produced for consumption needs. Chicken may either come from the household flock or it may be purchased. Pork nearly always must be bought for ceremonial purposes. Beef is very seldom used for the ceremonies, but if it is used it is bought for the occasion. In other words, for nearly every ceremony in which the Karen participate today, production is not sufficient for the requirements and there is dependence on money resources.

In the above discussion I have tried to present the evidence for the statement that the Karen are *forced* to enter the Thai economy. (They also may *desire* to enter the Thai market economy.) They must do so because Karen economic endeavors do not produce the consumption requirements. I have tried to make it clear that it is not a matter of using money merely because it is available from the Thai economy. The attempt has been to show that the Karen must have money because they cannot produce all that is needed in nearly every sector of the economy. The most important proof is in the rice production and consumption figures, although in other areas as well, consumption needs outstrip production and thus the Karen are bound to the Thai money economy in order to support and maintain the society. Now I wish to turn to a brief discussion of money consumption patterns.

THE USE OF MONEY

In the discussion of the above section, some consideration was given to the use of money while presenting the evidence for the need of money. In this section, however, I wish to turn to the specific uses of money in one typical household (H–15) in Ban Hong. The present discussion requires shifting the level of analysis from that of "the Karen economy" to that of "the household economy," the emphasis now being on household expenditure of money in the bazaar. Therefore, all the possible uses of money will not be discussed. The purpose of the present section is to give an indication of how much money is needed and what money is used for to maintain a particular level of everyday living.

The household represented is neither the richest nor the poorest in the village. It is an average household with a mother, father, four sons, and two daughters. The family does not own paddy land, but they prepare a swidden field yearly. The family maintains a tobacco garden and a banana garden near the river. This household owns the only coconut tree in the village, and they own several other fruit trees around the house as well as a couple of bamboo clumps. They do not own buffalo, but from time to time, they do speculate in cattle. During my stay in the village, the family bought and sold six head of cattle. They were raising a flock of ten chickens, and had one pig before the epidemic. As is typical, the women do a considerable amount of weaving, and the boys, one in particular, do wage labor occasionally. One son who was twenty-four years old was married but his wife died in childbirth. This son spends most of his spare time in wage labor and thus adds to the family larder. The summary (Table 15) presents the expenditures for an average year for this family.

The summary of the annual family expenditures contained in Table 15 includes at least the most frequent purchases. There are no doubt other items bought in the Wang Lung bazaar from time to time that were forgotton by the informant, and it is also possible that the average is a little high. The villagers were reticent to make such an estimate of expenses, since they keep no accounts and do not like to talk about money matters in specific terms (see Beardsley 1959:196 for a discussion of the problems of quantification). At any rate, the above is a fair average, and gives an indication of how money is used and how much is used for daily needs or desires. I would estimate that the village average per person is somewhere between 20 *baht* and 30 *baht* per month, or $12.00 to $18.00 per person per year. This is high according to the estimate by Young (1962:97). He suggests that, for the Sgaw, "An average of a thousand *baht* per year per family is probably a high estimate." However, the Sgaw, in Thailand at least, seem less well off than the Pwo, particularly those Pwo on Hod plain. My "average household" spends more than twice what Young estimates the income of a Sgaw family to be. However, Young's estimate is for all Sgaw, while mine is only for a single Pwo village.

TABLE 15 Annual Expenditures of an Average Household for One Year

Item	Price	Frequency of Purchase	For Family Estimate Per Yr.
A. FOOD			
Rice	18.00 *baht* thang[a]	6 *thang* per month	1,296.00 *baht*
Miang (fermented tea)	.50 *stg.*[b]	30 pkgs. per month	180.00
Salt	3.00 *baht* (*thang*)	1 *thang* per year	3.00
Fish	1.00 *baht* (pkg.)	4 per month	48.00
Tobacco	1.00 *baht* (pkg.)	4 per month	48.00
Peppers	10.00 *baht* (kilo)	1 kilo per year	10.00
Betel supplies	3.00 *baht* (set)	4 sets per month	144.00
Sweets and candy	1.00 *baht*	4 times per month	48.00
B. HOUSEHOLD			
Water jar	2.00 *baht*	1 every 2 years	1.00
Bucket	30.00 *baht* (pair)	1 every 3 years	10.00
Bowl	2.00 *baht*	1 per year	2.00
Spoons	2.50 *baht* (dozen)	1 dozen in 2 years	1.25
Lamp	1.50 *baht*	1 per year	1.50
Kerosene	.50 *stg.*	4–5 times per month	24.00
Water jar (another type)	2.50 *baht*	1 in 2 years	1.25
Cup	1.00 *baht*	1 per year	1.00
Rice cooker	37.00 *baht*	1 in 10–20 years	3.00
Pot to steam rice	2.50 *baht*	1 in 2–3 years	1.00
Tea cup	1.00 *baht*	2 per year	2.00
Betel box	6.00 *baht*	1 in 10 years	.50 *stg.*
Mat	15.00 *baht*	1 in 3–5 years	3.00

TABLE 15 Annual Expenditures of an Average Household for One Year—Continued

Item	Price	Frequency of Purchase	For Family Estimate Per Yr.
C. TOOLS			
Digging stick head	6.00 *baht*	1 per year	6.00
Hoe head	20.00 *baht*	1 per year	20.00
Plow share	6.00 *baht*	1 per year	6.00
Machete	14.00 *baht*	1 per year	14.00
Axe	14.00 *baht*	1 in 10 years	1.50
Small knife	4.00 *bhat*	1 in 2 years	2.00
D. CLOTHING AND ADORNMENT			
Cotton	7.00 *baht* (2 *vwai*)	10 *vwai* per month	420.00 *baht*
Shirt	25.00 *baht*	6 per year	150.00
Head cloth	6.00 *baht*	2 per year	12.00
Belt	6.00 *baht*	2 in 3 years	4.00
Buttons	1.00 *baht* (per 100)	4 pkgs. per year	4.00
Beads	2.50 *baht* (per string)	4 strings per year	10.00
Comb	.50 *stg.*	2 per year	1.00
Coconut oil (for girls' hair)	.50 *stg.* (bottle)	1 bottle per month	6.00
Hair oil (for boys)	8.00 *baht* (bottle)	1 in 2 months	48.00
Sandals	12.00 *baht*	2 pairs per year	24.00
Sandals (another type)	2.50 *baht*	4 pairs per year	10.00
Pants	10.00 *baht* (pair)	4 pairs a year	40.00
		TOTAL	2,597.00 [c]

[a] One *thang* = 20 liter of milled rice.
[b] There are 100 *stang* per one *baht*.
[c] The average per month is 216.42 *baht*, and the average per person per month is 27.05 *baht*.

THE ACQUISITION OF MONEY

Since the Karen cannot produce enough by traditional means in order to subsist until the next harvest, and since there are certain market goods that they need or desire, the people of Ban Hong carry out certain activities in order to acquire money. Money is part of the Thai economy, and the Karen are taking advantage of an alien culture trait but using it differently.[4] In the Karen case, the time spent in acquiring money is competing with rice production. What is important to the Karen economy is the money and often not the item produced to acquire the money. Or, to put it another way, money may be considered as stored rice in the Karen economy, while the item produced in acquiring the money (e. g., a fence, or a blouse to suit Thai taste) is often either not part of or not usable in Karen culture. The infusion of money into Karen economy has changed the culture, however, and just as there are techniques of rice production and catching fish, there are techniques for acquiring money.

There are various ways to acquire money; one way is to sell "surplus" subsistence goods.[5] Another way is to sell products not ordinarily used by the Karen but desired by the Thai and others. A third way is to work for the Thai for wages, and, finally, one may sell his land holdings. When these techniques of acquiring money are consistently included in an economy, there has been a true entrance into the market. The Karen are in the process of doing this, but have not fully achieved it yet. I will attempt now to describe this entrance into the market.

Selling Subsistence Products

Many of the items that are subsistence products are *sometimes* sold to the Thai (rarely to other Karen) in order to make money. Since the data on this has already been presented, the major categories of items sold which are ordinarily used for subsistence will merely be listed. These include everything cultivated except rice.[6] Some domestic animals are sold (pigs and chickens) and many items that are hunted or gathered are sold at times. Fish are sold in Wang Lung, as are certain products of domestic activities such as clothing, blankets, bags, rope, and some basketry items.

Besides these subsistence goods which are sold in the bazaar, certain services of Karen specialists are sought by Thai, and these individuals are paid for their services. These specialists include the curers, fortune tellers, black magicians, and even the midwife on rare occasions. The specialists do not ordinarily seek out business in the Thai community, however.

A Thai may at times "rent" a Karen buffalo or some implement to be used for short periods of time. The Karen are hesitant to engage in this activity, however, and will only do so in unusual circumstances; for example, if the Karen know the Thai well beforehand so that previous social relations have already been established, or if the Karen needs money badly for some purpose.

Cash Products and Crops

Besides the selling of subsistence products, a few items are produced specifically for the market. In this section is included a discussion of those subsistence products that are *altered* for the market, and those products sold on the market that are not used by the Karen for subsistence.

The major subsistence items that are specifically altered for the market are woven goods. The alterations effected make the woven clothing unacceptable for Karen use. These items must be sold, therefore, or the effort is wasted. Karen bags have also been altered in design and shape somewhat to make them more salable; this is changing the bag used by the Karen, because they will use these if they are not sold. Data has already been given above on selling these woven goods (p. 87, and see Appendix I), and it will not be repeated here. This is an important source of cash income because there is a constant demand for the goods, and because weaving can be carried on for most of the year. It is only forsaken at the peak seasons in the rice cycle.

Miscellaneous jungle products sold include stick-lac, collected once a year from trees owned by individual Karen and sold to Thai for from 2 to 10 *baht* per kilo. The Karen in the Hod area do not know what stick-lac is used for, but know only that the Thai will buy it. Children and sometimes women may from time to time cut weeds and grasses to be sold in Wang Lung to Thai to be used as pig food. One basket (about bushel size) is sold for 1 *baht*. This is not a regular activity and very little cash is realized.

Bark from the Chinese Box tree is collected in the hot season from which a face powder is made and which, it is said, makes one cool. This is sold to Thai, and at times Karen from Burma come to the Hod area to buy the bark to be taken back across the mountains and sold to the Burmese. The bark is sold for approximately 3 *baht* per kilo. A very small income is derived from selling the bark, and only a few individuals collect it.

One old man who recently moved into Ban Hong (H–33) receives part of his living by making and selling charcoal. He collects wood in the jungle and burns it underground. He is the only person in Ban Hong who has ever done this, but several people in Hui Sai, and one or two other small villages, also sell it. The standard price is 1 *baht* per five-gallon can.

This same man (and only he in Ban Hong) makes and sells brooms of local jungle wood and grasses. He sells these exclusively to Thai for 1 *baht* each. They are never used by Karen; the Karen, however, do have a kind of broom, but it is made differently and each household makes its own.

A few Karen, as has been indicated, buy and sell oxen as a means of making money. The Karen never use oxen, but the Thai use them to pull bullock carts; this is, therefore, purely a technique for making extra cash on the part of the Karen. Water buffalo are bought and sold for the same reason.

One or two Karen from other villages in the area grow and sell peanuts (many Thai do so). It was reported to me with some awe that one Karen made 1,000 *baht* in one year selling peanuts (this may be an exaggeration, of course).

There are several items which are bought in the bazaar by the local Karen and are sold to other Karen villagers in the mountains more distant from the Thai (or Burmese) markets. These include patent medicine of various sorts, beads for necklaces, buttons (used for making bracelets and to put on bags for decoration), and certain household goods (mostly metal spoons and bowls). The income from these items is quite small, and the trade is incidental to cattle trading between Burma and Thailand.

Wage Labor

Wage labor is an important means of supplementing the household income, especially for those households which have no or only a few ways of supporting the family, such as owning paddy, fruit trees, bamboo clumps, or even swidden fields. All households depend to some extent on income from wage labor; but some are more dependent on it than others, however, and there is a variety of activities engaged in to make money this way. The pay range for wage labor is from 2 to 15 *baht* per day; few individuals are paid either of these extremes, however;

the average pay being about 10 *baht* per day or a little less. The following is a sampling of labor activities and the pay received.

1. One young boy spent two days delivering three oxen to a Maeo village in the mountains west of Ban Hong. He received 15 *baht* for his efforts. This money was turned over to the family.

2. A group of Karen from Ban Hong and one or two other near-by villages spent six days cutting teak lumber for a Thai in Bô Luang, about forty kilometers away, and earned about 50 *baht* each.

3. Two men from the village worked for five days preparing a swidden field for a Thai, and each received 60 *baht*.

4. Another two men worked for seven days making a fence in Wang Lung for a Thai. Each received 35 *baht*, or 5 *baht* per day.

5. In another case, four men, two of whom were from Ban Hong, worked for six days hoeing a hill field for a Thai. Each had to spend 2 *baht* for a round trip bus fare. They earned a total of 65 *baht* each.

6. Two men were gone from the village for four days preparing a field for peanuts. The Thai owner paid them 60 *baht* each for this hoeing.

7. One old man, the head elder of Ban Hong, worked for a Thai helping to building a barrage across the river for a water wheel and paddy field. The Karen received 2 *baht* for this half-day.

8. One group of six Karen from two villages, Ban Hong and Dong Dam, worked for a month or more, making permanent wells in a couple of Thai villages. They were not paid a wage, but an amount was agreed upon for the job no matter how long it took or how many people were involved. The arrangements

for this work were made between the Karen *political* headman (who lives in Hui Sai and is the Thai-appointed headman for *muban* 4) and the Thai officials. The total pay was 2,900 *baht*, or 483 *baht* per man, which averaged around 16 *baht* per day. This is considered quite good pay, but the work of digging the wells was very difficult.

This is a good time to point out that the method of determining pay depends on the type of job to some extent. One cuts bamboo for so much, usually 50 *stg.* per pole (this is ordinarily carried on only once a year in making rafts for the Thai tourist trade). Making teak lumber is 1 *baht* per "arm" (tip of elbow to tips of fingers plus the width of three fingers. Some jobs, like making or repairing fences and helping to build Thai houses (general handyman work) are figured on the basis of so much per day labor. Another method, as discussed above, is to have a set amount for the job, always agreed upon beforehand. Finally, the job of doing the initial preparation of a field—for peanuts, soy beans, rice or garden—is usually paid by so much, 10 *baht* to *15 baht* per square *wa* (one *wa* is four "arms," or about one meter). However, all these methods of determining payment amount to about the same in terms of daily income.

Wage labor of these and other miscellaneous types goes on throughout most of the year. The peak season of rice work for Thai and Karen is about the same, so those Karen who do not own paddy or swidden fields are working in Thai fields while the Karen who do have fields are busily working their own. This tends to make a real division in the village work force. There is a physical separation of the two groups because often those Karen who are doing wage labor at the peak of the rice work period leave the village and may be gone for some time, sleeping away from the village. The Karen who have fields feel less obligation to share rice with the laborers later since there was no help received from them. This separation into two distinct groups is alleviated to some extent when some other member(s) of the household, usually women, can help in Karen fields. These are, nevertheless, two distinct groups, one group almost never involved in traditional Karen endeavors. This separation shows up in many subtle ways.

The solidarity of the household is maintained, however, because all members pool their resources no matter how they were received or what types of income, whether rice or money, are involved. The average yearly household income in *money* from wage labor surely does not exceed 1000 *baht*.

Land Speculation

The final drastic and sometimes desperate way of acquiring money is to sell land. The Karen are not land speculators and no Karen is a real estate broker, but sometimes a Karen will sell land to settle debts with the added desire or hope of making a profit besides.

Land has only recently become a salable item for the Karen since they began wet-rice techniques of cultivation. Before this time, land was never bought and sold. As pointed out earlier, much of the original paddy land cleared by the founder of the village has been sold. No one who sold his paddy land has bought more at some later date. There is, however, at least one individual in Ban Hong who bought land for both wet and dry-rice cultivation (H–19).

It is obvious, then, that the buying and selling of land is not a significant way of increasing resources or long-term income for the Karen. One who sells his land realizes a rather large sum of money (relatively), but when this is gone he is usually in a much worse position than before because he has no way to buy more land. Land may be sold for money, but it is easily lost with little possibility of gaining it back again. Paddy land is nearly irreplaceable for the Karen.[7]

HOUSEHOLD INCOME

I shall again shift to the household level and say a few words about income and the relationship between the two aspects of the economy, the subsistence and the market economy.

Unfortunately, I was unable to get accurate figures on the total money income of the various households in Ban Hong. On the basis of many examples of income and its source I would estimate, however, that about one third of the cash income of the households comes from each of the three major techniques of acquiring money: that is, one third comes from wage labor; one third from "cash" crops, products and services; and one third comes from selling surplus subsistence goods. Of course, these proportions vary from household to household, but all households in the village acquire money, and all use the three techniques mentioned.[8]

An important consideration for this discussion is the actual proportions of the economy which are involved in the subsistence sector versus those involved n the market/bazaar. Table 16 presents an estimate, in terms of percentages, of the average household income for one year. It is based on the few figures that I was able to get, some household inventory figures and observation and discussion with all the villagers. The ratio of subsistence income to income derived by the use of money is roughly sixty–forty. Even if we subtract the money income from consideration, since it is used to buy all the items in the last column, there is still 58.6 percent of the economy which is based on subsistence activities versus 41.4 percent based on the use of money. It is obvious, however, that money is *very* significant to the total economy, since 41 percent of the economy is based on it.

GENERAL CONSIDERATIONS OF DUALITY

One pole of the economy is based on kinship rights and duties, obligations, and privileges. The other pole is based upon supply and demand in the market, and profit and loss in money transactions. All three processes of production, distribution, and consumption are affected by this duality. It crosscuts the entire economy, and therefore it is not possible to describe efficiently the economic activities on the basis of duality. That is, it is not the case that some productive activities are entirely within the subsistence sectors, while others are only in the market sector. These, as stated earlier, are ideal polar extremes. Nearly every act of production, distribution, and consumption has both kinds of organization somehow involved. This fact is the cause of confusion, and possibly animosity, that develops in economic behavior of individuals and social units. At times a person may wish to act in terms of one set of principles or the other, kin or market, and he may not be sure which to apply. There might also be a dilemma, or he may apply the wrong set from the viewpont of the other party involved.

There are, of course, some activities that can be considered to be more in one sector than another. It is obvious to which pole belongs the act of collecting pig food to be sold in the bazaar, but even here there may be a conflict of interests. The person collecting pig food to be sold in order to buy rice may be asked by a relative to stop that task and help with some other; thus a kinship principle is involved. Or a relative may ask for some of the pig food, thus cutting into the expected income. In either case, a degree of animosity or ambivalence may be generated.

It is not intended to give the impression that there is complete confusion and breakdown of the culture; this is not the case. There are different organizing principles in the economy, to be sure, but the Karen generally understand them and know how to operate in a given situation. In terms of distribution, there is almost never a doubt or conflict. Everyone knows whether or not he is dealing with a relative or nonrelative, and it is obvious which rule of behavior is to be applied.

TABLE 16 Estimate of Average Household Income and Assets for One Year (in Percentages)

Item in the Economy: Income	% from the Subsistence (Internal) Economy	% from the Bazaar/Market (External) Economy [a]
I. FOOD		
Rice	25.00	75.00
Other plant foods	99.00	01.00
Meat (pork, beef, fowl)	20.00	80.00
Fish	95.00	05.00
Other	98.00	02.00
100.00%	67.00%	33.00%
II. HOUSEHOLD ITEMS		
Household utensils	10.00	90.00
100.00%	10.00%	90.00%
III. TOOLS AND IMPLEMENTS		
Work and household tools	20.00	80.00
Hunting implements	98.00	02.00
100.00%	59.00%	41.00%
IV. CLOTHING AND ADORNMENT		
Clothing items	90.00	10.00
Adornment and miscellaneous	10.00	90.00
100.00%	50.00%	50.00%

TABLE 16 Estimate of Average Household Income and Assets for One Year (in Percentages)—Continued

V. MATERIALS AND STRUCTURES

Building materials	80.00 (58.6% total economy)[b]	20.00 (41.4% total economy)[b]
100.00%	80.00%	20.00%

VI. MONEY

Money income [c]	67.00	33.00
100.00%	67.00%	33.00%
% of total economy [d]	59.00%	41.00%

[a] By *bazaar/market* is here meant items acquired by the use of money whether bought from Thai or other Karen.

[b] These two figures, 58.6 percent and 41.4 percent, are the proportion of the total economy represented by the two sectors of the economy if the category Money (Item VI) is left out of consideration.

[c] The *money income* under *subsistence* is that income derived from selling Karen products, and the income in the *bazaar/market* column is derived from various types of wage labor.

[d] The figures given here representing the proportion of the total economy were not prejudged or assumed. They were derived after the item-estimates were made. It is also true that the total percentage for each category were derived from the item estimates, and were not made first.

There are times, however, when the relation of distribution to consumption leaves some doubt or generates ambivalence. One man (the head elder) had great difficulty in deciding whether or not to sell some bamboo to his nephew. Who was to use the bamboo? The old man knew that his nephew was going to sell the bamboo to a Thai (thus, the reason for buying bamboo from a kinsman). The old man was finally forced to let the kin obligation take precedence since his nephew would not back down. As it turned out, the elder not only received some money, but he also had a return obligation due from his nephew. It was obvious, however, at the time of decision that he did not want to give up the bamboo. Other similar cases were noted in which the request was actually refused.

Money and the Economy: Kinship, Bazaar, Market 217

In terms of production, also, there is not a great deal of confusion. Subsistence production for food, shelter, and clothing is based on kinship principles and mutual aid. Social units within the society cooperate in producing rice, gardens, and so on. With paddy fields, however, since they are relatively new to the economy, there is again some division of interest. One must generally use more labor than his household can provide, so other Karen are "hired." Hired labor is usually a set of relatives of one sort or another. If the laborers working in a paddy field have their own paddy, there is no difficulty; there is merely reciprocity between the households which own paddy. Many workers do not own paddy, however, and so they are paid either in rice or money. If they are paid in money, however, this does not stop them from asking for rice later when their own is gone, since the paddy owner is a relative and is expected to give freely. It turns out, therefore, that even though only a few individuals own paddy fields, the yield is distributed to the whole village eventually, and sometimes beyond it to other kindsmen. This causes some difficulties, because there is no way to make a like return, or even an equivalent one, even though the ideal is to do so.

Conflicts in the general consumption patterns may occur due to differences of interest as discussed above. One person may wish to use a chicken as a sacrifice in a ceremony, while another may insist that the chicken be sold in order to buy some other good. Here again the conflict is between the kinship obligation and the market. The use of money is facilitated by and in the market, but it is almost never used in the internal economy. There is little or no lending and borrowing of money in the subsistence economy.

At any rate, the general pattern becomes clear: the internal economic processes are based on kinship principles and are imbedded in the general social organization. There is no exchange medium that can be strictly called economic. On the other hand, money may and most times must be used in the market, which has a separate social structure and is traditionally outside Karen culture. In this external economy, relations are based not at all on kinship, but on price, supply, and demand. However, these are not mutually exclusive categories in actual behavior, but intrude on each other in many situations. The final patterns have not yet been worked out.

HISTORY AND CAUSE OF THE DUALITY

To this point I have presented a synchronic analysis of the economic extremes, but how they came about is another important aspect of this study. I will, therefore, attempt to present an outline of what caused the Karen to become involved in the market.

The terms *kinship*, *bazaar*, and *market* represent the stages in the development of the present-day economy. At one pole of the economy is a situation where the social units are interdependent and interrelated in the processes of production, distribution, and consumption. At the other pole is a situation where kinship is a hindrance. At this pole there are attempts to outsmart and sometimes even to cheat, and there is always bargaining and maneuvering for better position. Magical powers, of which everyone has some, are used to gain advantage. Most transactions use money in some way. These two poles are the extremes; there is the intermediate step, however, which the Karen economy has gone through and which is still used.

It seems best to deal with the development of the stages of the Karen economy by discussing their probable history. The question becomes, therefore, what in general, set off the Karen involvement in the market and how was it accomplished? As long as the Karen had available land, could move freely, and there was little population pressure on natural resources, the internal subsistence economy was sufficient and efficient for satisfying

Building a waterwheel.

Karen work group building a water-wheel for irrigation. The workers in the water are attaching bamboo tubes which carry the water to the irrigation canals. The **barrage** crossing the river channels water to the wheels.

Repairing aquaduct to rice paddy.

Village girls planting rice.

Top: Work party eating a meal during swidden planting. Bottom: A work group thrashing paddy rice across the river from Ban Hong. The fence in background surrounds kapok and banana garden.

Family unit cleaning thrashing floor in preparation for measuring rice grain.

most needs of the society. There was always some outside contact, of course, and there were some economic relationships involved in these contacts due to need for knives and salt, and the desire for beads, betel nut, and a few other "luxury" items that could be acquired through trade. There have probably always been, therefore, some external economic relations with some precedent for an exchange value between items of trade. Exchange via trade, then, is the middle ground between subsistence activities and the market, and this kind of activity is carried on today.

As contact, land pressure, and restrictions became more intense due to inroads of the Thai and Burmese governments, however, these external economic relations became more important for sustaining the society. As time went on, more goods necessary for survival had to be obtained from the outside; or, more luxury goods were acquired and more efficient tools of production were necessary, thus changing the subsistence pattern and making the Karen more dependent. The relationship between the two types of economic organizations began to reverse. At this point, however, the "two economies" were only "internal," and "external"; they were not yet "market" and "nonmarket." That is, the Karen have been trading in bazaars in Burma and Thailand for a long time, but this involvement is not a true market with the factors of production on the market block of supply and demand. The Karen, no doubt, brought jungle products into the bazaars and traded them for knives, beads, cloth, and so forth. This trade probably had little effect on the basic subsistence economy.

The chain of causation which led to true market involvement and the development of the present dual economy seems to be as follows. There was, and still is, more and more intensive contact with a dominant culture. This involved greater population pressures on the land and other natural resources, and included as well more political restrictions and obligations of various sorts. Therefore, production levels began to decrease due to the inability to move easily and to land-use restrictions imposed by the Thai government. New swidden fields must now be kept secret from officialdom. These dry-rice fields, therefore, tend to be used too long, and production goes down further. There is, therefore, more dependence on the bazaars for subsistence goods, and thus many Karen are changing over to or adding wet-rice cultivation techniques. Changing to the use of paddy fields turned land into an item with a price for the Karen; it now must be individually owned, bought, sold, registered, and taxes must be paid in money. Land became an inherited item, as it had not been before. This new agricultural technique automatically involves the Karen paddy owners in the market not only because land now has a price, but because tools and buffalo must be bought on the market, and somehow labor must be paid. Therefore, the need for money grows as money becomes important for subsistence. Cash crops, or at least crops and goods that are salable, become significant for acquiring money, and new items become individually owned, sold, and exchanged in the bazaar or on the market. Labor begins to be sold as well, because not all individuals have paddy land; even those who do own it find that they cannot grow enough to support their households. However, this is partly due to kinship demands on the yield. At any rate, many items become commodities that were not in the past, and there is a price on the factors of production.

The bazaar and market involvement is tending to increase in intensity. This is due partly to the demand for consumption goods, which brings a greater demand for money, and necessitates more involvement for basic livelihood, causing, in turn, more and faster change. There is no equilibrium yet, since all of these changes cause other changes in the internal economy. In an attempt to maintain or increase productive levels and to raise the level of living, there is a desire for better or more production requisites. Therefore, an even greater involvement in the markets and need for money follow. Finally, the bazaar has many new goods available for which consumer-desire is being developed. The external economy has finally come to rival the internal one as the dominant form.

It is important to stress the extremes of Karen economy, because all, or nearly all, the market mechanisms are outside the Karen culture. The Karen would not and could not have a market economy if the Thai markets and market relations were not present. The relationship is a dependent one, but this new pole of Karen economy has had far-reaching effects on the whole of the culture. It is also important, I believe, to insist that there was a middle ground on the road to true market relations. If there had not been the bazaar mechanism and the precedent of outside economic contacts, then the necessity of economic change, if it had occurred as described above, would have required that these be developed first. Exchange between groups was the first step on the way to money and supply-and-demand schedules.[9]

NOTES

[1] These statements certainly have cause and effect implications, and I mean for them to have such implications. I will say more about cause and effect, and the articulation of Karen economy to that of the Thai on p. 266. However, I wish to make some general comments here: the chain of causation and its relation to changes in Karen culture are obviously complex. One might argue that the Karen *want* to enter the Thai market and therefore change results (e. g., production of subsistence crops goes down). I think that this is an anthropocentric argument for the cause of change in the general cultural situation. The Karen, as individuals, do "want" money and many of the consumer goods that money will buy. They do sell things in the bazaar in order to get money for luxury items; but essential items are purchased too!

However, the Karen do not *by choice* raise less rice because they can buy it in the market. They buy rice because they *must*. Each Karen household raises as much rice as it possibly can—given overuse and small plots of land. I have often seen the discouraged looks and heard the corresponding comments concerning the amount of yield at harvest time.

Be that as it may, even if it is argued and granted that the Karen enter economic relations with the Thai because it is advantageous to do so, the result is the same: due to contact with Thai markets, Karen culture is changed. I would only wish to add further, that as the contact increases and change becomes more profound in Karen culture, the situation become more irreversible. The Karen must be involved in the market relations now because of the heavy commitment made by the culture to market relationships. The argument that it is merely advantageous is no longer relevant. Of course, it was advantageous for hill Karen to trade in Thai and Burmese bazaars (otherwise they would not have done so), but this is not the cause of current market relationships and the resultant culture change.

In the present chapter I am not concerned with whether or not it is "good" or "bad," or "advantageous" or "disadvantageous," for the Karen to enter the market relations. My concern is to point out that they have entered market relations, that this has caused drastic change in Karen economy, and that they must now be involved in the Thai market system because of the environmental-cultural situation.

[2] Since female pigs may not be killed, the sows and female piglets would soon overpopulate the village if the Karen tried to raise litters. The ideological restriction on pig killing may, however, be a rationalization rather than a cause: given traditional productive activities and social structure, the labor, land, and capital required for serious pig production may not be available. There is also no large market demand for pork.

[3] In general, chicken is used, but, at the death of a lineage head, a duck is sacrificed in a special ceremony for the woman. Since ducks are not raised by the Karen, the bird is bought from a Thai.

[4] Boeke (1953:67) points out that: "A distinction must be made between money traffic and money economy. Money traffic means that money is used in trade by way of facilitating matters. Here the use of money is consumptive; it is employed to make payments to settle obligations; money is "bought" with commodities, labor or land when and in so far as it is needed for these purposes. But money economy means that the whole economic system is based on money; that money, mainly productive, is employed as capital, as the foundation and point of departure for profit making. In the first case the place of money can be indicated by the simple formula C-M (commodity-money) meaning that the commodity, ware or labor, is the foundation of the economic activity which brings the economic subject in the dualistic sphere, and that the purpose of this activity is the obtaining of an amount of money. With the obtaining of the money the economic ac-

tivity comes to an end. When the money is used to buy final goods the formula has to be extended to C-M-Cl, because then money, as a means of exchange, takes the middle place between the commodity sold and the commodity bought.

In the case the money economy has penetrated the society, however, the formula has to run thus: "M-C-M'C-M, etc., with money as capital at the base and at the end, including profit . . . . The formula is only a link in a progressing series, because the money, at every turn, is used again as capital."

[5] *Surplus* is defined as food items that will spoil due to inability to store them until needed, or other types of goods produced beyond the needs of a household. Sloan and Zurcher (1953:312) define *surplus* as "that which remains after immediate needs have been fulfilled."

[6] One or two Karen in Dong Dam do produce enough rice to sell some in the bazaar. This is unusual, however, and they do not do so regularly.

[7] All Karen in Ban Hong, and several other villages, are about to lose all their land due to the dam being built that is supposed to flood the area. The move will cause some drastic economic shifts for these Karen.

[8] The fourth technique, that of selling land, is so rare that it is not considered here.

[9] Concerning the time element for these changes, Hackett points out that it is very recent for the Pa-o, and I believe it is quite recent on the Hod plain too. The degree of involvement in the Thai market and the cultural shifting going on indicate this. Hackett says of the Pa-o:

> In recent years cash payment have come into vogue in a limited number of cases, but the village person usually prefers payment in kind to cash. Many Pa-o farmers are now raising cash crops, so that in the village nearest to Taunggi, a money economy is slowly replacing the barter economy. This is a very recent development however, for even in 1950 taxes were collected as a percentage of the crop (1953:173-74).

9

The Winds of Time and Change: The Past

INTRODUCTION

The focus up to this point has been on the social-structural and economic aspects of Karen culture at a given time. The "ethnographic present" so far has been 1959–60. However, there are two other ethnographic presents implicit in this work. One "present" is some hazy time in the past which I cannot pin down very well, but to which I have alluded from place to place. It is around seventy-five to one hundred years ago (if my headman genealogies are correct). The third ethnographic "present" is 1969–70. I am, therefore, talking about a continuum of structural relations, enviornmental change, and culture contact.

In turning my attention specifically to the issue of change, I will focus now on the period leading up to the 1959 "present," and then in the next chapter on the changes since that period up to the 1969 "present." Ordinarily (at least, in the past) not much happens to the groups studied by anthropologists over a ten-year period. However, the Karen situation in *Amphur* Hod has been characterized by contact, migration, change, and increased dependence upon the Thai throughout the time under consideration in these two chapters.

Contact and change occur in more than just the economic sphere, even though that has been a major emphasis in this study. I have attempted to deal with the problem of economic change in Karen culture by discussing the organization of the economy, and I have tried as I went along to show how economic change was effected diachronically. At the same time, I tried to show, mostly by implication, how this economic change causes change in the rest of culture. I have not yet, however, gone into other aspects of culture-change. Before doing so, I wish to discuss some theoretical issues concerning culture-change in general.

It is assumed that, first, culture is a system more or less integrated, but never in equilibrium because, second, the cultural system is constantly striving for better or new adaptation to a constantly changing natural and/or cultural environment. It follows that, third, culture-change is often effected by the factors outside the culture which affect that culture most drastically; that is, those factors which force a new adaptation. Before culture-contact, change may be caused by a changed natural environment (such as a decrease in water supply), or by a new relationship to the natural environment (such as an increased population density ratio), or by migration to a new environment. After culture-contact is established, change may be caused by adaptation to the new cultural environment or the natural environment as changed by the new cultural situation. The implication of the above is that the *impetus* for change comes from outside the system under consideration. If this is so, then the cause of culture-change in general comes from outside the system called culture. Culture consists of a number of functional subsystems, however, and at the level which defines the economy as the system of interest, the cause of change in the economy comes from outside of it, thus making other subsystems of culture part of the "environment" of the economy.[1] There are only three possibilities; first, change may be caused by a different natural environment or a new relationship to it. Second, change may be caused by economic contact with another culture, such as the Thai markets. Third, economic change may be caused by a change in some other subsystem of the culture (such as the political or religious) which was changed due to some outside factor. That is, it is possible that the original culture-contact or impetus for change was not through the economy at all, but through some other subsystem—for example, ideology as in the case of Christian missionary contact with the Karen. This type of contact may cause a change in the religious system as well as the others.

The above discussion brings up a further theoretical point: I would argue that there are two kinds of change, "content variation," and "structural rearrangement," or "elaboration." One might be called merely "change" and the other "evolution." It seems to me that structural rearrangement is crucial for change from one cultural type to another; in the case of the Karen, the change has been from tribal to peasant status. It is true that culture-contact may come from directions other than economic. However, these "other ways", such as religious, political, and social contacts, may involve merely cultural overlays or content variation that do not directly alter the basic structural features of the culture until the organization of the economy has been affected. It is possible too, of course, that content variation may occur in the economy due to contact, and that this does not alter the system structurally. I would argue this point by saying that it takes more than merely selling surplus subsistence goods in the Thai and Burmese bazaars to alter the structure of the economy (see footnote 4, page 228). In the case of the Karen, it took the placing of the factors of production on the market. Following is an example of this type of change. The Karen in Burma have been involved in a rebellion against the Burmese ever since the end of World War II. In addition, these Karen have been in contact with Christian missionaries for over one hundred years with the result that some Christian beliefs and ideas have filtered into Karen culture. Many of the Karen in Burma are still in isolated areas, however, and their animist beliefs prevail but with some interesting twists. One of the old beliefs is that with the proper rites or charms one may be made immune to physical attack, including that of bullets. One of my informants from Ban Hong who travels to Burma often on trading trips tells me that many of the Burmese hill Karen involved in fighting the Burmese are now using Christian rites and the cross, believing that these will make them superior to Burmese bullets. The culture is basically the same as it was, but content variation has occurred and Christian ideas and symbols have been substituted for traditional ones. Culture change in the sense of structural rearrangement had not occurred.

I would argue, then, that basic changes in the cultural system in general come with changes in the technological-economic system. If the economy does not change structurally, then the culture will not change structurally even though contact and content variation may occur in any of the subsystems of a culture. However, let the contact situation have important economic implications, and changes in the structure of the subsystems of the culture are imminent. As a matter of fact, the new ideas of all sorts that enter a culture are often brought first by economic agents. In the example above, there were religious agents, but the structure of the religious organization apparently did not change and the animist beliefs merely had a content change in these remote areas of Burma. It is important to note that I am arguing for the primacy of economic structural change, although all sectors of the culture may be changing at once, as indeed they usually do. Structural change in the economy must at least occur simultaneously with other changes, if it does not occur first.

FACTORS AND EVIDENCE OF CHANGE

Important changes have indeed occurred in Karen culture, and most important evidence that far-reaching changes have occurred is that the Karen themselves see differences between the recent past and the present. Many of the changes noted seem small and insignificant to the observer; to the Karen they are important, however, and they are symptomatic of deeper systemic changes in the culture. The systemic, structural changes will be discussed below in the appropriate section. Here will be listed only a few examples noted by the Ban Hong villagers.

It is well-known on the plains that the hill Karen men still wear their hair long and tie a turban-like cloth around their heads. There are a very few men in the Hod plain who still wear their hair this way. The head elder of Ban Hong pointed out to me that he did so until after he had two children. At that time he cut his hair short, like the Thai, "because it was in the way for work" and "it was not convenient to keep it long." The Karen have had scissors only since intensive contact with the bazaars, and could afford them only since there has been some excess money. It is also a fact that the Thai make fun of Karen men with long hair.

Another change of a similar type is seen in the Karen funeral dress and the dress of Karen youth in general. The funeral is a focal pont in Karen life (Hamilton in press) and is a time of courting for the unmarried. The marriageable boys and girls meet together and sing around the body for three days. During this time boys and girls are dressed in all their colorful splendor, but times have changed. In the past, the boys wore colorful turbans around their long hair, with just the short end beyond the hair-knot hanging rakishly over the turban. They wore earrings of silver with bright threads attached. The boys wore many strands of white, yellow, and black beads around their necks, and their bright dress was partially wrapped in colorful red and white striped blankets. To top it off, each boy carried a long cane of rattan with a crook at the upper end. The girls were colorfully dressed, too, in their long "sack dresses"—but apparently no so colorfully as today. Many aspects of the boys' dress have shifted to the girls' dress. Boys no longer wear bead necklaces, and the girls wear many more than they once did. Now a girl may wear as much as 100 *baht* worth of beads. Girls wear the blankets now, but did not before. The boys are still colorfully dressed, however, with some substitutions and some survivals of the past; they now wear a piece of market cloth around their short hair. Loosely-tailored "Chinese" pants are worn, sometimes with a Western-type, white dress shirt. The blanket, the earrings (often minus the silver), and the cane are still used. The Karen shoulder bag often has many buttons sewn on as part of the design. The effect of funeral dress is still there, but the older villagers bemoan the lack of traditional clothing that they remember.

In the past it was only "giants" and "demons" that had red mouths and finger tips, and Karen were afraid of them. Now, however, the girls are beginning to paint their mouths and fingernails red, despite the elders' protests. The girls are no longer afraid to use these "paints." According to the head elder, the children no longer "listen to or believe their elders." The children no longer obey so well, and it is "not good." The elders still say the children should not use lipstick, but they are often ignored. "Now, the Karen are not good," according to the headman of Ban Hong. Conflicts (sometimes actual fights) develop between the youths of various villages; this is particularly bad when it occurs at a funeral—as it did on one occasion that I observed. The head elder told me that some young men are becoming "lazy." One young fellow in particular was pointed out as lazy, because he loafs around the house and does not help his father with the work. It is true that this boy does not help with the swidden field or garden; however, the boy often spends his time in wage labor for Thai, and he always gives much of the income to the household. But because he does not often participate in "traditional" work, he is considered lazy. Those who do engage in traditional activities are not called lazy.

These brief examples provide some evidence that the Karen see change occurring even though they do not know the specific cause or results. The cause in general is the ever-widening contact with the outside world, and this, in turn, is widening the Karen world.

The Karen in the Hod area have been in contact with and impressed by different groups over the years. At one time this northern part of Thailand was under Burmese domination, but not during the life time of present villagers. At least by world of mouth, and sometimes by direct contact, the Karen know of the British and their culture in Southeast Asia.[2] The Chinese have left their mark in various ways, and, of course, the Thai have had intense contact in various capacities. During World War II, the Ban Hong Karen came into contact with the Japanese. Over a two-year period, the Japanese were seen going into Burma; later, as they began to lose the war, the wounded and hungry were again passing through Wang Lung. There were apparently friendly relations, but at least some Karen were conscripted to work in Chiengmai, building the airport for the Japanese. The head elder thus spent twenty days in Chiengmai and received a total of 5 *baht*. The school in Wang Lung was apparently a stopping over point for the soldiers. The Karen were frightened of the wounded, maimed, and dead Japanese soldiers because their "spirits" wer considered very "fierce." The Karen were impressed, however, with all the Japanese equipment, their large horses, their different eating habits, and so on.

As the Karen come into contact with these more dominant groups, the one thing that seems to impress them the most and which seems to them to be the cause of dominance or power is the fact that the Thai and others have a "country" and a "King." The Karen in Ban Hong have a vague idea of what the Karen rebellion in Burma is all about. One young man in Ban Hong told me in specific terms that their troubles stem from the fact that they do not have a country, but that they hope to have one some day. This general idea was expressed by others as well. However, the Karen in the Hod area do feel some small affinity to the Thai King. The year before I arrived in the area, the King came to Chiengmai and members of many of the hill groups were brought to see him at government expense. A few Karen from the Hod plain went to see him, and a young boy from Ban Hong sang a Karen song for the King. Also during the visit, many of the hill peoples were trying, at one point, to push forward to see and "pay respect" to the King, but they were pushed back by the police. Some hill person was heard to say, "He is our King too; he is not just your King." The personage of the King is held in awe and respect, but often the Thai officialdom is not.

From time to time, the Karen hear news broadcasts over the radio. Several villagers were also fond of hearing the Thai lottery results over my radio, which was the only one in the village (several Thai in Wang Lung have large, battery-operated sets). At any rate, the Karen have some idea of what is going on the world via the radio. They knew of the Berlin crisis because of a broadcast heard while I was in the village. Their world is still small, however, because even though they heard the names of countries such as America, England, France, Belgium, Germany, and Russia, when I asked what the broadcast said, I was told only that there might be a war between the Central Thai and the communists. Berlin was missed altogether. They know only that a communist is "bad" and has no religion. They know that America is across some water, but have no idea where or how far. I was asked how there could be a path through the water, and how I could follow it to get back to America if the water was so wide that one could not see the other side.

There are more immediate problems facing the Karen in the Hod area, however, and they are much more concerned with these. The most important problem, and the one likely to have the most far-reaching effects, is the fact that much of the Hod plain was to be flooded and many of the villages would have to be evacuated. The major villages of this study—Ban Hong, Vwang Kham, Vwang Mô, Mang Mêng, Hui Sai, Dong Dam—were all to be under water by about 1964. A dam has been built across the Ping River which is located north of Tak (see Figure 1) and roughly one hundred and fifteen miles south of Ban Hong, as the Thai, with American aid, develop a large irrigation project. Of the eight *Thambon* in *Amphur* Hod, five will supposedly be flooded. This means that even some of the Thai villages mentioned in this study—Ban Aen, Wang Lung, Ban Nong, Hod, and possibly Nakarya, will be inundated, although Nakarya may be far enough away from the river that it will not be so drastically affected. There is apparently still some doubt as to the boundaries of the proposed lake. However, whether or not the villages are actually flooded, they will be drastically affected by this project. The villagers, from the dam site all the way up to Wang Lung, have been paid for their land, trees, and bamboo clumps. The Thai government has also set aside some land for resettlement; nevertheless, the people are not happy about the impending move. Many of the Karen have said that they will not go to the government resettlement area. The Ban Hong villagers have found a site back in the hills a short distance that they believe is a good area to settle a new village. They probably could not have paddy fields there, however, and I suspect that they will either not go there, or that the village will split. Those that now have paddy land can get land for paddy at the government relocation area, and those that do not now have paddy fields probably will not be able to get such land since they will have only second choice. In addition, there will be the problem of paying for the new land. The money received for their present land was paid out three years ahead of the move, and it has not been saved for the move. The Karen, in particular, are indeed in a difficult situation, and what actually does happen will be crucial information for understanding the process of culture change a little better.

I will conclude this chapter with a brief discussion of some changes in the Karen techno-economic system, the social situation and the political structure; finally, some ideological-religious changes will be mentioned.

TECHNO-ECONOMIC CHANGE

Karen pre-market technology was relatively simple in the sense that it did not require many goods and materials that were not available to all. Most items were made of wood, bark, grasses, bamboo, leaves, and other jungle products. Rope was manufactured in the home, houses were made without nails and cotton was grown and clothing woven. Dry-rice fields were made with a digging stick and by burning. About the only tool needed from the outside world was a metal knife, and it lasted many years. The only food item necessary from the outside was salt. There were, however, apparently always some luxury items obtained such a drums (Marshall 1922:115), beads, and silver.

Much of the above description holds true today, but in an attempt to maintain productive levels, metal tools are now needed. Those who own paddy land must have tools for plowing, harrowing, watering (water wheels are made), and harvesting. The water buffalo itself has become an item of technology—with other technological requirements for its care. Changes in work time allotment mean that many items which were formerly produced are now bought. Therefore, items that were formerly used for direct consumption or for further production (investment) are now sold for cash. These changes have caused the technology to become considerably more complex.

The continuum of economic organization has long been in existence and is maintaining itself, but the market economy may become the dominant form. There are, therefore, conflicts today in interpersonal economic relations between villagers. The Karen are now dependent on the Thai for money and market goods, and this economic interrelationship tends to make the Karen more dependent in general.

SOCIAL CHANGE

Thai-Karen contact and social relations have been more or less intense for many years. During this time, and due to the attempts at accommodation, there have been significant changes in Karen social structure. Changes have occurred in house type (and therefore family pattern), residence, and the content of inheritance (which has had even further ramifications). Marshall reported in 1922 that the Karen in the hills of Burma lived in long-houses, but that on the plains they lived in individual houses as the Burmese do. I could find no long-houses in Thailand, nor could I find any Karen from the hills who lived in them or knew about this past, although there may still be some, of course. However, the linguistic evidence would indicate that the Thailand Pwo Karen lived in them also.[3] The characteristic pattern was, apparently, for one main lineage to form the nucleus of a village long-house with individual families occupying apartments.

As the Karen moved further into contact with the market and as the internal economy became less significant, the marital residence pattern began to change. Therefore, the house type changed as well as the pattern of ownership and inheritance. For example, of forty adult married women in present-day Ban Hong, nine do not follow the expected norm of matrilocality (H–3, H–5, H–6, H–10, H–13, H–22, H–26a, H–30, and H–34). The men in six of these marriages belong to the main lineage which owns most of the paddy held by villagers (H–3, H–6, H–10, H–13, H–22, H–34). In the seventh and eighth cases the couple lived with the wife's parents for a time and then moved to live in the husband's village to be near his father's paddy fields (H–5, H–26a). In the ninth abnormal case (H–30), the man and his wife moved to Ban Hong in order to benefit by aid from his relatives, and because the wife wanted to be closer to the Thai bazaar in order to sell her woven goods. However, just before I left the village this woman told me she and her husband planned to return to her home village. There is no paddy land in the husband's lineage.

Paddy land, originally cleared by Karen, has descended following traditional rules of inheritance for traditional items. It has, however, gone to men and women alike, and since it is nonmoveable, the owners stayed in the village after marriage in order to work the land. This new relationship of social organization to economy tends to break down the lineage effectiveness (men do not move out, and women do move in), and assuming that I am correct in postulating its previous existence, the long-house organization of residence is now gone. It must be remembered that previously land did not descend to lineage heirs, but was a "free" item, that is, a village resource. However, the old pattern of residence still persists in most cases, as with the woman mentioned above who will move back to her village with her husband.

Many other examples of social contact and change could be given. I will merely mention two. There is one case of what might be called "acculturation in reverse" in Ban Hong. A Northern Thai woman (H–6F) married one of the Ban Hong villagers. This woman has taken on many Karen traits, but it is obvious that she is Thai. She does not wear the complete Karen married woman's dress, but she does wear her hair in the Karen style. She always speaks in the Northern Thai dialect, and is always answered in Karen, even by her own children, who, by the way are being raised completely as Karen. In turn, however, this woman provides entree to the Thai community, in which she still has a place, and serves as a filter through which Thai ideas enter the Karen community. There are other such cases in a few of the Karen villages.

There are a few cases where Karen women have entered the Thai community, or have attempted to do so, but this situation is more difficult. In the first place, the Karen do not approve or sanction such behavior, particularly on the part of women. Secondly, the spirits may attack the woman or her relatives for such things as cutting the hair, removing the traditional Karen woman's dress and bracelets, or moving out of the village to marry a Thai. During my stay, one young divorcee (H–24 da) did leave the village to marry a Thai man. There was quite an uproar in Ban Hong over this. A short while later a young unmarried girl changed her dress, cut her hair, and moved into Wang Lung to live with and work for a Thai teacher and his wife. The Karen girl came from a large family, and her father was an opium addict; therefore, she left out of economic necessity. Nevertheless, when a short while later there was a series of events that were fearful or disastrous, including an elipse of the moon, a storm that ruined a few houses and rice bins, and the death of all the pigs in the village, the behavior of these girls was found, through the services of a Thai spirit medium, to be the cause. The families had to make amends by providing a sacrifice to the village spirits.

It is obvious that traditional social organization and relationships are changing. The residence pattern is changing due to economic pressures. Preferred marriage patterns are not always wise or possible, so people do take forbidden partners at times, including Thai mates. The effectiveness of the lineage segment is breaking down due to stronger interests outside of it or members being far away from lineage influence. Many conflicts (as described above) are developing in traditional social behavior.

POLITICAL CHANGE

There are many aspects of the political-social control organization that indicate contact, change, and dependence on the Thai bureaucratic system. On the other hand, traditional Karen political organization may have changed the least of all the aspects of the culture. From a formal point of view, there has been considerable change, but from a functional view, political and social control have not changed much from the old days. Structural changes are, for the most part, in external relations, even though there are probably more internal conflicts these days due to other kinds of changes.

The Thai-created position of headman is purely a political and secular one. The Karen man, who is elected to the position by his fellow villagers, wears his uniform, as do the Thai headman, when attending the monthly meetings at the administrative headquarters in Hod village. The function of the political headman is to report births, deaths, marriages, moves of people, land ownership, and infractions of the (Thai) law. In turn, he takes directives and information back to the village, as pointed out earlier. Not every Karen village has one of these political headmen; each Thai administrative unit called a *muban* does have one, however, and a single *muban* may include three or four Karen villages. In the present case, the headman in charge of Ban Hong lives in Hui Sai, but he has a brother and sister living in Bang Hong. The political headman has both a Thai and Karen title, although the Karen term is merely one of respect meaning "old uncle," and is a term applied to any oldster in the village that is respected.

The position is purely a Thai overlay, and the headman of *Muban* 4 has no structural position in traditional Karen ceremonies. He acts and is treated as any other adult in the community. The present headman is too young to be an important elder. However, he seems to be looked up to and respected by some of the younger adult men who have come somewhat under Thai contact and influence. In other words, he is beginning to take on the role of an official, and, in the future, he may be given a structural position in ceremonies. At present, he is usually ignored by the elders.

The Karen, however, have as little to do with Thai officialdom as possible. They often do not report the information requested by the Thai, although they do register paddy land, for their own protection. When they can get away with it, or if it is an internal problem, the Karen handle infractions in their own way. Practitioners of witchcraft are killed or run out with the threat of execution. Civil disputes are mediated by the elders, and decisions are voiced by the traditional politico-religious headman, which are lent weight by the elders. Sanctions are imposed on offenders of Karen custom by the traditional headman or in conjunction with the elders. For example, the unmarried and half-witted daughter of the midwife was known to be having sex relations with a number of different men. This behavior was frowned upon, but ignored, until she became pregnant and then it could no longer be ignored. She and her family had to make an offering to the village spirits which cost the equivalent of ten dollars; she also had to change to married women's dress, even though she still has no husband and is not likely to get one. Another case did involve Thai officials. A Karen man and his wife were killed during their sleep in the hills not far from Ban Hong. This was a complicated case involving witchcraft, property rights, and inheritance. Suspects were picked up and dealt with by the Thai higher officials, since the situation was reported to the *Amphur* headquarters rather than being handled by the Karen themselves as in the past. In this situation, as in many others, the case was finally dropped for lack of any proof or evidence. The Karen finally handled it to their own satisfaction: the suspected murderer was forced to flee from his village and is now living in a village closer to Thai influence.

Karen political organization, therefore, maintains the traditional headman who is both political and religious leader and who has power and authority through the village elders and the village spirits. He deals with intravillage problems ordinarily by traditional means. Problems or needed decisions are discussed by him and the elders at a political meeting at the headman's house where the sentence or decision evolves. The result is expressed through the headman. External political relations are handled by the secular headman who is officially appointed by the Thai, but who is "elected" by his own fellow villagers. This position is beginning to become more important as the Thai interfere in Karen affairs, or as the Karen ask the Thai to step into the situation. Generally, the Thai officials do not know who is the religious leader. At any rate, the Thai-appointed headman is usually not the traditional headman of his own village, and certain conflicts may eventually arise as these two positions compete for leadership.

IDEOLOGICAL–RELIGIOUS CHANGES

There has been a great deal of ideological contact and blending between Northern Thai and Karen. Both groups have animistic elements in their belief systems (see Brohm 1963:155 for a discussion of the false dichotomy between Animism and Buddhism), but the Thai are predominantly Buddhist and the Karen are Animists. In the Karen case, at least, it seems to be true that the shift going on from Animism to Buddhism is related to the greater involvement in Thai economic activities and involvement in the market. When checking my data to see which adult Karen go to the Thai Buddhist temple or regularly participate in other Buddhist ceremonies, I found that only those who own paddy themselves, or are likely to inherit it, are the ones consistently involved. The Karen seem to see a connection between economic activities and religious organization. This point was verbalized to me by the Headman of Ban Hong when he said that the Karen would become Christian if they knew it would improve their economic lot. There is a suggestion of a causal association in this correlation. It is at least true that when the Karen take over some economic task that is traditionally Thai, they also take on the ritual practices that go along with it. For example, there are certain Thai religious beliefs and practices that accompany the paddy cycle. The Karen who have paddy fields also carry out the Thai rites, as well as including some of their own. Leaving out the proper ceremonies is the same as leaving out some necessary technical activity. The religious beliefs and practices are part of raising wet-rice. This rule seems to apply in general: as the Karen take on more Thai characteristics in general, they also adopt the Thai religious practices and beliefs in general. There is recognition and adoption of the patterned connection between cultural elements.

One example of the relationship between economic and religious organization is from a village near Ban Hong. I saw several funerals while in the field, and the one which had Thai elements in strongest evidence was that given by two men from Dong Dam for their mother. These men owned several plots of paddy land, hired workers, and, in fact, produced a surplus of rice and sold some in the bazaar nearly every year. One of the men has a Thai wife. Their economic role was very unusual, and the mother's funeral was equally unusual. Thai priests attended and did half of the officiating, and the normal Karen procedures were carried out after the priests finished and left. These men were not obliged to spend extra money on a Thai ceremony. The fact that they did is significant and is correlated with the fact that they are more Thai-like than other Karen.

There are other kinds of evidence also that the belief system and ritual practices are changing. Thai spirit mediums and magicians are consulted by the Karen (as a matter of fact, the Karen magicians and curers are sometimes consulted by the Northern Thai). Christian missionary beliefs have filtered in also, even though there are no Christian Karen in the local area. The political headman living in Hui Sai remarried during my stay and had one of the local missionaries say a prayer and tie his wrists for the ceremony. However, Christian influence has been very slight in the local area.

At any rate, the religious organization and belief system are taking on a flavor of Buddhism. Traditional moral behavior is changing and conflicts are developing, particularly between the generations. Alien influences are coming in through Thai spirit mediums and through particular Thai priests. These Thai have magical powers to help the Karen solve problems with which their own animistic belief system can no longer cope.

NOTES

[1] This form of argument leads me to a discussion of the internal cultural environment, or the relationship between the subsystems of a culture in a search for causal factors. Maruyama (1963) has presented some interesting, provocative ideas concerning this type of causal process which he calls "the second cybernetics." I should note here, too, that since "individuals" are not included in the definition of culture, I leave undiscussed the question concerning their role in culture change.

[2] I learned the following Burmese Karen poem in Ban Hong: "The foreigners [British] will go home/The Burmese will die/The Karen will eat rice, eat rice."

[3] The Karen term for "house" in Ban Hong today is *daw'*; the current term for village is *gêing*; the general term for "house post" (poles which support the house above the ground) is *gêing thêng*, or "village post". According to Marshall, the term for an "apartment" within the old long-house is *dê* which involves only a vowel shift from the Ban Hong word for an individual house. This implies that the individual house today was the "apartment" of the past.

10

Ten Years Later

INTRODUCTION

This chapter focuses on the ethnographic "present" of the latter quarter of 1969, or roughly on the Karen in *Amphur* Hod as they were at the beginning of 1970. However, in order to understand the changes, I will also discuss the events leading up to that time which occurred during the decade of the 1960s.

When I left Thailand in late 1961, the Karen and Thai in five affected *Thambon* of *Amphur* Hod had been paid by the government for their registered land and property which would be inundated, and they had begun talking among themselves about the possibility of having to move their villages, and where they might go.[1] They were not convinced, however, that the flooding would actually occur. People carried on their daily activities as if nothing were going to happen. They planted trees, vegetables and rice, and were building houses in the villages. A few months before my departure, the Thai built a permanent market structure in Wang Lung. However, construction of a new *Amphur* Headquarters soon began on higher ground at Tha Kham, fifteen kilometers to the north on the Chiengmai highway. Officials were acting as if something would indeed happen, but this was hardly convincing to the Karen or even to the local Thai peasants.

For two additional years, the situation remained unchanged and the Karen continued their life uninterrupted. By this time, it had been approximately four years since the local people had been paid for their property, and of course, none of the money remained to be used for the move when it did come. In 1964, the flood came dramatically: the water level at the new dam reached 116 meters which raised the water level in the research area by 13 meters, thus flooding most of the villages. This forced both Karen and Thai villages to relocate on higher ground. The reservoir formed a lake in the *Amphur* for three seasons, 1964, 1965, 1966, and then it receded. By the beginning of 1970, it had not reached flood level again, and the river is back in its original bed at *Amphur* Hod, but is a little wider now. Nevertheless, the change has come and the area will never again be the same. The reservoir will fill and recede many times depending on the vicissitudes of rainfall variation.[2] Because the research area is located at the upper end of the reservoir, the fluctuation in water level is more noticeable and dramatic: there is either a "normal" river or there is a flood. Near the dam there is always a lake with minor rise and fall.

YANHEE AND THE ENVIRONMENT

The Yanhee Dam, officially known as the Bhumibol Dam, is located roughly sixty kilometers north of the city of Tak on the Ping River. The King of Thailand laid the foundation stone in June 1961, and he performed the dedication ceremony for the dam and power plant in May, 1964. Yanhee is a multipurpose dam with the potential of providing electricity to thirty seven provinces. At the time of this re-study it was providing power to twenty eight provinces and to one important *Amphur* in each of four additional provinces. The dam also provides flood control, fishing, and irrigation potential.

The "full" capacity of the dam is 123 meters, and at that level the reservoir just reaches Tha Kham where the new *Amphur* Hod headquarters are located. The maximum length of the reservoir is 207 kilometers reaching from the dam in Tak Province to Tha Kham in Chiengmai Province, and the maximum width is 7.5 kilometers. It covers a total area of 300 square kilometers in size. However, the reservoir has a general but rough hourglass configuration with lakes at both extremes, and with a narrower channel connecting them. The upper lake, of interest here, extends from Myd Ka, 135 kilometers north of the dam, to Tha Kham at the extreme northern end of the reservoir. The upper lake is, therefore, 72 kilo. long, and in places it reaches the maximum width of 7.5 kilometers.

Reservoir shape and extent are only theoretical and potential, however. They will only be realized when there is 120 or more meters of water at the dam, which has not yet occurred. The maximum water depth reached during the five years from 1964 to 1968 was 116 meters, and the minimum was 92 meters. In July, 1969, it was at the 98 meter level. The high point of 116 meters was sufficient to flood the research area for three seasons, thus affecting the natural environment and the socio-cultural situation to such an extent that natural and cultural ecological shifts were effected and noticeable. One informant said, "Before the flood I was an adult; when the flood came it was as if I died; now it is as if I have been born again as a young boy; I must relearn how to make a living." At any rate, since the completion of the dam, the gross changes in the environment are easily identified, and the resultant changes in human use of the environment can be traced.

1. Since it is already some distance into the reservoir area at the Hod—Wang Lung—Ban Hong area, the flow of the Ping river has slowed down somewhat, which has resulted in some additional silting. This slowing and silting has altered the use of water wheels which were used to irrigate the paddy fields (discussed further below). There has been little, if any, major

FIGURE 8   Upper Reservoir Area

change in the main river course, but it is wider and some new islands have developed which are sandy and overgrown with bush. The river is navigable by small power boats from the dam to Wang Lung where fish are brought daily by boat to be sold and transferred to buses and taken to the Chiengmai market.

2. Ten years ago the Karen caught many small and medium-sized fish with their traps, throw nets, surrounds, and by sand-diking. Currently, the fish are generally much larger, up to fifty kilo in weight, which has caused a change in fishing technology. There was a dramatic increase in the number of fish caught after the reservoir filled in 1964, but then a decrease occurred in the fish population. Still, however, there are more fish now than before the dam was built since the government is stocking the reservoir. This was paralleled by an increase, then decrease, in human population in the *Amphur* (see footnote 5). The local people have noted the difference in the quantity and size of fish and in the resulting income. In fact, there is currently competition between Thai and Karen in the fish market. The Karen are catching fish to eat and sell, but they cannot compete well with the more advanced technology of the Thai. Karen say that fishing is now very poor, but in many cases the fish are larger than the Karen traps can handle. However, the amount of fish being taken has decreased since the first period after the dam was finished, even though more fish are caught now than before the dam was built. Karen difficulty with fishing has to do with fish viewed as a commodity, and Karen inability to buy expensive nets, boats and motors—all of which are used by the Thai. Before the dam, fish were seldom sold by the Karen, and certainly were not a significant source of income, as they would like to make them now.

3. There have apparently been some changes in the weather if the local people are correct. Everyone is convinced that their well-being is to a great extent determined by adequate water, mostly in the form of rain. People are also convinced that since 1964, the year of the first flood, there has not been adequate

rain. In 1964, they believe there was a great deal of rain which brought a good rice crop and the filling of the reservoir. Since that time, it is believed there has been less rain and less rice each year. The people are convinced that before the dam was built, there was, in general, more annual rainful. Ergo, before the dam was built, life and times were 50 percent better (by local estimate) than now. People recognize and admit that, before the dam was built, it sometimes happened that too much rain fell and over-filled the paddy fields, but it would always go down in a few days and did no great damage to the rice crop. Now, however, when the fields flood, the water does not recede and the crop is ruined.

There may be some truth in what the people say, but it is clear that they are reacting to a general change that they do not like and imputing a cause-and-effect relationship that may not be the case. On the other hand, people who live in and are closely dependent upon an environment do know something more about its fluctuation and characteristics than mere uninformed guesses. One difficulty is that their knowledge may be very short term. Unfortunately the rainfall records of *Amphur* were somewhat disrupted by the moving of the headquarters, but a look at Table 17 summarizing days of rainfall does indicate that there was a trend for significantly fewer rainy days around the time of the flood in 1964 and thereafter. Surely the Karen would notice this and impute to it the notion of less rainfall. However, Table 18 indicates that there is no significant trend in annual quantity of rainfall over the ten-year period. However, the number of days of rainfall may be quite significant to Karen gardens and swidden rice fields. At any rate, it is as yet unclear whether or not there has been an alteration in the weather that is significant over a long period.

4. Land contours have changed due to the flooding which has had a drastic effect on agriculture: ten years ago the Karen were able to use water wheels to raise the water about twenty feet to irrigate paddy fields. However, with the flood, the rath-

er sheer banks of the river have been eroded in most places so that water wheels can seldom be used. Water is now brought to the fields by gasoline pumps owned by Thai. Thus the Karen who rent the pumps are able to grow two crops per year, whereas before the dam was built, they could get only one crop per year. However, paddy fish, crabs, etc. are no longer found in fields irrigated in this way.[3] Furthermore, the pumps draw sig-

TABLE 17 Days of Rainfall*

	1 Annual Days of Rain	2 Jan.–July Days of Rain [a]	3 Aug.–Dec. Days of Rain [b]	4 May–Oct. Days of Rain [c]
1960	107	46	61	92
1961	131	71	60	111
1962	109	51	58	100
1963	121	52	69	102
1964	?	?	?	?
1965	85	38	47	78
1966	77	42	35	71
1967	(77)[h]	(34)[h]	(43)[h]	(60)[e]
1968	(109)[h]	(58)[h]	(51)[h]	(93)[f]
1969 [d]	(110)[h]	57	(53)[h]	(90)[g]

* This data is based on *Amphur* records maintained by local Thai officials. Unfortunately there is no data for 1964, the year of the flood.

[a] This set of seven months includes the first three months of the rainy season.

[b] This set of the five months includes the second three months of the rainy season.

[c] This is the rainy season. Its onset and termination is dramatically characterized, throughout the ten years for which I have data, by large increase in rainy days during May and decrease after October.

[d] Since I left the field in 1969, I do not have complete data.

[e] This figure had some missing data for two months. It was completed by averaging on the basis of past performances during the same months.

[f] This figure had missing data for one month, and was completed as for e above.

[g] This figure had missing data for three months and was completed as for e and f above.

[h] This figure may be inaccurate since some data seems to be missing from local records.

TABLE 18 Rainfall

	Annual Rainfall (cm)	Jan.–July Rainfall	Aug.–Dec. Rainfall	May–Oct. Rainfall
1960	87.4	37.3	50.1	76.4
1961	109.3	55.5	53.8	82.0
1962	105.3	30.7	74.6	102.4
1963	100.1	31.1	69.0	90.2
1964	?	?	?	?
1965	93.4	33.8	59.6	77.0
1966	100.0	48.7	51.3	95.2
1967	92.3	35.5	56.8	74.9
1968	98.3	53.1	45.2	85.9
1969	99.3	41.3	58.0	81.3

nificantly less silt and nutrients, thus lowering paddy soil fertility. There were many comments that the soil is not as fertile as it was ten years ago. In addition, use-rights of the pumps can cost as much as half the yield. In spite of an additional crop per year, the farmers are realizing less rice than before the dam was built. The cost of water is high, net yield is lower; insecurity is widespread due to the possibility that crops may be ruined by flood so most Karen are not planting paddy today.[4] Thai have relocated their fields through purchase (which the Karen cannot afford to do) or have taken up new pursuits made possible by their generally higher income.

5. In the previously flooded areas, a thorn-bearing scrub bush eight to ten feet tall has invaded the land. The plant is quite dense and makes passage difficult. It must be cut back to reclaim paddy fields and gardens. However, bees gather the flower pollen and are producing honey in quantity which many Karen are now collecting and selling in the Wang Lung market providing a new scource of income in the Karen economy.

6. Access to Thai and Karen villages, on both sides of the river, has become very difficult due to soil erosion. A new dirt road has been built since the construction of the dam to provide access to the newly opened settlement areas on the east side of

the river. However, there is as yet no bridge across the river connecting that area to the Chiengmai highway. All roads in the Hod area are in bad repair and most bridges across the many streams have been entirely washed out. All of this has important repercussions on market access for goods, services, and labor going into and out of the research area which has, nevertheless, become more dependent on the market. However, the highway connecting Chiengmai to Tha Kham, the new *Amphur* Hod Headquarters and turn off point for Mae Sarieng, was completely paved in 1968. Ten years ago it was a poor, rough dirt road beyond Chom Thong, the halfway stop and market, between Chiengmai and Wang Lung. Wang Lung was the market center for old *Amphur* Hod and is fifteen kilometers south of Tha Kham which has become the new market center; thus the market is removed from the Karen area. Old Wang Lung is, however, still a fish market terminus for the old Hod area even though much of Wang Lung is now deserted due to the threat and actuality of flood. Only those houses and shops on high points remain. Thus, the whole center part of the village has been abandoned. Mostly due to the fish market, there are approximately thirty bus-lories that travel between Chiengmai and Wang Lung daily, about fifteen originating at each end of the line. Fish catches from all over the reservoir are brought to Wang Lung daily by boat, transferred to buses and carried to Chiengmai.

Taxis also travel back and forth today which was made possible by completing the paving of the highway between Chiengmai and Tha Kham in 1968. Today it costs only an additional 2 *baht* to take a taxi rather than a bus to Chiengmai, so people, mostly Thai, however, going to buy and sell often go by taxi. There are about thirty taxis between Chiengmai and Chom Tong (14 *baht* round trip); there are ten between Chiengmai and Wang Lung (24 *baht* round trip). These taxis cannot reach Wang Lung in the rainy season, however, and therefore will not replace the older buses.

DEMOGRAPHY AND SOCIAL STRUCTURE

Most, if not all, of the recent demographic and attendant social and economic changes in *Amphur* Hod are directly related to the Yanhee Dam. There are eight *Thambon* in *Amphur* Hod and, at present, fifty-six "villages" with a total population of 37,120 people as of July, 1969.[5] As indicated earlier, these fifty-six villages are often made up of several "natural" villages that are geographically and socially distinct entities, but are merged for administrative purposes. The villages are an administrative fiction and thus not very useful for the kind of analysis attempted here. Therefore, the villages discussed are the natural villages, and are only partially related to the Thai administrative *Muban*.

The total population of *Amphur* Hod during the ten years 1960–69, had an overall increase of only 1,031 individuals. However, the internal population movement is significant. Comparing the population of 1960 and 1969, the following occurred:

Thambon Hod. There was an overall loss of 367 houses and 1,498 individuals. These were probably mostly from the Thai village of Wang Lung, and Luang Hod.[6] Many of the people from Wang Lung formed a new village, Ban San, in *Thambon* Hang Dong to the north and they moved and rebuilt *Wat* (temple) Wang Lung in the new village. Old Wang Lung still has about seventy-eight houses on high ground, however. Luang Hod, the old administrative center of the *Amphur*, has now been completely abandoned and reformed at the edge of the *Thambon* just north of the (Thai) village of Khwae Moh Kok.

Thambon Hang Dong. This *Thambon* has gained in houses and individuals just a little more than *Thambon* Hod lost. Hang Dong contains the site of the new *Amphur* Headquarters. Thus officials have moved to this village of Tha Kham which brought shops and services, and most of the losses from *Thambon* Hod. Tha Kahm is also the turnoff point on the highway leading to Mae Sarieng, which was paved just ten years ago, and it is thus an important bus and truck stop. Before being paved the road to Mae Sarieng was impassable in the rainy season.

Thambon Ban Tan. This is the most stable of the *Thambon*, losing thirty-six houses but gaining nine individuals. The populated areas of Ban Tan are so far away from the area affected by the dam and reservoir that little change has occurred.

Thambon Ban Aen. There has been a substantial loss of population here and this is no doubt almost entirely due to the fact that the large village of Ban Aen was forced to relocate, some people going as far away as Mae Sarieng. The major portion of the population moved to four different villages in relocation areas. The more populous areas of this *Thambon* were all in the reservoir basin.

Thambon Ta Dya. This *Thambon* had an even larger loss of population than Ban Aen, but this is not surprising when it is realized that the government relocation area is across the river in *Thambon* Doi Tao. Ta Dya people could easily relocate their houses and still return to work their old fields when not flooded.

Thambon Doi Tao. This *Thambon* has had a significantly larger increase in population than any other *Thambon* in the *Amphur*. This is entirely due to the fact that the government relocation areas for all *Thambon* are in Doi Tao. Since this area was chosen by the government to be developed for people dislocated due to the dam, a north-south road has been built through the *Thambon* which connects to the Lampoon-Li highway; it will connect to Tha Kham when a planned bridge is built across the River at that point. Currently, the road is in extremely poor condition, however. Besides Doi Tao, *Thambon* Ban Tan will be linked to the Chiengmai highway. These areas were extremely isolated before, Doi Tao having no roads at all, but now potentially linked to the major northern Thai centers.[7]

Thambon Myt Ka. This *Thambon* has been little affected by the dam and is relatively stable in population, losing only 640 people over the ten years. It was the least populous *Thambon* ten years ago, and is now only slightly more populated that *Thambon* Hod which had a large loss of people. Myt Ka has no access roads, and it is located in the channel area between the two lakes of the reservoir. Its lack of population shift is due to lack of influence from the dam.

Thambon Boh Luang. This is the only *Thambon* in the *Amphur* that does not touch the Ping River. If there has been any influence from the dam in this *Thambon*, it has been to receive refugees from the affected areas. Indeed, Boh Luang has had a slight population increase, but this may be due merely to normal population growth. This is the *Thambon* that is the most mountainous and which has the largest Karen population (Hinton 1969).

There is some indication that the total *Amphur* has lost people in the figure showing a decrease in houses by 282 over the ten years. The total population however, has increased by 1,031 which probably represents children and normal growth trends. There is the probability that the loss in the houses represents Thai movement, and that the population increase represents Karen. The census is not broken down so that one can be sure. But if we turn now to the villages of concern to this study, there is some evidence for this surmise.

The Thai villages of interest are Ban Aen, Ban Nong, Ban Den, Luang Hod, and Wang Lung. Of these villages, only Ban Nong and Ban Aen are outside *Thambon* Hod, being located in *Thambon* Ban Aen. The individuals from Ban Nong, Ban Aen, and Ban Den have all migrated, merged, and split in various ways. Some moved to the relocation area; some stayed in the *Thambon*; some went in other directions. The few remaining Thai from old Ban Den (across the road from New Ban Hong) are counted in *Thambon* Ban Aen for census purposes. Individ-

TABLE 19 Amphur Population

Thambon	Number of Villages	Number of Houses 1960	1965	1969	Gain/Loss Over 10 yrs.	Population 1960	1965	1969	Gain/Loss Over 10 yrs.
Hang Dong	6	868	986	1,211	+343	3,614	4,757	5,262	+1,648
Hod	4	761	419	394	−367	3,444	4,638	1,946	−1,498
Ban Aen	7	1,207	1,087	1,007	−200	5,593	5,939	4,376	−1,217
Mut Ka	4	589	436	412	−177	2,775	5,198	2,135	− 640
Bau Tan	5	701	717	665	− 36	3,231	6,867	3,240	+ 9
Bo Luang	14	1,243	1,498	1,304	+ 61	6,504	4,533	7,631	+1,127
Tha Dya	8	1,209	816	906	−303	6,030	6,481	4,268	−1,762
Doi Tao	8	984	1,469	1,381	+397	4,898	4,219	8,262	+3,364
TOTALS	56	7,562	7,428	7,280	−282	36,089	42,632	37,120	+1,031

uals from these three Thai villages have formed four new villages in *Thambon* Ban Aen, the largest consisting of 942 individuals in 315 houses.

Hod village, which was the seat of the *Amphur* headquarters, has been completely abandoned. Some families moved to the new *Amphur* headquarters which was established in 1962 at Tha Kham, which now has 328 houses and is located at the edge of the *Amphur* in *Thambon* Hang Dong. However, most families joined together to form a new Luang Hod, which now has 155 houses, and is located a short distance north of old Hod, but on higher ground away from the river. Thus they are still in *Thambon* Hod.

Most people from Wang Lung moved to *Thambon* Hang Dong to form a new village of Ban San with 804 individuals in 82 families. These people moved *Wat* Wang Lung with them when they were paid for the old *Wat* by the government. The remnants of old Wang Lung, which involves 348 individuals forming 82 families, maintains its viability through its economic functions. Wang Lung is the end of the boat line coming north with fish for the Chiengmai market, and it is the end of the bus/truck line going north to deliver and pick up various goods and products and crops, including the fish. Currently, Wang Lung has three noodle shops, four general stores, and three small vegetable and fish market areas. As mentioned, it is the terminus for about thirty buses daily. It is the market outlet for Karen goods, and the point at which Karen buy. If it were not for these economic functions, Wang Lung would, no doubt, have disappeared. As it is, the center part of the old village is completely abandoned. The northern end includes the market area, and the southern end has the remaining houses and a couple of small shops. These two ends of the village were on high ground that did not flood.[8]

The important point of this discussion is that most Thai villages moved at least out of their former *Thambon*. There is no accurate figure on how far they moved, but it is known that some went as far as Mae Sarieng, and many went to relocation sites, thus suggesting a loss of Thai houses to the research area in and around *Thambon* Hod. On the other hand, the Karen villages merely moved to higher ground, and none migrated outside the *Thambon*. Yet all the Thai and Karen villages were within the potential flood area. Therefore, nearly 100 percent of the population loss to *Thambon* Hod was Thai movement. There were a few Karen families that moved away from the area, mostly to surrounding Thai villages, and a few went to the government relocation area. Many Thai, however, continued to maintain their former paddy fields after changing residence. There was thus a labor vacuum left in *Thambon* Hod and Ban Aen which the Karen have filled, to their economic advantage.

The Karen villages of special concern in the 1969 re-study are Ban Hong, Dong Dam, Vwang Kham, Öelaphi, Hui Sai, and Mang Mêng all of which are in *Thambon* Hod.

From 1960 to 1963, there was no change and no shifting of Karen villages, but from 1964 to 1966, there was a period of shifting of both village location and economic pursuit in order to survive. (During this period, the Karen sold fish, peanuts, vegetables, jungle crops, and labor in order to buy rice.) From 1967 to 1970, there was a period of settling down to new microadaptations during which some paddy was grown again, but using a new system of irrigation. The villages were attempting to stabilize themselves and establish their new locations for the future.

Ban Hong first merged with the people from Vwang Kham (see figure A page 13), on higher ground, and stayed there for three years, yet maintaining its separate identity. Then Ban Hong separated into several splinter groups over a short period of time:

a. Five houses, which have important paddy interests, merged into Dong Dam (H–4; H–5; H–16; H–16 son, H–17).[9]

b. Three households migrated to the Thai relocation area near the Karen village of Nong Pu to the south (H–22, H–22, da., H–26) where they were given the right to claim some land.

c. One household moved into Nong Pu (H–31).

d. Two households merged into separate Thai villages along the highway to Chiengmai. These have been lost to Karen culture through assimilation, but were probably the least successful members of old Ban Hong, one (H–12) being a hopeless opium addict, and the other (H–29) with few kinship connections and no land, unable to support his family.

e. Five households disappeared due to death (H–3, H–8, H–14, H–25, H–33).

f. The Thai village of Ban Den, which had always included a few Karen families living across the road, absorbed four houses (H–24, H–24 da., H–27, H–30) when the Thai from there merged and migrated with Ban Nong people.

g. Another group of nine houses (H–6, H–6 sons, H–15 son; H–11; H–34; H–15, H–25 da., H–26 son; H–28) formed New Ban Hong just southwest of the upper village of old Ban Hong.

h. Öelaphi is the new, successor village to old Ban Hong. It is located a mile or two southeast of Dong Dam on a forested, secluded hill, and it, like old Ban Hong, is divided into a lower village of five houses (H–19, H–20, H–6 son; H–7, H–13), and an upper village of twelve houses (H–1, H–1 da, H–1 son; H–2, H–2 son; H–8a, H–9, H–10; H–15 son; H–21, H–18; H–23).

This total of forty-five houses is larger than the original number in old Ban Hong due to the formation of new households by the marriage of children who grew up.

There is basically a four-way split that occurred in old Ban Hong (ignoring deaths) with those more involved in paddy production going to Dong Dam (*a* above); the more traditional and conservative group forming the new village of Öelaphi (*h* above); a group that assimilated into Thai culture (*b* and *d* above); and an amorphous group some of which are successful but less traditional, and some of which are less able or more depressed (*f* and *g* above) who are merging into a new village (see New Ban Hong, Vwang Kham, below).

Turning to a broader view of the reearch area, the village of Hui Sai was inundated when the reservoir filled in 1964, and so it moved west a short distance further from the river on higher ground. Currently, there are over seventy houses remaining in Hui Sai, and thus only a few were lost to other areas. Dong Dam moved a short distance further east away from the river, and was probably the least disrupted of the villages in terms of loss of individuals and distance moved. It currently consists of over twenty houses. Before the flooding Mang Mêng had more than twenty houses. Now there are just over ten. The village was moved a short distance because the people feared flooding. In fact, its site was not flooded, but in the disruption several houses were lost to the area by migration to a location along the Mae Sarieng road out of the research area. Currently Mang Mêng is separated from Dong Dam only by a stream, and is almost an appendage of Dong Dam. However it is administratively part of Wang Lung (*Muban* 3). The small village of Vwang Mô has disappeared, the people going to Ban Den. The Karen from Ban Den have merged physically with Vwang Kham, and together constitute fifteen houses (see above for those from old Ban Hong); in turn, this group has merged with New Ban Hong consisting of seventeen houses, to form a two-part village with the Dang Khaw of old Vwang Kham acting as headman to both. The two halves of the village are separated by a primary school serving the remaining local Thai. The resulting viable Karen villages, then, are Hui Sai, Öelaphi, Dong Dam with its appendage Mang Mêng, and possibly the as yet unstable village of New Ban Hong-Vwang Kham. This latter village, however, will surely change its composition, and maybe its location, over the next few years.

When it was decided that Ban Hong had to be moved, the *Dan Khaw* (H-1) searched around for an appropriate site. Once a likely spot was found, he invited a spirit medium to the village in order to consult the village spirits. Since there were no adverse signs, it was decided to move. At this point the village splitting became pronounced (H-4, H-5, H-6, and H-17 had already left). Since the *Dang Khaw* cannot, by tradition, be the first householder on a new site, he and three others moved together. After a few days, the rest of the households moved that intended to do so. This left the rest free to do as they chose. When Öelaphi was established, a special all-village ceremony was held which involved moving the village spirit. The *Dang Khaw* made an offering to the spirit in old Ban Hong, then carried it across the river to its new home at Öelaphi. A sacrifice and feast was held which included one pig plus one chicken per household and liquor. This ceremony must be repeated every three years.

Ban Hong was one of the "original" Karen villages in the *Amphur* Hod area, others being Hui Sai, Mae Phraphai, and Mae Ngut. Two main daughter villages had separated from Ban Hong in the past. These were Vwang Kham and Dong Dam. When Ban Hong had to be moved there was a ceremonial shifting of village spirits to maintain the ideological and social arrangements that had developed over the years. The spirit of Ban Hong had two sons which were the spirit protectors of the two daughter villages of Vwang Kham and Dong Dam. The spirit of Dong Dam was moved with the village, and the *Dang Khaw* of Vwang Kham, with proper ceremony, moved his village spirit back to the abandoned spirit house in old Ban Hong and incorporated the people of New Ban Hong and Ban Den into a single village. Thus, the spiritual and social relationships between the villages were retained with Öelaphi still in position of parent village.

ECONOMY

The ecological and demographic changes discussed above have led to a further shift in the Karen economy from subsistence to a cash orientation, and this in turn has led to interesting ecologic-economic variation among the Karen villages in their individual adaptations to the natural and social environmental changes: (1) New Ban Hong in combination with Vwang Kham has turned to fishing, honey collection, and wage labor as major economic activities; (2) Öelaphi, which became more isolated in moving across the river, is dependent upon field crop wage labor, jungle crops, and weaving; (3) Hui Sai now sells charcoal, some woven products, and engages in wage labor; (4) Mang Mêng has turned entirely to wage labor; (5) Dong Dam is the only village that has maintained paddy production by nearly every household. Very few villagers anywhere are now making swidden rice fields, whereas nearly all were before the flood. Nearly all are still planting vegetable gardens, however.

These important variations are determined by proximity to one or some of the following: the river (New Ban Hong-Vwang Kham), the Thai market of Wang Lung (Hui Sai) intense Thai influence and contact (Mang Mêng), a new paddy labor market (Öelaphi), and old established Karen paddy fields (Dong Dam). It is often the case, of course, that more than one influence is affecting any particular village.

Karen economy is still bicentric, with both subsistence and market elements. However, it is shifting more towards a market orientation. Land has become a very limited commodity. Paddy land may be bought, sold, and loaned, but more Thai than Karen are involved in the land market.[10] Labor is the major factor of production that has affected Karen culture. More and more Karen are entering the labor market, and this is having important repercussions on the social structure in general. Capital accumulation is almost impossible for the Karen, but a few have acquired some in the form of boats, motors, and large fish nets. The Karen do not accumulate savings whether or not they are able to do so. Whatever money comes in is spent on goods of one sort or another. Wealth, then, is expressed and observed in material goods.

Shifts in economic activities have caused some additional personal and social upsets. Karen culture has an ideological orientation revolving around rice production, but new modes of livelihood are based mostly on the labor market and a few "cash crops." The Karen have not, therefore, adjusted to the changes wrought in their lives even though they are generally more affluent today than in 1960. Income and expenditure are both unpredictable and thus breed insecurity. Several informants told me that the Karen, in general, were less well-off today than ten years ago. It is true that there is a wider gap in wealth among the population. Nevertheless, several have built Thai-style all wood houses with tile roofs, whereas before all were living in thatch and bamboo houses.[11] Many now have battery-operated radios and flashlights; before, no one had a radio or flashlight.[12] Money income is noticeably higher and is more in evidence in the villages. More market goods are in use today. Some of the increased material affluence may, however, be based on the temporary labor shortage being filled by the Karen in the area, which may evaporate with time. Currently, few Karen have any paddy land of their own, and nearly all have sold their water buffalo. Income is now based on some paddy, a few swidden fields, fishing, vegetable gardens, selling jungle products, and a few specific cash commodities. Thus, in 1960, at least 60 percent of the Karen were dependent upon subsistence activities, but by late 1969, about 75 percent of them have switched to dependence upon wage labor and the cash received from selling local products. This turnaround is a 35 percent shift toward a cash economy.

Ten years ago, the Karen were active subsistence rice cultivators. Although not all Karen owned or had use rights to paddy fields then, most at least worked on paddy fields being planted by other Karen, usually kinsmen. Some individuals had both paddy and swidden fields, and some merely planted swidden. Even then, however, few could grow all the rice needed. The organizing principle for production, distribution and consumption was kinship and friendship obligation. Today, the Karen tell me that they must and do think in terms of market and price much more than kinship and ethnic identity. Only a very few Karen claim ownership of paddy land: the twenty or more households in Dong Dam claim ownership and plant the fields. In Öelaphi there are four or five households that claim paddy ownership, but only one that plants it regularly (there are a couple of other households that plant abandoned Thai fields from time to time). In Hui Sai seven households claim land, but only four or five plant it. In New Ban Hong, one man still claims his land, but does not plant it. The size of these plots range from 3 to 13 *rai*, most being around 4 or 5 *rai*.

This is not yet a stabilized situation, however. During the years of flooding virtually all rice production stopped, and since everyone had been paid for their land holdings, no one has an official claim to any land. The land is not now registered, and no taxes are paid for its use. It officially does not exist. However tradition is stronger than legality, and people are beginning to reassert their land claims since the reservoir has receded. As one might expect, since people have moved or migrated, there is some shifting of ownership or use claims occurring. In fact, some individuals are buying and selling this officially non-existent land (e. g., H–7 sold his 2+ *rai* to H–17 for 500 *baht*. One may even "lend" his paddy. The user takes the plot for five years, maintains it and digs the irrigation ditches. If the lender wants it returned to his use before the five-year period, he must pay the user 100 *baht* for improvements. At the end of five years the land reverts to the "owner." No rent is paid during the period of use. Very few are doing this, however. Most people have given up claim to land and are not attempting to plant, partly due to the fear and risk of new flooding. Individuals are rather selling their labor to work on Thai-claimed fields, thus avoiding the risk of crop loss. Since the current concern is to acquire money, Karen do not ordinarily "work" for Karen. Cooperative endeavors are lessening, therefore, since the Karen cannot afford to pay for labor. Thus social relations are affected, and so is plot size. One cannot attend a large plot with only family labor. Until 1968, many people attempted to maintain swidden fields, but yield became less and less as soil became exhausted due to over-cropping. One could do better to work for cash to buy rice. Currently, only two households in Öelaphi and ten households in Hui Sai are planting swidden. Most people in other villages have decided against it.

Those few who do cultivate paddy rice can now realize two crops per year. Since the fields are now irrigated by a gasoline pump owned by a Wang Lung Thai, the people are not dependent upon rainfall or high river water required by the old water wheels. Indeed, where the water wheels cannot be used, an individual must plant two crops in order to reap about as much rice as he did ten years ago with one crop. This is partly because it is extremely expensive to rent the use of the pump to irrigate, which is an additional reason why many Karen are not now attempting paddy rice. The pump was purchased in 1967 for 70,000 *baht* and installed with the agreement from the paddy owners that they would rent its use for five years and pay about 13 *thang* (182 kilo) of rice grain per *rai*, per harvest (i. e., twice a year). Cost per *rai* is 156 *baht*, since a *thang* sells for 12 *baht*.[13] If buffalo must be rented they cost 10 *thang* per animal per season. Rice yield, however, may range from about 14 *thang* to 40 or 50 *thang* per *rai* at most. Water and buffalo cost is not proportional to yield. The water arrangement turned out to be an agreement between Dong Dam Karen and the Thai pump owner, other villages deciding against it.

Now I would like to compare the experiences of two brothers during the first cycle of the 1969 season. One of them (H–17, now living in Dong Dam) planted 4 *rai* using water from the pump. His yield was a little more than 18 *thang* per *rai* (1,021 kilo). He claimed it was a poor yield due to worms in the rice. He had to pay the pump owner just over 13 *thang* per *rai* (744 kilo). The remaining 276 kilo will feed his family for about a month. Even with two crops per year, this man must still spend about 1000 *baht* on rice every year, buying at least eight sacks of 120 kilos each. The younger brother (H-6 son, now married to H-19 da and living near her family in Öelaphi) took over an abandoned Thai field further down the river toward Ban Aen where he could built a water wheel. He planted 3 *rai* with a yeild of 120 *thang* of rice, or 40 *thang* per *rai*. The water wheel cost him 500 *baht* or the equivalent of just under 42 *thang*.

The difference between the two brothers was not in the cost of water. In fact, the younger brother paid the equivalent of 3 *thang* more than his brother (although he did not pay it in rice, which makes a difference for food in hand). The important difference is in yield. There is great fluctuation in yield from year to year any way, but the Karen say that yield in the area where the pump is used has decreased by about one-third. The complaint, then, is not merely about the cost of water, but also that fertility has decreased because of the pump. It is claimed that oil deposits from the pump are left in the fields, that acquatic life such as fish, crabs, shrimp and water snails which were important food supplements, are not brought into the fields watered by the pumps, that soil nutrients are not brought into the fields by the pump, and that water level in the fields is too low for good yield.

In the case of the two brothers, the younger did not plant a second crop because he feared the reservoir would rise during that period. But, then, he did not need to plant since he had nearly enough for he and his wife for the year. and he could earn enough cash to buy the rest. The older brother had to plant a second crop, and still he must buy rice for about four months of the year. Ten years ago people had to buy rice for two to five months a year. Therefore, the older brother is maintaining himself about where he was before, but he must work harder to do it. He is more fortunate than most, however, who must now buy rice for from ten to twelve months per year. Only two men in the local area, both in Dong Dam, do not need to buy rice. For a family of four, nearly 2000 *baht* is necessary for the annual supply of rice.

I will turn now to a discussion of other major economic activities from which food and income are derived. There is great variability in the economic activities pursued by the Karen, and individuals engage in them differentially. It is therefore, difficult to calculate a household income. However, several informants independently volunteered the information that every household receives a minimum of 10 *baht* per day, per year, and that one able-bodied man will average that much. Therefore, the minimum household income is 3650 *baht* per year. This figure is to be multiplied by the number of laborers per household. The range in cash income is 5 *baht* to 30 *baht* per person, per day, per year, or from 1825 *baht* to 10,950 *baht*. This range of 9125 *baht* is clearly much broader than anything ten years ago.

Table 20 gives a summary of the annual round of activities in which the Karen are involved, and Table 21 presents the income derived form the various activities. It must be realized, of course, that all Karen are not engaged in all the activities because of their overlappoing nature; therefore, choices must be made on the basis of time, resources and household labor available. One thing is quite clear which is that all Karen are much more involved with the Thai and the market than ten years ago. A few Karen at least would like to see more involvement by having a Thai "capitalist" enter the area with loans, and seed, and who would buy the crops. Some local Karen are experimenting for the first time with raising castor beans and peanuts. They have an idea that oil is extracted from the beans, but have no idea what it is used for—and do not care; they merely want the cash to be received. There is a Thai middleman that comes annually to collect their castor beans and peanuts.

A middleman is also involved in the firewood and bark market. The firewood is for the Thai railway which pays 10 *baht* for a unit measuring 2 x 2 x 1 meter. This is a two-man job, and they may cut four or five such units per day, but it is very hard work. The bark collecting is done during four months of the year: The middleman comes to collect the people and gives each 100 *baht* in advance. They are then taken in his truck to the bark-collecting area. They are paid 1 *baht* per kilo and may make from 20 *baht* to 50 *baht* per day. They do not make that much everyday, however, during the season. At the end of the period they must return the 100 *baht* advance. The bark is eventually resold by the Thai and is chewed with betel nut. No long-distance trading is carried on today since the money from Thai middlemen has dried up.

There is a great deal of collecting and gathering activity going on now in order to make money, and it goes on year round, often done by women and children; but men, when not otherwise engaged, are involved too. People collect and sell bamboo shoots, bees wax, mushrooms, frogs, ground crickets, and honey. Bees are not domesticated, but wild honey is collected for about ten months of the year. However, it is in abundance for only two months. Ten years ago, it was a rare luxury. A large variety of vegetables are grown in the hope of a surplus so that some may be sold. These include melons, tomatoes, onions, beans, lettuce, cabbage, bean sprouts, and corn. Crops grown specifically for cash are peanuts, castor beans, cotton, soy beans, tapioca, and tobacco.

Animals have become much less important to the Karen than they were ten years ago. Many people in Dong Dam still have buffalo used in the paddy cycle, but most Karen in the area have sold their buffalo for the cash to be realized. No one in New Ban Hong or Öelaphi now has buffalo. A few people are still raising zebu cattle for sale, but only five households in Öelaphi, with a total population of twenty head, are doing so.

None are being raised in Hui Sai or New Ban Hong. About ten Karen in Öelaphi are raising pigs for use and sale; very few chickens are being sold now.

Weaving for sale is still being carried on, but has decreased in quantity. The Karen say they have lost much of the market that they had due to the dam; that is, it is more difficult to make contact now since the villages have dispersed, roads are very poor and flooding is unpredictable. Thai from many areas formerly ordered woven goods. Currently, there is one man in Öelaphi who acts as salesman-middleman for the four households in the village who still weave for the market in Wang Lung.[14]

Ten years ago, the Karen sold very few fish in Wang Lung for the Chiengmai market, and those that were sold went for 1 *baht* to 2 *baht* per bunch of a dozen or so small fish, or about 6 *baht* per kilo in Wang Lung and resold in Chiengmai for 12 *baht* per kilo. Fish are now averaging about 10 *baht* per kilo in Wang Lung and are generally much larger in size than before. Most sellers and all buyers are Thai, with most fish coming by boat from Ban Aen and south. Karen do, however, bring fish to Wang Lung along with thier charcoal and honey.

Before the dam was built the fish were uniformly small, about six to twelve inches in length. Now a single fish may weigh from 15 to 50 kilo or more. When the dam was completed the Thai government began stocking the reservoir and the yield at the Wang Lung market was over a metric ton per day during the rainy season. The yield soon began to decrease and has apparently stabilized over the last three years between 100 to 700 kilo per day during the four or five months of the rainy season. The Karen, although generally peripheral to this market, have profited from it both in diet and cash.

Most Karen are using their traditional techniques of catching the fish, but some are too large for the fish traps and are lost. A very few Karen are trying to enter the market using the more advanced technology of the Thai. The large fish nets which are usually used in conjunction with a motor boat cost from 50 *baht* to 500 *baht* depending on size and type. The smaller nets may be used by staking, and therefore do not require a boat. A few Karen are trying it, but the cost and risk keeps most from attempting the technique. A boat and motor bought by one Karen cost 6000 *baht*. The nets can be used for about two months of the season and last three to four years. During the high water season, this technique will yield a minimum of 50 *baht* per day. Last year, H-17 realized 700 *baht* and his younger brother, 1,170 *baht* on one day.[15]

A most important source of income is wage labor in Thai-owned fields. Karen may receive from 30 *baht* to 90 *baht* per *rai* for hoeing a field (if hoeing is done, there is no need to plow). . . . It takes from one to four days per *rai*. Four people can do 1 *rai* per day. One may receive several 100 to a 1,000 *baht* or more per season for this work. The hoeing season is short, but there is much additional paddy work to do and there are a host of additional odd jobs that one can do to make some cash working for the Thai, some of which have already been mentioned.

There has been some noticeable inflation over the years, but according to the local Karen, it has become dramatic since the advent of the Yanhee Dam. Wages today are about twice what they were ten years ago, and most Karen believe they have more cash now. However, the amount of wage labor engaged in has not doubled, but certainly has increased. I am told that thirty to forty years ago (i. e., in the decade of the 1930s, just before World War II), people who worked received 30 *stang* (100 *stang* per *baht*) per day; before the dam, they received 5 *baht* per day; now they receive 10 *baht* per day. On the other hand, thirty to forty years ago a sack of rice cost 6 *baht*; before the dam a sack cost about 80 *baht*; and now rice is up to as much as 180 *baht* per sack, and the people must buy more of it since they grow less.

TABLE 20 Economic Scheduling in the Annual Round

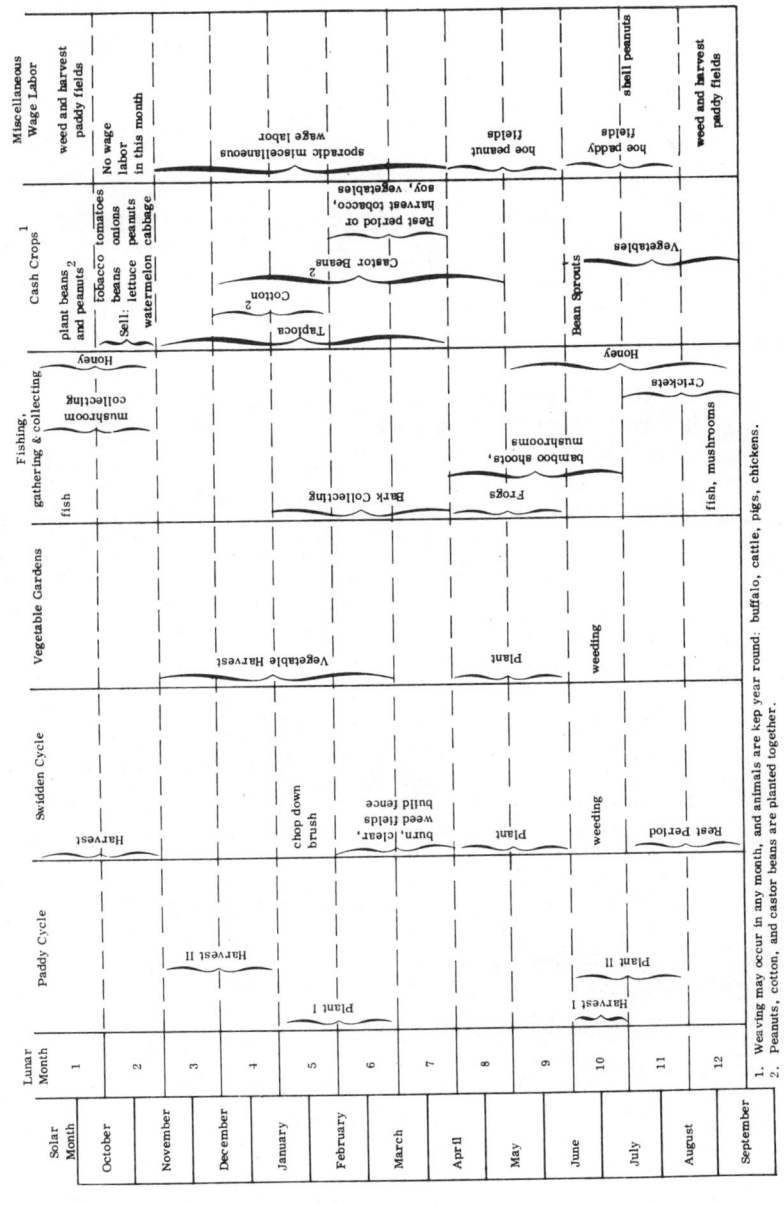

TABLE 21 Income

Activity	Pay	Comments
A. CROP FIELDS		
1. Hoeing rice and peanut fields	24 *baht* per day, avg.	30–90 per *rai*; about 4 days per *rai*; up to 1000 *baht* per season; individual is paid per *ngan* (= ¼ *rai*, 1 day work)
2. Harvest peanuts		
3. Weed peanuts	5 *baht* to 10 *baht* per day	
4. Weed paddy		
5. Harvest paddy		
6. Shell peanuts	6–7 *baht* per day	1 *baht* per basket
7. Castor beans	2–3 *baht* per kilo	Up to 2000 *baht* per season; average 200–300 *baht* per season
8. Peanuts	2.50 *baht* per kilo, or 10 *baht* per 5-gal. can, or 12 *baht* per *thang* (basket) unshelled	As much as 1000 kilo per season
9. Soy beans	28–29 *baht* per *thang*	
10. Tobacco	8–20 *baht* per kilo	Up to 100 kilo
11. Tapioca	1 *baht* per 4 kilo	
12. Cotton	2.5 *baht* per kilo	200–300 *baht* per season
B. VEGETABLES (all grown or collected for home consumption; surplus resold)		
1. Bamboo shoots	6–7 *baht* per small bag	Occasional, 1 bag per day
2. Bean sprouts	2.50 *baht* per kilo	
3. Corn	1 *baht* per 6 ears	
4. Mushrooms (various kinds)	1 *baht* per 2 handfuls 5 *baht* per liter; 1 *baht* per 10 pieces	
5. Misc. vegetables	2–4 *baht* per measure; 8 *baht* per kilo	Variable

TABLE 21 Income—Continued

Activity	Pay	Comments
C. ANIMAL AND AQUATIC		
1. Ground crickets	5 *baht* per 100 crickets	
2. Frogs	1 *baht* per 5 frogs	
3. Bees wax	25 *baht* per kilo	
4. Honey	10 *baht* per qt.	Some collected year-round, two months are best
5. Chicken	2–5 *baht* per chicken	Not often sold
6. Fish	8–20 *baht* per kilo	Daily during rainy season
7. Buffalo, cow, pig	25–500 *baht* per animal	Raised over several months; may sell 2 per year
D. MISCELLANEOUS		
1. Occasional labor	10 *baht*–20 *baht* per day	Variable seasonal
2. Cutting firewood for Thai railway	20 *baht*–25 *baht* per day, per man	2-man job
3. Collect bark (to be chewed with betel nut)	1 *baht* per kilo	20 *baht*–50 *baht* per day, 4 month season
4. Weaving	8 *baht*–100 *baht* per item	Up to 1000 *baht* per year; usually much less; only 4 active houses

RELIGION

I pointed out above how social structural relations were maintained through the religious-symbolic system in the face of ecological adjustments, demographic splitting, merging and migration. Now I will turn to some changes in the religious system brought about by the dam or increased contact with the Thai. However, I must point out that the traditional Karen ceremonies, discussed in earlier chapters, are still being carried out. The lineage head is still important and lineage ceremonies are being conducted. In fact, there are heads of two lineages living in Öelaphi, whereas, none were living in old Ban Hong. The village spirit of Öelaphi, in charge of the *Dang Khaw*, is considered to be one of the most fierce in the local area.

New changes are, however, occurring and older trends of change are continuing. For example, all the local Karen villages had a second spirit house, besides the one mentioned earlier, to honor C_o *Ti*, the Thai spirit of the land. When the villages moved, however, there was no ceremony to move him since he is all-pervasive. A new house was merely built for him next to that of the main village spirit. In Dong Dam, however, which is less traditional due to its greater emphasis on Thai-style paddy cultivation, the two spirits have been merged into one; thus, Dong Dam has only one spirit house, and part of the spirit ceremony is conducted in northern Thai, and part in Karen. In this process certain of the traditional Karen customs are being lost such as the ability to "read" chicken bones (see Marshall 1922: 280 ff.). There is only one local Karen that can still perform this fortune telling technique, and he lives in Dong Dam.

Thai spirit mediums were consulted by the local Karen before the dam was built, but the practice seems to have increased somewhat since the completion of the dam, and an interesting amalgamation is occurring. When old Ban Hong was faced with the necessity of the impending move, the *Dang Khaw* found a likely spot, as mentioned above. Then a Thai Spirit medium was brought in in order to consult the Karen village spirit. Determining that the area was acceptable to the Karen village spirit, through the Thai medium, and making the move, the Karen next reported to the local Thai headman to make the new location official with the secular Thai administration.

More formal Thai Buddhism has continued to invade the Karen villages as well. A temple (*Wat*) has been constructed in Dong Dam, which is little more than a bamboo-and-thatch rest house (*sala*), for the purpose of holding Buddhist ceremonies for the local Karen. From time to time, a Thai priest comes and officiates at Buddhist ceremonies. These are attended by Karen from all the local villages, but mostly by those living in Dong Dam. Local Karen, however, are not entering the priesthood as yet.

When *Wat* Hui Sai, which was in Wang Lung and served both Thai and Karen, was moved due to the flooding, the Wang Lung Thai and Hui Sai Karen who did not migrate built a new temple for the area. It now has one Thai priest and four novices to serve the local area, but most Karen outside Hui Sai now attend the *Wat* in Dong Dam.

Christian influence is still almost nonexistent, but there has been one convert now living in New Ban Hong who was a Hui Sai Karen and son of old H-8. There is, however, still no general interest in conversion. This is partly because Christians cannot drink liquor, which automatically puts one beyond normal behavior for most Karen ceremonies. It is also partly because Karen feel a Christian is vulnerable in a crisis since he cannot turn to the spirits for protection, and cannot call upon the magical powers of the "White Priest" (see below). The local Pwo Karen have equated Christianity with being Sgaw Karen. Thus there is an identification problem for Christian conversion, as well.

Finally, a religious cult has developed over a period of years and is centered around a "White Priest" generally residing in *Amphur* Li in Lampoon Province. This Thai priest has taken on white robes since being derobed from the regular Thai priesthood. His following includes Thai and many hundreds of Karen

Top: Thai teak-loggers with their elephant passing between the head elder's house and rice grainery in Ban Hong. *Bottom*: An elephant caravan passing through the Thai market-town of Wang Lung.

Thai provincial government officials informing the Karen that their lands will be inundated by the Yanhee Dam.

from all over the plains and hills in a wide area of northwestern Thailand. His influence and following are much wider than that of the local research area of *Amphur* Hod, and they antedate the building of the Yanhee Dam. His importance to the Karen in *Amphur* Hod was enhanced because of the dam, however. The priest is considered to be superhuman with supernatural powers. He commands both awe and respect.

One may receive great religious merit from making a donation to the White Priest for his good works projects, such as schools, of which he has financed many in Northern Thailand. This merit will help both in this life and the next, according to the Karen.

One may also receive various forms of protection from a photo of the priest, or from an object made sacred by his blessing. His photo may sell for as much as 100 *baht* and is in great demand. The sacred objects, often a small figure of the Buddha or a medallion with an impression of the teacher of the priest, into which he has infused magic may provide magical protection against enemies, spirits, or accidents. There are many stories told of how his magic has saved lives.

It is also possible to receive information and predictions from the priest through his ability to foretell the future. One informant told me of a prediction made about twenty years ago when the informant was fifteen years old to the effect that a dam would be built, that the Hod area would be flooded for about three years, that after that time the people would be able to plant rice again, and that the dam would be impermanent. It is said that many of the difficulties encountered by the builders of the dam were caused by the White Priest through his ability to manipulate events.

The White Priest, therefore, satisfies many needs of the local Karen who are insecure about the dam and its effects. The time that I made the pilgrimage to see him with the Karen from Ban Hong involved a three-day walk over the hills. Several hundred Karen were in attendance, and many goods as well as money were donated for the merit received.[16] One man, originally from old Ban Hong, spent 200 *baht* on a single trip.

POLITICAL ADMINISTRATION

The two political structures, mentioned earlier, are still in operation. I will summarize their characteristics and their interrelationships today.

In the Karen structure, the largest political entity is the village, as mentioned before. This makes any larger organization somewhat difficult for the Karen because the traditional *Dang Khaw*, or head elder, has no authority outside his village. To the Karen, the village redundancy feature has very strong ideological support and legitimacy since the *Dang Khaw* is both political and religious leader at the same time. His relation to the village spirits and proper propitiation thereof sanctions his political decisions and maneuverings—as long as things go well for the village. He is, therefore, no autocrat. He must work in conjunction with the village elders, and consensus is the mode of decision-making.

The Thai system, however, is otherwise. It is strongly centralized and operates only one direction (from top to bottom) for the most part. This Thai structure has been imposed on top of the indigenous one, and there has been slight attempt to articulate the two. Karen see the Thai structure as alien, but they tolerate it, partly because it seems to impose little burden on them. The Thai political and administrative officials have access to the Karen, and control over them, through the Thai-appointed and Thai-supported Karen headman. The one of concern to the research area is the same man as ten years ago, and he still lives in Hui Sai. He is in charge of "village" (*muban*) number 4 which now includes Hui Sai, New Ban Hong, Öelaphi, and Dong Dam.

This is a somewhat unwieldy situation for three reasons. First, as previously stated, he is not the traditional headman of even his own village. Second, his authority extends beyond the bounds of his village of residence with no precedent in Karen culture for such a situation. Third, the Karen villages lumped in this administrative fiction are not all related to each other through traditional spiritual ties. Hui Sai and Mang Mêng are related traditionally, but Mang Mêng is lumped with the Thai village of Wang Lung and therefore under intense Thai influence. On the other hand, Mang Mêng, as previously pointed out, is becoming a nonviable village, and some of its people will probably merge with Dong Dam while others assimilate into Wang Lung Thai life. Öelaphi, New Ban Hong, and Dong Dam do belong together, but they are not represented as a unit in the Thai system. In fact, the Karen are somewhat confused about how they are combined by the Thai administration. Several informants could not tell me the complete and proper list of Karen villages in their Thai *muban*. This has caused difficulties when orders are passed down or when requests are made. The secular Thai-appointed headman, then, is little more than an administrative errand boy for the *Amphur* officials. However, he is beginning to acquire some political and economic power by virtue of his connection with Thai authority and favor.

NOTES

[1] By local estimates and consensus, the government gave the people less than 50 percent of the worth of their property. At least parts of the following *Thambon* in *Amphur* Hod are considered worthless because of the flooding and loss of land rights: Hod, Hong Dong, Ban Aen, Mydka, Tha Dya.

[2] An American geologist teaching at Chiengmai University, Malcom Shouls, informed me that it may take a hundred years for the Yanhee reservoir to stabilize and that all the rivers and streams included will build deltas as their flow slows upon entering the reservoir area.

[3] The headman of Wang Lung has some paddy that may be irrigated from a stream. Consequently, he does have aquatic life in his fields which indicates that their absence in other fields is truly caused by use of the pump to irrigate.

[4] Most local people feel that they were much happier before the flooding; that if they could use water wheels again they would be better off; that because of their tampering with the environment,

government water officials will not be reincarnated as men; that everyone must work harder now.

⁵ The population of the *Amphur* has not yet stabilized however. In 1960, it was 36,089. By 1965, it increased to 42,632. Then it began a decline, and in 1967, it was 41,698. The population has continued to decrease following the receding of the reservoir.

⁶ The population of *Thambon* Hod in 1960 was 3,444. By 1965, it increased to 4,638, probably due to expectation of economic gain from the reservoir. However, by 1969, the population was only 1,946. This is almost entirely movement of Thai and not Karen.

⁷ A superhighway connecting Chiengmai and Lampang was completed in 1969, and another superhighway connecting Lampang and Tak is under construction. Thus the whole of Northern Thailand will soon be easily accessible year-round.

⁸ The present headman of Wang Lung has held the position for four years and has a Karen mother. He owns a shop and some paddy land.

⁹ House numbers are those from Old Ban Hong and my original study (see Figure 3). H–4 and H–5 had moved to Dong Dam before I left the field in 1961. These are given here again for completeness. (The houses are grouped, between semi-colons, to indicate household clusters based on the old system.)

¹⁰ In fact the "land market" is nearly all illicit. Since the building of the dam the local people were paid for their land and therefore lost claim to it.

¹¹ The Thai-style house of H–17 cost 6000 *baht*; that of H–19 cost 3000 *baht*; that of H–1, without the tile roof, cost 470 *baht*. Compare costs of ten years ago, page 000.

¹² There are eleven houses in Dong Dam that have radios, and about twenty houses in Hui Sai that have them, but only one house in Öelaphi claims one.

TABLE 22   Various Weights and Measures

MILLED RICE

1 *tang*	=	20 + liter
1 *thang*	=	20 liter
1 liter	=	1.25 *baht* (2–2.50 *baht* in Chiengmai)
1 *thang*	=	27 *baht*–30 *baht* (20 liters)
1 sack	=	6 *thang*
1 sack	=	100 kilo
1 sack	=	120 liter
1 sack	=	150 *baht*–180 *baht* (buying price)
1 liter	=	.83 kilo
1 kilo	=	1.2 liter

UNMILLED RICE   GRAIN

1 *thang*	=	12 *baht* (when selling)
1 *thang*	=	8 liter (after milling)
1 *tang*	=	10 liter (after milling)
1 *thang*	=	14 kilo
1 sack	=	84 kilo
1 sack	=	72 *baht* (selling price)

CONSUMPTION
1 person eats about 2 *baht* of rice per day
Minimum of 1 liter per person

1 family of 4 needs 200 *thang* (unmilled, 8 liter per *thang*) per year.
1 family of 4 needs 12–13 sacks (milled, 100 kilo, 120 liters) per year.
1 family of 4 spends between 1000–2000 *baht* per year for rice.

YIELD
H–1 = 30–70 *thang* (unmilled) from swidden
H–6 son = 120 *thang* = 40 *thang* per *rai*   (3 *rai*)
H–1 = 50 *thang* from paddy   (4 *rai*)
Paddy yield, range = 14–30–50 *thang*, *rai*

Cause of low yield = oil in water, worms, 2 crops = poor soil

EXPENDITURE
12–14 *thang* (unmilled) per *rai* for water (pump)
10 *thang* per buffalo rented
Pay workers in cash = on smaller Karen plots

[14] The thread and yarn used in weaving costs the same as it did ten years ago. Current selling prices are as follows:

TABLE 23

White dress (adult)	75–100 *baht*
Shirt (boy's, small red)	8–10 *baht*
Skirt (married woman's)	40–60 *baht*
Skirt (man's)	30 *baht*
Bags (shoulder, various size)	8–30 *baht*
Blouse (married woman's)	65 *baht*
Blanket	25–30 *baht*
Shirt (man's red)	10–20 *baht*
Shirt (man's white with sleeves)	45 *baht*
White dress (child's)	50–60 *baht*

[15] In the off season, this enterprising younger brother of H–17 used his 6000 *baht* motorboat to carry passengers and Thai tourists along the reservoir just after it filled. He charged 4 *baht* to 6 *baht* per person, depending on the length of the trip, and made about 100 *baht* per day during the season. He was only able to do this for two years, however, before the reservoir subsided and he lost the trade. The boat now sits in a shop in Ban Den.

[16] I was allowed to take photos of the priest and received from him a sacred necklace. The photos were later stolen when I attempted to get the film developed.

11

Conclusion: The Beginning

In this study I have tried to present a picture of Karen culture, using both a synchronic and a diachronic perspective with the hope of analyzing in particular the social structure and economic organization as they were and as they are now and showing how they came to be this way through culture-contact and ecological changes in the environment caused by the Yanhee Dam. I have tried to show how Karen society came to be partly articulated to the Thai market through required adjustments and through personnel whose special roles increase market transactions. Consequently, changes have resulted in total economic behavior of Karen communities, with variations among them, which in turn have caused change in the totality of Karen culture. Specific results of the contact between Karen and Thai have been presented.

Karen culture in *Amphur* Hod shows no evidence of "breaking down" in the sense of becoming disorganized to the extent that it cannot cope with the situation. Rather, the society shows reorganization toward a new stability in the process of adapting to the changing natural environment and to Thai political and economic requirements or possibilities.

The Karen descent system is still basically matrilineal, but the matrilocal residence pattern is changing due to economic contingency. More often now males bring in their wives rather than moving to live near the wife's parents. The cooperative work groups are no longer so viable, and there is a movement toward individualism as money becomes more important. Religion is taking on an even stronger Buddhist orientation, but Karen Animism is still very strong even though modified by Thai peasant Animism. Economic organization has changed the most as the Karen are being more and more incorporated into the Thai money-market economy, particularly as wage laborers. There has been a quantitative shift in the economy that is leading to a qualitative change in the culture toward northern Thai peasantry. The political system is so far maintaining a balance between traditional modes of decision-making and problem solving on the one hand, and the use of Thai law and procedures on the other hand.

It is true that some Karen individuals are moving out into the Thai community and thus are losing their cultural base, contact, and identity with Karen culture. However, many of these "acculturating" individuals are still visably Karen and are distinct because they continue to wear traditional clothing and speak Karen. There are no Karen attending Thai schools in *Amphur* Hod even though in one case a Thai school separates two parts of one Karen village.[1]

However, significant changes in the local natural environment and in the cultural response to the environment are not yet stabilized. Karen cultural traditions are changing and Karen society is adapting to these new environmental requirements. At the same time Karen culture is accommodating itself to the more dominant northern Thai culture and society. These recent changes are noticeable, and are basically economic in origin and nature, but at the same time Karen culture is maintaining an integrity of its own. While changing, Karen culture is continuing to be distinct from northern Thai culture. There is no evidence that Karen culture will soon disappear. There is little evidence of conflict between Karen and Thai in this interactional process. The Karen and Thai farmers in *Amphur* Hod understand each other, at least in their economic pursuits, and they are dependent upon each other. The only local conflict is over the price of water for irrigation: Karen are in agreement that the Thai owner of the pump is charging too much since his entire investment has been returned after two years; yet he insisted on a five year contract from the users. Both Karen and Thai in *Amphur* Hod feel that the Thai government has taken the responsibility of causing change, but not that of dealing with the resulting problems arising from the changes such as crop loss when the floods come. Both Karen and Thai who have remained in the flood area believe that they have been abandoned by the government. A contributing factor is that the people do not now have ownership rights to the land. However, they are not now paying taxes on the land either. At any rate, their feelings could be partially counteracted by the completion of the proposed bridge across the Ping River at Tha Kham linking the new population centers with the Chiengmai market.

Both Thai and Karen cultivators who remained in the flood area would like assistnace in the process of adapting to the changes brought by the Yanhee Dam which would include improved transporation links, market facilities, and loan arrangements for seed and capital improvement.

What are the general consequences for the Karen and their future? The most obvious consequence is further loss of autonomy. Many Thai elements are being incorporated into the Karen view and way of life, as has been shown above, and various internal conflicts have developed. The Karen are becoming even more dependent upon the Thai as change and adaptation continue. However, despite the loss of autonomy, the Karen seem unlikely to become completely Thai for some time. They appear to be maintaining themselves as an ethnic group even though they are becoming a subculture of the Thai state. It is expected that additional study in the area will determine more detailed reasons or forces for maintaining ethnic identity and the modes of doing so, even while losing cultural autonomy (see Spicer 1971). It is hoped that the present study has shed some light on this problem.

My assertions and data concerning the causes and directions of culture-change should lend themselves to cross-cultural testing in other situations where tribal groups like the Karen are moving into the orbit of a more complex socio-cultural system such as the Thai state. I have focused on social structure, ecology, economic organization, and the market as motivating factors for this change. In a wider context, however, this is a case study of the transition from tribal to peasant status, a transition in which market involvement is a prerequisite and in which the steps are definable.

The steps so far discernable are: first, more intense Thai-Karen interaction, particularly economic; second, demographic pressures and changes; third, Thai laws and regulations concerning land registration, taxes, and prohibition on cutting forest; fourth, new economic adaptation due to changed natural and social environment; fifth, cultural adjustments in social structures, residence, politics and religion; and, sixth, lack of homeostasis, and, therefore, increased local innovation.[2] All of this implies that Karen culture is now at the beginning of a new role in the Thai national life.

NOTES

[1] Some Karen say the children do not go to school because of the language problem, and this may be partly true, particularly if the central Thai language is the medium of instruction. H-17, whose mother is Thai says he would like to see his youngest daughter attend

school, but he knows that if she does, she will be soon lost to Karen culture. He does not insist that she go. Nevertheless, there are a few more Karen women and girls that are changing to Thai dress and language without the drastic results that occurred ten years ago in Ban Hong.

[2] Spicer (1961) has an interesting and provacative discussion of various "processes" of culture change due to differences in culture contact, but does not consider ecological factors to any extent. An even more relevant discussion of both persistence of ethnic groups—such as the Karen—as well as changes in them through time is the book edited by Barth, *Ethnic Groups and Boundaries* (1969). The introduction by Barth, which I did not read until after the present book was completed, also discusses the issue of ethnicity as a status distinction. The argument is similar to my notion of "Karenness" discussed above (p. 115).

Appendixes

APPENDIX A RESEARCH PROCEDURES

The following is the chronology of my field work:

My wife and I arrived in Bangkok on October 22, 1959, to begin a full two-year's residence in Thailand. Full-time language study occupied most of my time during the first five months. We were able to live as part of the family in the household of a wealthy Thai Buddhist from our second to fifth month in the country. Our benefactor is a well-to-do man who owns several private schools in Bangkok, and he is the former Lord Mayor of Dhonburi, the twin city of Bangkok. During this early period, besides living in Thai culture and studying the language, I met many Thai officials, obtained letters of introduction, established myself, and made by proposed purposes known. I also visited the various libraries in Bangkok. The purpose of this was to refamiliarize myself with the literature and to discover the resources available in the country. Much of the material I had read before, but during this procedure I met *Phya* Anuman Rajadhon, a Thai scholar who probably knows as much about the history and culture of his country as any Thai. *Phya* Anuman (Thai do not ordinarily use last names) gave me many useful suggestions and tips on where to carry out my research and which officials to see for help.

I began to make excursions, long and short, into the country, looking for an appropriate area in which to conduct my research. For this purpose I hired a young Thai college student who acted as guide and interpreter in my reconnaisance trips looking for "a village." During the first three months of 1960, I visited thirty villages in ten provinces, coming into contact with five ethnic groups in three of the four geographical-cultural areas of the country. My research concern was to find a non-Thai group with the intent of studying its culture and its relationships to the Thai nation-state. I was also hoping that considerable travel would give me a feeling for the country and how the various regions and groups fit together. I am satisfied with the results.

After this period of travel, I decided upon the Pwo Karen area in Chiengmai Province in the north of Thailand. One of the several reasons for the choice was that in the near future some of the villages will be flooded because of a dam being built across the Ping River. I originally thought that I would see the move that the Karen would be forced to make, but the area was not yet flooded by the time I left the field. Another reason for the choice of area was that there are many villages, in a relatively small area, in different states of contact and change.

On April 21, 1960, after about a month making arrangements, moving, and settling into the area, my wife and I moved into a rented house in Wang Lung, a Thai market village for the local area. After a period of surveying the local Karen villages, I picked one, Ban Hong, to study intensively. This village was chosen because it was long established, somewhat isolated and therefore a little more traditional, and because of its size (thirty-five households) and its importance to other villages in the area. We commuted about two miles daily by bicycle between our Thai and Karen villages. This afforded a view of contrast as well as contact between the two, but it was also necessary because of the problem establishing rapport with the Karen: we were not allowed to live in their villge because the villagers feared that they would be harmed by their village spirits if they permitted it. After living in Wang Lung for ten months and establishing the necessary trust, as well as propitiating the Karen spirits, we moved into our new house in Ban Hong on February 22, 1961. the house was a modification of the Karen style, and was built by the villagers whom we hired. We lived in the village for the next seven months, until September 12, 1961, when we left and began preparations for our return home. During a short rest in Chiengmai, I checked over my data, and then we made one final trip to Ban Hong on September 28. Upon returning to Bangkok, we stayed with our "Thai family," while we made final preparations to leave Thailand on October 19, 1961 —almost two years to the day from our first sight of Bangkok.

The field problems were as follows:

As stated above, I studied Central Thai during the initial stay in Bangkok, and this dialect was my principal means of communication for about the first year in the country. I studied the Pwo Karen language with my interpreter, developing my own language materials, and using some of those of the local missionaries. During the second year in Thailand, I communicated almost entirely in the Karen language, and for the last six months of research I did all work in Karen with no interpreters. The Northern Thai dialect is the language used in the market by the Karen, but this dialect is not easily understood by a Central Thai speaker, and I learned just enough to function in the market.

To solve our initial language problems in the north we hired a Sgaw Karen girl who had learned some English in a mission school as an interpreter for my wife. This girl also acted as a servant in the early period. With some difficulty I selected a young local Pwo Karen who had been taught Central Thai by the missionaries. He spoke no English, so Thai was our common language. This man acted as my interpreter for both Northern Thai and Karen, and he was my principal language teacher for the local Karen dialect.

Rapport was a serious problem, but it manifested itself in different ways between the Thai and Karen. There was a marked contrast in the welcome accorded us by the two groups. The Thai peasants were friendly, cordial, and curious—but also somewhat superficial when it came to getting serious or complicated information. They would tend to give the "easy answer," and if one were not careful, he might take this easy answer to be the real answer. The tribal Karen, on the other hand, were apprehensive and suspicious—they wanted to be left alone, but they tolerated us. The Karen became alarmed in new or nontraditional situations, which caused many problems as time went by. Karen spirits are "fierce" and retaliate in various disastrous ways for breaking customs. The presence of my wife and me in the village was a departure from custom, and our questions were often frightening to the Karen. Since there were these two variant situations, I had to work differently with the two groups. When the Thai asked why I was there and what I was doing, I could answer, "I am making a degree" (*tham prinjaa*). This was a perfect answer, and it meant to them that I would get a promotion and more money when I returned home, which is worth doing something odd such as studying the Karen language and customs. In working among the Thai, therefore, I could usually ask questions directly and record the answers in my notebook while interviewing. I received the information desired even though I had to ask the same question several times and of different people. I did have to answer many questions about America during the interview.

Among the Karen, however, I had to be more indirect and could not record answers in the presence of my informants until near the end of the field work. The answer given to the Thai concerning my presence and purpose did not work for the Karen. Of the several answers that I tried among the Karen, the one that worked best was the following: I told them that I was a teacher, that Americans were curious people, that I would go home and teach about Karen customs. The pictures in Marshall's book on the Sgaw of Burma made it a little more concrete, but they never really understood why anybody cared about Karen customs. However, my interest in them and their language was flattering, and familiarity began to bring trust. Long before the Karen came to trust me, however, they knew that I wrote down information, but they did not know what I wrote and they were not comfortable if I recorded data in their presence. I learned to avoid this difficulty by carrying a "language notebook": learning the language was an important rapport builder. As the Karen began to accept us, they were quite anxious for me to learn their language. To the delight of the Karen, I often had a Northern Thai who wished to converse with me use a Karen as interpreter. When collecting information from the Karen, I constantly asked them to give me the names of things, or to repeat something so that I could write it down. I took these opportunities to write a great deal more than the words I was eliciting. There was still the rapport problem, however, but by the time I was "adopted" by the head elder as his "last son," and by the villagers as the "youngest brother" to the Karen, I no longer had trouble with rapport, or with recording information in the presence of most people. This kinship connection was the only "real" solution to the rapport problem. Indeed, my "problem" then became finding time to record all the information that was received.

Another difficulty of the field situation involved our own living conditions, including housekeeping, supply lines, food, and disease. In order to have free time for both my wife and me to collect data in the village, we hired a Thai man and his wife, after two months in Wang Lung. The Thai woman was our cook and housekeeper, and did the laundry. Her husband became my man Friday: he collected information among the Thai villagers and officials and carried out time-consuming official business from time to time. He shopped for food, clothing, and medicine in Chiengmai, and picked up our mail, and money, and so on. Most importantly, however, he became a member of the research team. He spoke very good English and when I got into difficulty with translation he could help me. He was able to use the typewriter and so did much of the recording and filing of data at home while my wife and I were in the village collecting further information. I am greatly indebted to this man as a worker, an assistant, and as a friend. He was also a good informant and apologist for Thai culture. Our housekeeping problems were not "solved" by hiring this couple, but they were greatly alleviated. There were still difficulties in finding enough food locally for the everyday needs of two foreigners—and their staff. There were times when we could find only rice, duck eggs, and peppers in the Wang Lung bazaar. There were also problems of maintaining health. We tried to drink only boiled water, but this was not always possible. At any rate, we made an adjustment to our food and health problems that was "satisfactory."

My wife worked with me in collecting data, and field reserach was accomplished in the following way. At first we went almost daily to the Karen village, each with his own interpreter. We spend half a day going from house to house developing rapport and getting basic information on genealogy, property holdings, daily activities, and so on. The second half of the day was usually spent in studying the language and reviewing information with my interpreter. Later we worked separately, my wife with her interpreter and my Karen and Thai assistants with me. When we returned home, I would hold a staff meting to collate all information gathered that day and to plan the questioning and strategy for the next day. I tried to keep the two groups collecting all of one kind of information until the "area" was filled in as much as could be done with this technique. I collected the subtle points and missing links myself later. When there was a shift in major type of information to be collected, I held a staff meeting and explained thoroughly what the information was that I wanted and generally why I wanted it. We would then discuss the best ways to go about collecting it—what questions to ask, what questions not to ask, who should or must be asked, and so forth. These rather formal staff meetings were followed by very informal, casual questioning in Ban Hong.

There were days when we did not go to the village. At these times a variety of things were done. I might study the language (both Thai and Karen, at different times) or transfer data. Sometimes we just loafed because we were tired, because it was too hot, or raining. However, always when we were home, someone, Karen or Thai, would stop in and much casual data gathering was done in our house.

On some days I went to a Thai ceremony, visited shops, went to the administrative headquarters, talked to Thai farmers, interviewed specific Thai specialists such as rice mill operator, turpentine factory manager, nurse, school and government officials. The purpose of this was, of course, to get information on the Thai community as it related to the Karen. As time passed and people became accustomed to our curiosity, individuals would come and tell me that something had happened or was about to happen, in both communities: a death had occurred, a marriage was going to occur, the harvest was about to start, a group was going off on a trek across the mountains to gain merit, and so forth. This aided in collecting new or verifying old information.

The order of collecting data was roughly as follows. First, we worked on the kinship system and on collecting genealogical data. I needed to know who was related to whom so activities made sense. I was also mapping the village and lands at this time and getting information on technology. Before these time-consuming tasks were done I started in earnest on the economic system, collecting information on crops, yields, distribution, and so on. At this time, also, I began making tape recordings of stories, songs, and so forth, both as data and as a way to study the language. Then I began working on the political organization and power structure of the village. At this time, I started work

on residence history of all adults in the village. Then I began to
work on the religious organization and belief system. Finally, I
worked on individual development and socialization. While I was
translating the tape recordings, I worked intensively on the beliefs and customs, and ceremony content.

The above is a rough outline of the collection schedule. When
I started on something new, I did not stop on previously started
areas of inquiry. I made the decision to start something new
when I felt I understood the outlines of a subject. I also must
note that I had to take data as it came. The first death, funeral,
and village ceremony all came very shortly after we arrived on
the scene. I did not understand all that I had recorded about
these events until long after.

The formal methods of work noted above lasted for about
eight months. As my language ability developed, as rapport improved, as data categories filled, the staff became top heavy. I
did not need all these people and they began to be a hindrance to
the casual and more intimate relations that would give me the
subleties of Karen life. So the Karen girl left us in December,
1960. At about the same time I began to have my Thai assistant do less in the village and more typing and filing at home.
When we moved into the village in February of 1961, the Thai
assistant came to the village twice a day to pick up typing or filing work to do in his house in Wang Lung, to bring our food,
and to pick up the laundry. He did no translating in the village
now. I kept the Karen interpreter for one month after we
moved into the village and worked on the Karen language with
him all day, every day. Then I let him go too. For the last seven months, we employed only the Thai and his wife, but they did
all their work in Wang Lung. No one lived in the village with
us from the first day on.

The Karen accepted my policy of never paying directly for information. I was afraid this would formalize the relationship
too much, that individuals would always talk to us with the hope

or expectation of getting paid for it, and therefore friendships and mutual trust would not develop. I would also have the problem of validity: were they telling me this bit of data just to get some money? We did, however, compensate people for their time. We made it a public policy that since the villagers were helping us, we would help them. Since all villagers were respondents, and all were potential informants, we gave medicine to all villagers when they needed it. We also gave gifts of tobacco, betel supplies, and fermented tea (*miang*) nearly every time someone on the staff returned from Chiengmai. We gave extra and special gifts to our main informants.

When we first started field work, I carefully explained to as many people as possible that I wanted to learn their language and customs, and that I wanted to know all, see all, and hear all about their life. I wanted to participate in ceremonies and work. During the early "get acquainted" period, I was watching carefully for future informants. When I finally developed a few, I tried to train them to know what kind of information I wanted, that accuracy was important, and that I did not wish to accept "easy answers." It took some time on my part to realize that the work was hard and tiring for the informant too.

As I said all villagers were respondents, and for many kinds of data I was able to cover the village completely. At different times, and for different subjects, I used different informants, but the main ones were:

1. The head elder, a man of sixty-seven, and by far the most important informant.

2. His wife, aged sixty-six, who was very friendly to my wife, and from whom much important information came.

3. This woman's brother, the headman, who was fifty-seven.

4. A young man of twenty-eight, who was a widower, now living at home again.

5. A married man of thirty, whose mother is Thai, and who is coming up in the power structure of the village.

6. Finally, the midwife, a vivacious woman of fifty.

I should mention a young couple here. They were not informants in the strict sense, but were my most important "case study." During our stay we got to know the couple well. We saw them courting. We went to their wedding. We watched them break the residence rules and then reinstate them. We saw them build their own house and move into it. In short, we observed the founding of a new family.

My techniques of eliciting information were as follows. When we first started working in the village, our contacts were very casual and informal. I might go up on a porch and chat with someone, asking general questions about what they were doing, and so on. I always, however, had in mind some information that I wanted and would get around to it leisurely. If someone was going to work in the fields, fix a fence, and so forth, I would go along and help if I could. I always used the present activity, whatever it was, as a starting place for information that day. Sometimes, therefore, I did not get the information that I went for. This is the technique that I used with all villagers. There were always, therefore, two means of gathering data going on simultaneously: (1) participant observation, that is, learning about what one accidentally runs into; and (2) deliberate, non-accidental attempt to get specific information through the interview. I had to make the collection of information seem casual and conversational.

As I trained informants to know what information I needed, how to answer questions, and so on, I could use more direct methods. We would sit on a porch and there would be a question and answer period—an interview if you will, but I was careful not to make it too formal. These periods would often be interrupted or continued at a later time. Often someone would come up, and depending on the situation and/or the person,

I would do one of two things. I might carry on the questioning with either myself or the informant inviting the new person to help with the answers; or, I might stop and change the subject to fit the new situation. I was always collecting information one way or another while in the village.

We participated in the life and activities of the village as much as we could or as much as the Karen would let us. In the latter part of December, 1960, I was assessed two chickens and a bottle of whiskey like any villager for the all-village ceremony. From that time until we left we were considered villagers even though we had not yet moved to the village. At any rate, a great deal of my data and understanding of Karen culture came from participating in, observing, and later questioning about ceremonies, work activities, and so on. I am convinced that one cannot really understand an alien culture without living in it for a considerable time. Merely questioning an informant is not sufficient. I tried both techniques.

There is always a question of verification in anthropological work. My first test of validity of information was always consistency—was this bit of data consistent with what I already knew? Probably there are no data in my files that were not checked with at least one person other than the original informant. I tried to keep the informant consistent with the type of information desired. For example, I used women to tell me about women, or my wife obtained the information. Sometimes I used informants from different status groups for a bit of data to get a contrast: I got sex information from young adults, married and unmarried, and I got the same information from the head elder. This did provide an interesting contrast between what people say is ideal sex behavior (from the elder) and what people actually do (from the young adults). I also tried to get some idea of who knew what, and what changes were occurring. For example, I asked the head elder about religious ideas and beliefs. He had the reputation of knowing more about this than anyone. But, I also asked the young man whose mother was

Thai. He interestingly included Buddhist ideas which were entering the belief system in general. I also asked some others and found that not all Karen know the belief system equally well.

This is enough on verifications. The recording techniques that I used were as follows. I kept a small diary, approximately five by eight inches, purchased in the Thai market, in which to record in outline form daily events in the life of the Karen, what I did each day, weather, personal feelings, attitudes, and other miscellaneous information. (I felt it important to use this Thai diary because Thai holidays are given, lunar calendar is recorded, and so on. In this way I could correlate Karen activities with the Thai calendar, which is followed by the Karen.) Then, once a week I transferred the information from this diary to my journal in a great deal more detail. By setting aside a special time to record in the journal once a week, I was more sure of keeping it up to date, and by not recording immediately, I was able, usually, to record the details of an event that I did not know or understand when first learning about it.

Besides this running record of day to day events and activities, I always carried a stenographic notebook for recording words and phrases of the Karen language, as I mentioned above. From this a dictionary was compiled, translating from Karen to English, and English to Karen, on one and one-half by five-inch cards (three by five cards cut in half). Sometimes the equivalent Thai word, as well as a phrase showing word usage, is recorded on the back of the cards.

A separate stenographic notebook was kept in which were recorded long ceremonies, events, technical processes, and so on. These were then typed on regular typewriter-sized paper.

All specific technical information which was observed or elicited in interview (e. g., rice consumption, size of paddy holding, information on magic, people participating in an activity, etc.), was recorded on five- by eight-inch sheets of paper with a date, a title, and the name of informant. There was only one piece of datum on each sheet of paper. These were later collated according to type of information and then typed on five- by eight-inch edge-punch cards. These cards were not punched in the field, but filed roughly by major cultural category (individual development, economics, political organization, etc.), and by minor category within these (rice yield, pregnancy, magic, etc.). That allowed me to keep close track of what information I had, and sometimes suggested new leads and lines of approach.

A genealogical chart was made for each household in the village on typewriter-size paper. These were cross-referenced to certain "key" charts. On the back of these charts were recorded specific data about individual persons (miscarriages, causes of death, etc.). From these a large village genealogy chart was made which goes back to the founding of the village.

Special files and collections that I found useful to compile while in the field were as follows:

1. File of black and white photos pasted on three by five cards with descriptions, data, and negative number.

2. File of black and white negatives in individual envelopes with descriptions, date, and number on the envelope.

3. Index file, of color slides, on three by five cards with description, date, and number.

4. File of names, ages, lineage affiliation by household of all people in the village on five- by eight-inch sheets.

5. Residence history of each adult villager on five- by eight-inch sheets.

6. A set of tape recordings of songs, stories, ceremony texts.

7. Flora and fauna lists with Karen, Thai, and scientific names, classified in Karen categories for an understanding of their ethno-biology.

8. Sketch map of each household showing and listing all property holdings.

9. File of rice production and consumption by household, both wet and dry, for two years, on five- by eight-inch cards.

10. Property lists of each household on five- by eight-inch cards.

11. Chart showing lineage affiliation of all married adults and where lineage head is living.

12. Generalized kinship and lineage charts.

13. Local weather conditions for two years, collected from Thai administrative headquarters in Hod village.

14. Local calendars for two years.

15. Various language materials: phonemic system, morphology, syntax, word lists, texts of nearly all "prayers."

16. Soil samples from paddy, garden, hill field.

In conclusion I will say a few things about evaluation of the field work. As pointed out in the beginning of this appendix, I visited many areas before making a final decision on the general area of field research and on the group to be studied. I am satisfied that the choice was a good one, and I am convinced that I would have made a wrong choice for my purposes if I had gone to the Karen area in the south near Bangkok. Those villages were too changed, and I would have learned little of Karen culture, but I only had an impression of this before the field work was undertaken. In terms of actual village choice, I also think I made the right decision. Other villages were a bit easier to reach than Ban Hong, and the people were more friendly in the initial period, but these are the very factors that steered me away from those villages. It turned out that Ban Hong had a longer and more important history than some of the others, that it was an important parent village for several others. I might not have understood Karen social structure as well if I had picked a smaller, or larger, or younger, or more friendly village. The choice of Ban Hong was based on the impression that "here is a village where I will find out more about Karen culture." This impression did gain weight from visiting several villages and finding out a little about them before making a final decision. I do, however, wish that I had done some more comparative work in more distant villages such as Mae Ngut, Mae Phraphi, and Nong Pu.

The impact that my wife and I made on the Ban Hong villagers was complex. We did not affect the kinship system, or the economy, or the religion, but we did affect the lives of certain individuals, and we did introduce some new ideas and impressions. In some cases this could not be avoided, and in others it was quite conscious on our part. We tried very hard not to upset village social relations, but at times even the Karen tried to get us to interfere. I soon learned the village power structure, and tried to work through the headman when necessary, but the Head Elder was the most friendly to me and the best informant. The Head Elder was already in competition with the headman as a village leader, and I am afraid I did aggravate the situation to some extent. I maintained satisfactory relations with the headman, but had excellent relations with the Head Elder. In a couple of cases of "crisis," my opinion was asked. I tried to have no opinion, but of course this was impossible. I, therefore, acted in a conservative way in an attempt not to upset the situation. For example, when three girls in the village decided to "Thaiize," they tried to get our approval. We maintained a "neutrality" but this was interpreted, as I knew it would be, pro-traditional Karen behavior and against the new ways. In a couple of instances, I was held up as a "good Karen." This endeared me to the conservative elders, but did not make friends with those individuals who wished to accept Thai ways. However, no strong animosities developed between any of the villagers and us.

We quite consciously introduced Western medicine into curing techniques, but always told the Karen to use both their methods as well as ours. They already know about our medicine, but now anxiously asked for it. As a matter of fact, we learned a great deal about the Karen medicine and curing techniques by always asking about them while we were administering our medicine. My wife became noted in the local area as a curer with Western medicine, and she gathered much useful information in the process. The Karen also became aware that there is medicine specifically for children, and this had an effect on ideas concerning the death of small children. Before it had been taken quite pessimistically.

There were other kinds of influences, too, some so subtle that I do not know the effects. Many questions were asked of us about all kinds of things such as spirits in America, communism, farming techniques in the United States, whether or not we had matrilineages in our home country, how some specific customs differed from those of the Karen such as marriages and funerals, and so on. I tried to answer these as honestly as possible, but at the same time tried to find parallels to Karen ways in order not to interfere with my data gathering concerning their ways and beliefs. In short, my wife and I had an effect on the life of Ban Hong, but we tried always to direct it and control it. We tried to blend into the stream of Karen life as much as was humanly possible without compromising our field work.

The above should give an idea of my field methods and the extent of data collected, as well as how it was collected, and our impact on the village is indicated. At this point, I must make two comments: I could not have completed all the files and collections if it had not been for the help of a dedicated team of people. Among this group was my wife, Donna, who took to field work like a professional. Especially after our move to the village, Donna set about adjusting to Karen life by raising chickens, learning to weave, cooking Karen dishes, and visiting with the Karen women on our porch or on theirs, and so forth. In short, Donna was an asset as a field assistant, and at the same time she made us more human to the Karen. All of my assistants contributed in particular ways to the research. The second point that I wish to stress is that in spite of every effort to do a complete and accurate study of Karen culture, there are still some things I do not know or understand completely, and I am sure that I have made some mistakes in data collection or understanding. I hope, however, that these have been kept to a minimum.

The above statements and discussion of field methods all refer to the first field session 1959–61. The second field period in 1969 was organized differently since I already knew a great deal, had already established rapport with the people, and was to be in the field a much shorter period of time; from the beginning of March through the middle of August, 1969.

My wife and I quickly re-established our contacts with friends in Chiengmai, and we rented a house there for a permanent base since we now had a school-aged child. I found and was able to rehire the Thai couple who had worked for us previously as assistant and cook-helper. Thus I not only had a ready-trained assistant, but one who was well acquainted with the previous research. I bought a car and rented a small house in Tha Kham, the new *Amphur* Hod Headquarters, which was about fifteen kilometers from old *Amphur* Hod. I thus could drive from my field base of Tha Kham to new Ban Hong in a very few minutes. Since time was short and people were dispersed, I did not have a house in the research area. Besides, it would now be difficult to choose a village in which to locate, and it might have caused some antagonism if I had chosen only one. There was some competition among the Karen for my place of residence. My strategy was to visit the various Karen villages during the day, but to sleep in Tha Kham, except on these occasions when something important was happening such as a political meeting (always in the evening) or a ceremony. At such times, I was invited to sleep on someone's porch, and I accepted.

I generally returned to Chiengmai on the weekends to rest and go over my notes. My wife and son lived in Chiengmai, but visited the Karen on several different weekends. These were times of fun, friendship, and visiting old friends. The Karen were very happy to learn that we now had a child. Several had worried about our being childless ten years previously.

My first field task was to locate or account for all the Ban Hong Karen, which I did very quickly. Next I gathered census-demographic data on marriages, births, deaths, and residence changes over my ten years absence. I then turned to economic and environmental data in earnest. This occupied most of my time. I gathered data from government officers in Wang Lung and Tha Kham, visited the completed Yanhee Dam to acquire data on its construction, operation, and local affects, went to the relocation areas, and talked to Thai peasants about all that was happening. The bulk of my time was spent with the Karen gathering systematic data on attitudes, physical changes, economic activities, quantifying changes in "wealth" and ideology and ceremonial activities.

APPENDIX B   LINGUISTIC NOTE

The orthography used for both Thai and Karen words is a modification of that used by Mary R. Haas in *Spoken Thai* (1945). The alterations made for present purposes are as follows:

1. Thai words that have an accepted English spelling are not changed.

2. The glottal stop symbol has been dropped from all Thai words since its use is not significant in the present work and since Thai scholars disagree on its phonemic status (personal communication from William J. Gedney). However, the glottal is retained for Karen words.

3. Both Thai and Karen are tone languages, but tone markers have been omitted since they are not crucial.

4. The long vowel in Thai is represented by reduplicating.

5. Final *b*'s, *d*'s, and *g*'s in Thai are changed to *p*'s, *t*'s, and *k*'s, since those seem to be voiceless in final position.

6. Pwo Karen has at least phonetic degrees of nasalization, but this is ignored for present purposes.

7. The phonemic inventory, and the symbols used, are as follows:

THAI

CONSONANTS:

p		t	c	k	
ph		th	ch	kh	
b		d			
	f	s		h	
w			j		
m		n		ng	
				(n)	
		l			
		r			

VOWELS:

i	y	u
e	ê	o
ae	a	ô
(æ)		

KAREN

CONSONANTS:

p		t	c	k	'
ph		th	ch	kh	
b		d			
	f	ö	sh	x	
	v			ĝ	h
w			j		
m		n	ny	ng	
				(n)	

VOWELS:

i	y	u
e	ê	o
ae	a	ô
(æ)		

APPENDIX C HOUSEHOLD COMPOSITION

House Number	M Adults Who Have Been Married	F Adults Who Have Been Married	M Persons Never Married	F Persons Never Married	Household Total	Nuclear Family Only	One Parent and Child	Single Adult	Couple and Related Children	One Adult and Related Children	One Adult and Related Nuclear Family	Older Couple and Related Nuclear Family	Nuclear Family and Divorced Child	One Adult, Child Who Was Married, Her Children	Couple Only
H–1	1	1	3	6	11	x									
H–2	1		1	3	5		x								
H–3		1			1			x							
H–4	1	1	3	4	9	x									
H–5	1	1	2	2	6	x									
H–6	1	1	3	1	6	x									
H–7	1	1		1	3				x						
H–8	1	2	1		4							x			
H–9	1	1	1	1	4	x									
H–10	1	1	2	4	8	x									
H–11	1	1	2	5	9	x									
H–12	1	1	3	3	8	x									
H–13	1	1	3	2	7	x									
H–14		1			1	x									
H–15	2	1	2	2	7									x	
H–16	1	1	3	4	9	x									
H–17	1	1	1	3	6	x									
H–18	1	1		3	5	x									
H–19	1	1	3	2	7	x									
H–20	1	1		3	5	x									
H–21	1	2	1	2	6									x	
H–22	2	2	2	1	7							x			
H–23	1	1	2	2	6	x									
H–24		1		2	3	x									
H–25	1	2		2	5									x	
H–26	3	2		4	9									x	
H–27	1	1	3	1	6	x									
H–28	1	1	1	3	6	x									

APPENDIX C HOUSEHOLD COMPOSITION—Continued

House Number	Adults Who Have Been Married M	Adults Who Have Been Married F	Persons Never Married M	Persons Never Married F	Household Total	Nuclear Family Only	One Parent and Child	Single Adult	Couple and Related Children	One Adult and Related Children	One Adult and Related Nuclear Family	Older Couple and Related Nuclear Family	Nuclear Family and Divorced Child	One Adult, Child Who Was Married, Her Children	Couple Only
H-29	1	1	3	3	8	x									
H-30	1	1	1	1	4	x									
H-31		2	1	2	5									x	
H-32	1	1	1		3	x									
H-33	1			1	2				x						
H-34	1	1	1		3	x									
H-35	1	1			2										x

APPENDIX D MARRIAGE PATTERNS—MALE

Household	Number of Marriages	Divorced	Spouse Dead	Living
H–1	1			1
H–2	1		1	
H–3 *	1			1
H–4	1			1
H–5	1			1
H–6	1			1
H–7	1			1
H–8 *	1			1
H–8a **	1			1
H–9	4	1	2	1
H–10	1			1
H–11	1			1
H–12	1			1
H–13	1			1
H–14 *	1			1
H–15	1			1
H–15a	1		1	
H–16	1			1
H–17	1			1
H–18	1			1
H–19	1			1
H–20	1		1	1
H–21	2			1
H–21a *	1			1
H–22	1			1
H–22$_a$	1			1
H–23	1			1
H–24 *	1	1		1
H–24a	1	1		
H–25	1			1
H–25a	1	1		
H–26	1			1
H–26a	1			1
H–27	1			1
H–28	1			1
H–29	1			1
H–30	2		1	1

* Person now deceased.

** The letter "a" after a number signifies a person living in the household of a parent or parent-in-law who is not yet, or is no longer, forming a separate household.

APPENDIX D MARRIAGE PATTERNS—MALE—Cont'd

Household	Number of Marriages	Divorced	Spouse Dead	Living
H–31	2		1	1
H–31a	1			1
H–32	1			1
H–33	1		1	
H–34	1			1
H–35	1			1
43	49	4	8	38

APPENDIX D (CONT.) MARRIAGE PATTERNS—FEMALE

Household	Number of Marriages	Divorced	Spouse Dead	Living
H–1	1			1
H–2 *	1			1
H–3	1		1	
H–4	1			1
H–5	1			1
H–6	1			1
H–7	1			1
H–8	1		1	
H–8a	1			1
H–9	2		1	1
H–10	1			1
H–11	1			1
H–12	1			1
H–13	1			1
H–14	1		1	
H–15	1			1
H–15a	1			1
H–16	1			1
H–17	1			1
H–18	1			1
H–19	1			1
H–20	1			1
H–21	1			1
H–21a	1		1	
H–22	1			1
H–22a	1			1
H–23	1			1
H–24	1		1	
H–24a	1	1		
H–25	1			1
H–25a	1	1		
H–26	1			1
H–26a	1			1
H–27	1			1
H–28	1			1
H–29	1			1

* Person now deceased.

APPENDIX D (CONT.) MARRIAGE PATTERNS— FEMALE—Continued

Household	Number of Marriages	Divorced	Spouse Dead	Living
H–30	2	1		1
H–31	1		1	
H–31a	1	1		
H–32	1			1
H–33 *	1			1
H–34	1			1
H–35	1			1
43	45	4	7	34

* Person now deceased.

APPENDIX E BIRTHS AND DEATHS OF CHILDREN FOR WOMEN OVER 40

Female	Present Age	Age at Birth of Last Child	Number of Pregnancies	Miscarriages	Live Births		Deaths			Living Offspring	
					Male	Female	Male	Female	Total	Male	Female
H–1	40	40	9	?[a]	3	6	0	0	0	3	6
H–3	82	36	5	?[a]	5	0	0	0	0	5	0
H–6	51	39	7	0	4	3	0	0	0	4	3
H–7	66	?	12	?[a]	?	?	?	?	8	2	2
H–8	62	42	15	3	5	7	2	3	5	3	4
H–11	41	41	23	10	4	9	2	3	5	2	6
H–13	40	39	9	0	6	3	3	1	4	3	2
H–14	74	39	7	0	3	4	2	0	2	1	4
H–15	46	37	6	0	4	2	0	0	0	4	2
H–16	49	45	11	0	5	6	1	1	2	4	5
H–19	42	38	8	0	4	4	0	1	1	4	3
H–21	50	41	2	0	0	2	0	0	0	0	2
H–22	65	39	8	0	1	7	1	2	3	0	5
H–24	56	37	7	0	1	6	0	0	0	1	6
H–25	56	38	9	0	3	6	0	1	1	3	5
H–26	44	37	16	6	3	7	1	1	2	2	6
H–29	40	37	9	0	4	5	1	1	2	3	4
H–31	62	37	6	0	4	2	0	0	0	4	2
18			169							48	67

[a] Data from these women were not available.

APPENDIX F HISTORY, LOCATION, AND USE OF PADDY LAND BY HOUSEHOLD

The headman of the previous generation in Ban Hong had the following children (those not living in Ban Hong are omitted): H–1M (present headman), H–6M, H–7F, H–8F, H–22M, H–25F. All of these individuals inherited paddy land, but only H–7F and H–24F of this family retain their land which is located in the large paddy claimed by the founder of Ban Hong. The others sold their plots to Thai.

Currently, the two men of H–1 and H–4 are co-managers of the land belonging to the father of H–4M and H–1F. The father of these two people, besides the father-in-law of H–1M, is also his first cousin (the mothers of the two men are sisters). The land is located in the large paddy area across from Ban Hong, and was apparently inherited through a daughter of the village founder. (However, the situation may be a bit more complicated. It is possible that there was some land transfer between the foothill area—around Mae Phraphai—and the Ban Hong paddy area; see H–2 below.)

H–1M and H–4M alternate using this land in the following way: one year, both work half the land; the second year, one of them works all the land and the other works none; the third year, both work half again; the fourth year, the other one works all the land by himself, thus completing a four-year cycle. The 1961 season was the year H–1M did not work the land of his father-in-law. A new relationship was instituted that year, however: on the western side of the river (same side as the village) and north of Ban Hong a short way, is a paddy field that had not been worked for a few years. This land belongs to a Karen from Mae Phraphai. H–1M arranged to work the land in 1961 on a trial basis to see if he could get a profitable yield. If successful, he may work the land every year. Getting sufficient water for irrigation is the problem with this land. A water wheel cannot be used for the same reason that H–19 (see below) cannot use one, the land slopes toward the river. So H–1 must depend on sufficient rainfall that can be dammed and regulated into the field. If this endeavor is successful, presumably the relationship between H–1 and H–4 will be altered for the future use of H–4's father's land. When both H–1 and H–4 work the land in the same year, they each take half of it. The total land area is not worked jointly by the two men. They probably cooperate only in building a single water wheel. H–1 usually has enough labor supply in his own household and requires only one or two other women at planting and harvesting time. He owns two buffalo, but sometimes borrows another from his brother's son, H–17. On the other hand, H–4 does not own a buffalo and has a small family, so he must borrow or hire buffalo (see below H–21, H–14) and must get more outside help in the work. He does have relatives in Dong Dam who help when needed.

The land of H–2 is also across the river, but it is at the other side of the large paddy area and is surrounded by land owned by villagers from Dong Dam. The land was, no doubt, originally that of another daughter of the founder of Ban Hong. There is nothing unusual about H–2's land, labor, or capital outlay. He owns his own buffalo, and has a large enough family that he needs little extra help.

H–2M received his paddy from his father (a brother of the mother of the present headman), but this land was near the foothills around Hui Fang. H–2M exchanged his land with a Thai for his present location in the large paddy field.

H–3M is the father of H–2M and H–21M, but H–3M is no longer alive, and H–3F is supported by her sons (this woman died during my residence in the village). The land of H–3M descended to only one or two of his sons (other sons do not own paddy land). It is important to mention, however, that H–3M and the mother of H–1M were brother and sister. Both had paddy land in the foothills area so were apparently inheritors of paddy land from the original paddy in that area. It must be noted in this regard that the lineage head of the present headman (H–1M) lives in Mae Phraphai, a foothill village.

H–5 works on his father's land which is near that of H–2. The father of H–5M is a resident of Dong Dam and received his lands through a daughter of Ban Hong's founder. There is nothing unusual about H–6. He is the brother of H–1, owns buffalo and uses few people outside his immediate kinsmen. The next parcel of paddy land is owned by H–7F (sister of H–1). This land is worked by H–7 and H–13 (his son). H–7 owns two buffalo. In spite of the fact that this land is worked by two households, they cannot supply nearly enough labor. This is because H–7F is too feeble to help, but the children of H–13 are still too young. Therefore, people from several nonmanagerial households work at planting and harvesting time.

H–12M owned some paddy, but did not work it for several years, then sold it, and I could not determine its exact location or size. He says there is not enough water to use it now. However, this man is an opium addict and possibly did not work the land because he is physically not able. At any rate, he may have gotten it in a similar fashion to H–16M, since he also came from Hui Sai. Or he may have gotten it the same way H–19 and H–28 got their paddy.

The male at H–14 died several years ago, and the land now owned by H–14 is worked entirely by a Karen from Dong Dam because H–14 is too old to be of any help, and she does not have buffalo for plowing or harrowing. The manager of her land is responsible for all the work. His pay is a set amount of the yield no matter what the total is, but usually is a little more than half.

H–14F may have gotten her land from her husband or through her father, but either way it descended from the founder of Ban Hong: her husband was a great-grandson of the founder, and she is a greatgranddaughter. In other words, she and her husband are second cousins.

H–16M and H–16F both own paddy in two separate plots. H–16F is a daughter of another son of the past generation's headman and received her land from her father. It was impossible for me to trace H–16M completely, but he has relatives in Hui Sai and therefore the original Ban Phae. He is probably related somehow to the founder of Ban Hong, and his land probably came through a daughter. Or he may have received his land in the same way as H–2M.

H–16 is probably the most wealthy in the village. They own several buffalo, but do use extra labor too, usually their son or daughter-in-law, H–18.

There are four households who help in working paddy land regularly (H–5, H–13, H–18, H–20), but these are merely helping on the land of a parent. However, a fifth household is a special case: H–17M is the son of H–6 (who is a brother of the present headman), and H–17 owns no paddy of his own. Every year, however, he works the plot of his father's sister, H–24F, the plot that belonged to H–8F (his aunt), and the plot that belonged to another aunt who now resides in Vwang Mô (she is the wife of the headman there). These three plots are adjacent to each other so H–17 works them all together (but keeps yield separate). The latter two plots now belong to a Thai and H–17M acts as foreman or labor boss on the three plots of land. He owns a buffalo, and gets labor from the village, often from his father's household (H–6).

The land belonging to H–19 is on the same side of the river as the village. H–19M and his sister, H–16F, inherited from their father who is the older brother of H–1M. The father of H–19M was the headman of Ban Hong for a time, but had to leave the village because of an attempt on his life (he now lives in Nông Pu). When this man and his wife left the village, he sold some land and gave some to his daughter, H–16F. H–

19M inherited enough resources to buy buffalo and land. He bought six *rai* of land, but only one-half *rai* had been cleared for paddy. H–19 cleared the rest over the years, plus two *rai* of illegal land (it is not registered or taxed) which he now works with labor from the village.

H–20 works on his father's land, who lives in Dong Dam and who probably received the land through a daughter of Ban Hong's founder. The land owned by H–21M is located near that of his brother, H–2, on the Dong Dam side of the large paddy area. H–21, like H–14, does not own buffalo, so he must hire someone to do the plowing and harrowing for him. He is able to manage all the rest of the labor required so he pays less than H–14, which amounts to less than one-fourth of the total yield. There are no buffalo owned by H–25 either, and since this couple is getting beyond their peak physical capacity, the land owned by H–25F is managed by H–6 and H–17.

The last paddy-field owner to be discussed is H–28M. His is not a success story. This man took it upon himself to clear a small plot of land and make his own paddy field beside the H–19 plot. This is another case of an illegal unregistered paddy. However, there is no way of irrigating the field properly, so the yield was very poor. The plot was planted in 1959 and 1960, but not in 1961. The household does not own buffalo, and has now abandoned the land.

Currently, there are twenty households which neither own nor work Karen paddy land consistently. Two of these, however, H–12 and H–28, owned land as mentioned above but one sold his and the other abandoned his. There are, therefore, fifteen households in Ban Hong that own or work in the paddy fields of Ban Hong. There are twenty households which either do not work in paddy fields at all (for one reason or another—such as being too old), or whose members are part of the labor force for Thai (more rarely, Karen) fields.

APPENDIX G SUMMARY OF VILLAGE USE AND OWNERSHIP OF PADDY LAND

Household	Current Paddy Owner	Previous Paddy Owner	Manage or Work Paddy	Little or No Paddy Work
H–1		M	x	
H–2	M			
H–3		M		x
H–4			x	
H–5			x	
H–6	M			
H–7	F			
H–8		F		x
H–9				x
H–10				x
H–11				x
H–12		M		x
H–13			x	
H–14	F			
H–15				x
H–16	M, F			
H–17			x [a]	
H–18			F	
H–19	M [b]			
H–20			x	
H–21	M			
H–22		M		x
H–23				x
H–24				x
H–25	F			
H–26				x
H–27				x
H–28		M		x
H–29				x
H–30				x

[a] This man is a "labor boss" in managing paddy for both Thai and Karen.

[b] This is the only successful paddy owner who does not have his plot in the large paddy area across the river from Ban Hong.

APPENDIX G SUMMARY OF VILLAGE USE AND OWNERSHIP OF PADDY LAND—Continued

Household	Current Paddy Owner	Previous Paddy Owner	Manage or Work Paddy	Little or No Paddy Work
H-31				x
H-32				x
H-33				x
H-34				x
H-35				x
TOTAL	8	6	7	20

APPENDIX H TREE AND GARDEN OWNERSHIP

Household	Vegetable Garden	Tobacco Garden	Fruit Tree (Banana) Gardens	Pepper Gardens	Bamboo Clumps	Other Trees	Vegetable Garden with Swidden
H–1	x	x	x	x	x	x	...
H–2	x	x	x	x	x	x	...
H–3	...	...	...	...	...	...	...
H–4	x	...	...	x	...	...	x
H–5	...	x	...	x	...	...	...
H–6	x	x	x a	x	x	x	...
H–7	x a	x	x	x	x	x	...
H–8	...	x	...	...	x	...	x
H–9	...	...	...	x	x	x	x
H–10	...	x	x	x	...	x	x
H–11	x	...	...	...	x	x	...
H–12	x	...	...	...	x	x	...
H–13	x	x	...	...	x	x	...
H–14	...	x	...	...	x	x	...
H–15	...	x	x	x	x	x	x
H–16	x	x	x	x	x	x	...
H–17	...	x	x	x	x	x	x
H–18	...	...	x	x	x	x	x
H–19	x	x	x	x	x	x	...
H–20	...	...	...	...	...	...	...
H–21	...	x	...	x	x	...	x
H–22	x	x	x	...	x	x	...
H–23	...	...	...	x	...	...	x
H–24	x	...	...	...	...	...	...
H–25	x	...	...	x	...	...	x
H–26	x	...	...	x	...	...	x
H–27	x	x	...	...	...	...	x
H–28	...	...	...	...	...	...	...
H–29	...	...	...	...	...	...	...
H–30	x	...	...	...	...	...	...

a These households each had two of the gardens indicated.

APPENDIX H TREE AND GARDEN OWNERSHIP—Continued

Household	Vegetable Garden	Tobacco Garden	Fruit Tree (Banana) Gardens	Pepper Gardens	Bamboo Clumps	Other Trees	Vegetable Garden with Swidden
H-31	...	...	...	...	...	...	x
H-32	...	...	...	...	...	...	x
H-33	...	...	...	...	...	...	...
H-34	...	...	...	...	...	...	x
H-35	...	...	...	...	...	...	x

APPENDIX I WEAVING IN BAN HONG

Item	Material	Price	Work Time	Asking Price	Average Sale Price
Married woman's blouse [a]	1 vwai,[b] red 1 vwai, yellow 2 vwai, black Job's tears	3.50 baht 3.50 baht 7.00 baht 1.00 baht ——— 15.00 baht	±20 days total time	60–70 baht	35 baht
Married woman's skirt	2 vwai, red 1 vwai, yellow 1 vwai, black 2 pe, green 2 pe, white dye	7.00 baht 3.50 baht 3.50 baht 1.50 baht 1.50 baht 1.00 baht ——— 18.00 baht	± 3 days	25+ baht	23 baht
Skirt variation A (for market)	3 vwai, red 1 vwai, yellow 1 pe, green 2 pe, black	10.50 baht 3.50 baht .75 stg. 1.50 baht ——— 16.25 baht	± 3 days	22 baht	20 baht
Skirt variation B (for market)	4 vwai, red 1 pe, green 1 pe, yellow 1 pe, white 1 pe, black	14.00 baht .75 stg. .75 stg. .75 stg. .75 stg. ——— 17.00 baht	± 3 days	23–25 baht	23 baht
Man's blouse (red)	2 vwai, red 1 pe, yellow 1 pe, white 1 pe, green	7.00 baht .75 stg. .75 stg. .75 stg. ——— 9.25 baht	± 2 days	15 baht	13 baht

[a] This information came from H-11F who must do a great deal of weaving for the market because her husband is an opium addict. She believes that about 2 baht per day for labor is proper profit above cost of materials.

[b] 1 vwai = 5 pe, or 1 skein; 1 pe = .75 stg.; 1 vwai = 3.50 baht; 1 package of Job's tears = 1 baht; 1 package dye = 1 baht.

APPENDIX I WEAVING IN BAN HONG—Continued

Item	Material	Price	Work Time	Asking Price	Average Sale Price
Man's jacket (white)	2 *vwai*, white 1 *pe*, red 1 *pe*, black	7.00 *baht* .75 *stg.* .75 *stg.* 8.50 *baht*	± 3 days	Not sold in market	
Man's jacket variation	2 *vwai*, black 1 *pe*, green 1 *pe*, yellow 1 *pe*, white	7.00 *baht* .75 *stg.* .75 *stg.* .75 *stg.* 9.25 *baht*	± 3 days	15 *baht*	14 *baht*
Man's skirt	2 *vwai*, red 3 *vwai*, black 1 *pe*, white	7.00 *baht* 10.50 *baht* .75 *stg.* 18.25 *baht*	± 4 days	Not sold	
Unmarried girl's dress	3 *vwai*, white 1 *vwai*, red 1 *pe*, green 1 *pe*, yellow	10.50 *baht* 3.50 *baht* .75 *stg.* .75 *stg.* 15.50 *baht*	± 6 days	50 *baht*	25 *baht*
Blanket	5 *vwai*, red 1 *vwai*, white	17.50 *baht* 10.50 *baht* 28.00 *baht*	± 4 days	35 *baht*	30 *baht*
Shoulder bag (decorated)	½ *vwai*, red 1 *pe*, yellow 1 *pe*, green ½ *pe*, black ½ *pe*, white	1.75 *baht* .75 *stg.* .75 *stg.* .50 *stg.* .50 *stg.* 3.25 *baht*	± 4 days	12 *baht*	11 *baht*

APPENDIX J RELATIONSHIP OF MARRIAGE PARTNERS

FAMILY	Connecting Link Sisters	Connecting Link Brothers	Connecting Link Brothers and Sisters	Same Generation Marriage	Different Generation Marriage	2nd Cousin Marriage	3rd Cousin Marriage	4th Cousin Marriage	Unknown Marriage Connection	Probably No Connection	Male Marries Cousin's Child 1st	Male Marries Cousin's Child 2nd	Female Marries Cousin's Child 1st	Female Marries Cousin's Child 2nd	Legal Marriage	Illegal Marriage	Certain of Connecting Link
H–1M Parents		x	x		x										x		
H–1F Parents	x		x		x										x		
H–1	x			x					x						x	x	x
H–2		x		x					x	x					x		x
H–3						x	x								x		
H–4	x		x	x											x	x	
H–5						x									x		
H–6 *						x	x								x		
H–7	x		x	x											x		
H–8						x	x								x		
H–8a **						x									x		
H–9						x	x								x		
H–10						x									x		
H–11						x									x		
H–12						x									x		
H–13						x	x								x		
H–14		x	x		x										x		
H–15	x		x		x										x		

* The wife in this marriage is Thai.

** A letter "a" following a number signifies that a separate household is not established; rather the family lives in the household with the same number.

APPENDIX J RELATIONSHIP OF MARRIAGE PARTNERS—Continued

FAMILY	Connecting Link Sisters	Connecting Link Brothers	Connecting Link Brothers and Sisters	Same Generation Marriage	Different Generation Marriage	2nd Cousin Marriage	3rd Cousin Marriage	4th Cousin Marriage	Unknown Marriage Connection	Probably No Connection	Male Marries Cousin's Child 1st	Male Marries Cousin's Child 2nd	Female Marries Cousin's Child 1st	Female Marries Cousin's Child 2nd	Legal Marriage	Illegal Marriage	Certain of Connecting Link
H–15a									x						x		
H–16									x						x		
H–17	x			x							x				x		x
H–18		x		x									x		x		x
H–19	x			x									x		x		x
H–20		x		x								x			x		x
H–21	x		x		x										x		
H–21a						x									x		
H–22						x	x								x		
H–22a						x									x		
H–23		x		x								x			x		
H–24						x	x								x		
H–24a						x									x		
H–25						x									x		
H–25a		x	x										x		x		x
H–26						x	x								x		
H–27	x		x	x		x	x								x		
H–28						x	x								x		
H–29						x	x								x		
H–30						x	x								x		
H–31						x	x								x		

APPENDIX J RELATIONSHIP OF MARRIAGE PARTNERS—Continued

FAMILY	Connecting Link Sisters	Connecting Link Brothers	Connecting Link Brothers and Sisters	Same Generation Marriage	Different Generation Marriage	2nd Cousin Marriage	3rd Cousin Marriage	4th Cousin Marriage	Unknown Marriage Connection	Probably No Connection	Male Marries Cousin's Child 1st	Male Marries Cousin's Child 2nd	Female Marries Cousin's Child 1st	Female Marries Cousin's Child 2nd	Legal Marriage	Illegal Marriage	Certain of Connecting Link
H-31a									x						x		
H-32		x	x		x											x	x
H-33									x								
H-34		x		x							x				x		
H-35		x		x								x			x		x
45	7	3	9	9	11	6	2	1	26	12	4	3	1	2		4	11

APPENDIX K MARITAL RESIDENCE PATTERN

Woman of Household	Mother in Ban Hong		Mother-in-law in Ban Hong		Husband Changed Village Residence	
	YES	NO	YES	NO	YES	NO
H–1F	x		x			x
H–2F	x		x			x
H–3F		x	x			x
H–4F	x		x			x
H–5F	x			x	x	
H–6F		x	x			x
H–7F	x		x			x
H–8F	x			x	x	
H–8aF	x			x	x	
H–9F	x			x	x	
H–10F	x		x			x
H–11F	x			x	x	
H–12F	x			x	x	
H–13F		x	x			x
H–14F	x		x			x
H–15F	x		x			x
H–16F	x			x	x	
H–17F	x		x			x
H–18F	x		x			x
H–19F	x		x			x
H–20F	x			x	x	
H–21F	x		x			x
H–21aF	x			x	x	
H–22F		x	x			x
H–22aF	x			x	x	
H–23F	x		x			x
H–24F	x			x	x	
H–24aF	x			x	x	
H–25F	x			x	x	
H–25aF	x		x			x

APPENDIX K MARITAL RESIDENCE PATTERN—Cont'd

Woman of Household	Mother in Ban Hong		Mother-in-law in Ban Hong		Husband Changed Village Residence	
	YES	NO	YES	NO	YES	NO
H–26F	x			x	x	
H–26aF	x			x		
H–27F	x		x		x	
H–28F	x			x	x	
H–29F	x			x	x	
H–30F		x	x			x
H–31F	x			x	x	
H–31aF	x			x	x	
H–32F	x		x			x
H–34F	x		x			x
H–35F (41)	x (36)	(5)	x (22)	(19)	(19)	x (21)

APPENDIX L FAMILY RESIDENCE PATTERNS

Family	Residence Near Wife's Parents (1)	Residence Near Husband's Parents (2)	Residence Near Neither Set of Parents (3)	Present Residence [a] (4)	Previous Residence Village Other Than Ban Hong (5)
H–1 [b]		x	x	2	x
H–2	x			2	x
H–3	x	x		2	x
H–4	x		x	3	x
H–5 [c]	x	x		2	x
H–6 [d]	x	x	x	2	x
H–7	x	x		1	x
H–8	x		x	3	x
H–8a	x	x		1	x
H–9	x			1	
H–10	x	x		2	
H–11	x			1	
H–12	x			1	x
H–13	x	x	x	3	x
H–14	x	x		2	x
H–15	x			1	
H–15a	x			1	
H–16	x		x	3	
H–17	x	x		1	
H–18	x			1	
H–19	x		x	1	x
H–20	x			1	
H–21	x			1	x
H–21a	x			1	
H–22		x	x	3	x

[a] Figures in this column (4) refer to Columns 1, 2, and 3 of this table.

[b] Wife's parents moved out of Ban Hong about three years ago: H–1M, H–1F born in Ban Hong.

[c] His parents were in Ban Hong, but moved to Dong Dam. Now he and his wife have also moved to Dong Dam.

[d] Wife is Thai. He lived in wife's village, Ban Nong, for one year.

APPENDIX L FAMILY RESIDENCE—Continued

Family	Residence Near Wife's Parents (1)	Residence Near Husband's Parents (2)	Residence Near Neither Set of Parents (3)	Present Residence [a] (4)	Previous Residence Village Other Than Ban Hong (5)
H–22a	x			1	
H–23	x			1	
H–24	x			1	x
H–24a	x			1	
H–25	x	x	x	3	x
H–25a	x			1	
H–26	x		x	3	
H–26a	x	x		2	x
H–27	x			1	
H–28	x			1	x
H–29	x			1	x
H–30		x		2	x
H–31	x		x	1	x
H–31a	x	x		1	x
H–32	x			1	x
H–34	x	x		2	x
H–35	x	x		1	
42	39	17	11		25

[a] Figures in this column (4) refer to Columns 1, 2, and 3 of this table.

APPENDIX M SWIDDEN YIELD, 1960

Household	Size of Field		Seed Rice			Total Yield		
	Rai [a]	Acre	Ma [b]	Kilo	lbs.	Ma [b]	Kilo	lbs.
H–1	2	.8	1	15	33	3	45	99
H–2	2	.8	1	15	33	7	105	231
H–6	2	.8	1	15	33	12	180	396
H–7	2	.8	1	15	33	10	150	330
H–8	4	1.6	2	30	66	20	300	660
H–10	2	.8	1	15	33	30	450	990
H–15	3	1.2	1.5	22.5	49.5	8	120	264
H–16	2	.8	1	15	33	4	60	132
H–19	3	1.2	1.5	22.5	49.5	18	270	594
H–21	2	.8	1	15	33	9	135	297
H–22	5	2.0	2.5	37.5	82.5	60	900	1980
H–23	2	.8	1	15	33	30	450	990
H–25	3	1.2	1.5	22.5	49.5	30	450	990
H–26	3	1.2	1.5	22.5	49.5	7	105	231
H–27	3	1.2	1.5	22.5	49.5	21	315	693
H–30	2	.8	1	15	33	7	105	231
H–31	2	.8	1	15	33	10	150	330
H–32	2	.8	1	15	33	7	105	231
18	46 [c]	18.4 [d]	23	345	759	293	4395	9669

[a] One *rai* = .4 acre.
[b] One *ma* = 15 kilo (Approx.), or 33 lbs.
[c] Average yield per *rai* is 6.36 *ma*, 95.5 kilo, or 210 lbs.
[d] Average yield per acre is 2388 kilo, or 525.4 lbs.

APPENDIX M PADDY YIELD, 1959

Household	Size of Field Rai	Size of Field Acre	Ma	Seed Rice Kilo	Seed Rice lbs.	Ma	Gross Yield Kilo	Gross Yield lbs.	Ma	Net Yield Kilo	Net Yield lbs.	Distribution
H-1	8	3.2	4	60	132	220	3,300	7,260	113	1,695	3,729	103 *ma* to *Fa-in-law*
H-2	4	1.6	2	30	66	95	1,425	3,135	93	1,395	3,069	0
H-4 [a]	0	0	0	0	0	0	?	?	0	?	?	0
H-6 [b]	?	?	?	?	?	?	?	?	?	?	?	0
H-7	4	1.6	2	30	66	50	750	1,650	18	270	594	15 *ma* to H-13
H-14	2	.8	1	15	33	30	450	990	8	120	264	21 *ma* to manager
H-16	8	3.2	4	60	132	110	1,650	3,630	?	?	?	?
H-17	7	2.8	3.5	52.5	115.5	100	1,500	3,300	46.5	697.5	1,534.5	50 *ma* to Thai owner
H-19	6	2.4	3	45	99	45	675	1,485	42	630	1,386	0
H-21	2	.8	1	15	33	46	690	1,518	35	525	1,155	10 *ma* for plowing
H-25	2	.8	1	15	33	40	660	1,320	19	285	621	20 *ma* to manager H-17
H-28	2	.8	1	15	33	4	60	132	3	45	99	0
TOTAL	45 [c]	18.0 [d]	22.5	337.5	742.5	740	11,100	24,420	377.5	5,662.5	12,457.5	

[a] This household plants paddy every other year. It did not plant in 1959 (for details of the arrangement, see Appendix F).

[b] I was unable to get any information concerning this household, but they do plant and harvest paddy rice every year.

[c] The average gross yield per *rai* is 16.4 *ma*, or 246.6 kilo, or 542.6 lbs.

[d] The average gross yield per acre is 616.6 kilo, or 1356.6 lbs.

APPENDIX M PADDY YIELD, 1960

Household	Size of Field Rai	Size of Field Acre	Seed Rice Ma	Seed Rice Kilo	Seed Rice lbs.	Gross Yield Ma	Gross Yield Kilo	Gross Yield lbs.	Net Yield Ma	Net Yield Kilo	Net Yield lbs.	Distribution
H-1	4	1.6	2	30	66	102	1,530	3,366	60	900	1,980	40 *ma* to *Fa-in-law*
H-2	4	1.6	2	30	66	75	1,125	2,475	73	1,095	2,409	0
H-4	4	1.6	2	30	66	90	1,350	2,970	48	720	1,584	40 *ma* to *Fa*
H-6	4	1.6	2	30	66	86	1,290	2,838	48	720	1,584	36 *ma* to H-17
H-7	4	1.6	2	30	66	30	450	990	13	195	429	15 *ma* to H-13
H-14	2	.8	1	15	33	40	600	1,320	9	135	297	30 *ma* to manager; 1 *ma* to H-19
H-16	8	3.2	4	60	132	209	3,135	6,897	146	2,190	4,818	58 *ma* to H-18
H-17	7	2.8	3.5	52.5	115.5	101	1,515	3,333	47.5	712.5	1,567.5	50 *ma* to Thai owner
H-19	6	2.4	3	45	99	30	450	990	27	405	891	0
H-21	2	.8	1	15	33	29	435	957	18	270	594	10 *ma* for plowing
H-25	2	.8	1	15	33	54	810	1,782	33	495	1,089	20 *ma* to H-17
H-28	2	.8	1	15	33	5	75	165	4	60	132	0
TOTAL	49 [a]	19.6 [b]	24.5	367.5	808.5	851	12,765	28,083	526.5	7,897.5	17,374.5	

[a] The average gross yield per *rai* is 17.4 *ma*, or 260.5 kilo, or 573.1 lbs.
[b] The average gross yield per acre is 651.2 kilo, or 1432.8 lbs.

Bibliography

Barth, Fredrik, ed.
    1969   *Ethnic Groups and Boundaries.* Boston: Little, Brown and Company.

Beardsley, Richard K., John W. Hall, and Robert E. Ward
    1959   *Village Japan.* Chicago: University of Chicago Press.

Benedict, Paul
    1942   "Thai Kadai and Indonesian; A New Alignment in Southeastern Asia." *American Anthropologist* 44:576–601.

Blanchard, Wendell
    1958   *Thailand (Country Survey Series).* New Haven: Human Relations Area Files, Inc.

Boeke, J. H.
    1953   *Economics and Economic Policy of Dual Societies.* New York: Institute of Pacific Relations.

Bohannon, Paul
    1963   *Social Anthropology.* New York: Holt, Rinehart and Winston.

Brohm, John F.
    1963   "Buddhism and Animism in a Burmese Village." *The Journal of Asian Studies* 22(2):155–167.

Buckley, Walter, ed.
    1968   *Modern Systems Research for the Behavioral Scientist: A Sourcebook.* Chicago: Aldine Publishing Co.

Burling, Robbins
   1962 "Maximization Theories and the Study of Economic Anthropology." *American Anthropologist* 64:802–821.

Cooke, J. R., J. E. Hudspith, and J. A. Morris
   1967 "Phlong (Pwo Karen of Amphur Hod)." In *Phonemes and Orthography in Eight Marginal Languages of Thailand*, William A. Smalley, ed. Chiang Mai. pp. 148–197. Mimeographed.

Dalton, George
   1961 "Economic Theory and Primitive Society." *American Anthropologist* 63:1–25.
   1965 Review of *Capital, Saving and Credit in Peasant Societies*, R. Firth and B. S. Yamey, eds. *American Anthropologist* 67:121–122.

deYoung, John E.
   1955 *Village Life in Modern Thailand.* Berkeley: University of California Press.

Dobby, E. H. G.
   1958 *Southeast Asia.* 6th ed. London: University of London Press.

Durkheim, Emile
   1964 *The Division of Labor in Society.* New York: Free Press

Firth, Raymond
   1946 *Malay Fishermen: Their Peasant Economy.* London: Kegan Paul, Trench, Trubner and Co., Ltd.
   1950 *Primitive Polynesian Economy.* New York: The Humanities Press.
   1951 *Elements of Social Organization.* London: Watts and Co.
   1956 "Function." In *Current Anthropology*, edited by W. L. Thomas, Jr. Chicago: University of Chicago Press. pp. 237–258.
   1959 *Economics of the New Zealand Maori.* 2d ed. Wellington, New Zealand: R. E. Owen, Gov't Printer.

Firth, Raymond, and B. S. Yamey, eds.
1964 *Capital, Saving and Credit in Peasant Societies.* Chicago: Aldine Publishing Company.

Fortes, Meyer
1959 "Descent, Filiation and Affinity." *Man* 59:193–197; 206–212.

Haas, Mary, and Heng R. Subhanka
1945 *Spoken Thai.* New York: Henry Holt and Company.

Hackett, William D.
1953 *The Pa-o People of the Shan State, Union of Burma: A Sociological and Ethnographic Study of the Pa-o (Taungthu) People.* Ph.D. dissertation, Cornell University.

Hamilton, James W.
1960 Unpublished Field Notes on the Karen.
1963a "Effects of the Thai Market on Karen Life." *Practical Anthropology* 10(5):209–215.
1963b *Karen Social Structure and Social Relations: Anatomy and Physiology.* Paper presented at the annual meeting of the American Anthropological Association.
1965a *Ban Hong: Social Structure and Economy of a Pwo Karen Village in Northern Thailand.* Ph.D. dissertation, University of Michigan. Ann Arbor: University Microfilms.
1965b *Kinship, Bazaar, Market: The Karen Development of a Dual Economy as an Aspect of Modernization.* Paper presented at the annual meeting of the Association for Asian Studies.
1966 *Political Behavoir, Structure, Organization, and Function: A Karen Case in Northern Thailand.* Paper presented at the annual meeting of the American Anthropological Association.
1968 Unpublished Field Notes on the Bakuria.
1969a *Karen Culture Change Due to the Yanhee Dam: Ten Years Later.* Ms.

1969b Unpublished Field Notes on the Karen.
In Press *Structure, Function, and Ideology of a Karen Funeral in Northern Thailand*. Paper presented at the 9th International Congress of Anthropological and Ethnological Sciences. The Hague: Mouton Company.

Haudricourt, A. G.
 1942 "Restitution du Karen Community." *Bulletin de la Societe Linguistique de Paris* 42:103–111.
 1953 "A Propos de la Restitution du Karen Community." *Bulletin de la Societe Linguistique de Paris* 49:129–132.

Henderson, E. J. A.
 1973 "Karen Languages." In *Encyclopaedia Britannica*.

Hinton, Peter
 1969 *The Pwo Karen of Northern Thailand—A Preliminary Report*. Chiengmai: Tribal Research Center. Mimeographed.

Ijima, Shigeru
 1965 "Cultural Change Among the Hill Karen in Northern Thailand." *Asian Survey* 5(8):417–423.

Jones, Robert B., Jr.
 1961a *Karen Linguistic Studies*. Berkeley: University of California Press.
 1961b "Laryngeals and the Development of Tones in Karen." *Fiftieth Anniversary Publication*, no. 1 Rangoon: Burma Research Society. pp. 101–106.

Judd, Laurence
 1964 *Dry Rice Agriculture in Northern Thailand*. Data Paper 52. Ithaca, N.Y.: Department of Asian Studies, Cornell University.

Keyes, Charles F.
 1969 *Thai Tribal Relations in a Frontier District of Thailand*. Seattle: University of Washington, Department of Anthropology. Mimeographed.

1970 "New Evidence on Northern Thai Frontier History." In *In Memoriam Phya Anuman Rajadhon*. Bangkok: The Siam Society. pp. 221-249.
1971 *The Karens in Thai Histroy and the History of the Karens in Thailand*. Paper prepared for the symposium, "A Pivotal or Marginal People: The Place of the Karens in Southeast Asia."

Kingshill, Konrad
    1960 *Ku Daeng, A Village Study in Northern Thailand*. Chiengmai, Thailand: The Prince Royal's College.

Kunstadter, Peter
    1964 *Research on the Lua' and S'Kaw Karen Hill People of Northern Thailand*. Bangkok: Mimeographed.
    1965 *The Future of Upland Tribal People in the Nations of Southeast Asia: Lua' and Karen Hill Peoples of Northeast Thailand*. Paper prepared for the American Anthropological Association meetings, Denver. Mimeographed.
    1967 "The Lua" and S'Kaw of Maehongson Province." In *Southeast Asian Tribes, Minorities and Nations*, Peter Kunstadter, ed. Princeton, N.J.: Princeton University Press.
    1971 *Karens in Northwestern Thailand: An Outline of Relations Between Ethnic Categories*. Paper prepared for the symposium, "A Pivotal or Marginal People: The Place of the Karens in Southeast Asia."

Kunstadter, Peter, ed.
    1967 *Southeast Asian Tribes, Minorities, and Nations*. 2 vols. Princeton, N.J.: Princeton University Press.

Leach, E. R.
    1954 *Political Systems of Highland Burma*. Cambridge: Harvard University Press.
    1973 "Karen." In *Encylopaedia Britannica*.

Lebar, Frank M., et al.
    1964 *Ethnic Groups of Mainland Southeast Asia*. New Haven: Human Relations Area Files.

Leclair, Edward E., Jr.
   1962 "Economic Theory and Economic Anthropology." *American Anthropologist* 64:1179–1203.

Lehman, F. K.
   1959 *Some Anthropological Parameters of a Civilization: The Ecology and Evolution of India's High Culture.* Ph.D. dissertation, Columbia University.
   1963 *The Structure of Chin Society.* University of Illinois Anthropological Series, Number 3. Urbana: University of Illinois Press.
   1964 "Typology and the Classification of Sociocultural Systems." In *Process and Pattern in Culture. Essays in Honor of Julian H. Steward,* Robert A. Manners, ed. Chicago: Aldine Publishing Company.
   1965 *Report of a Preliminary Survey of the Position of the Kayah (Red Karen) of Thailand.* Mimeographed.
   1967a "Burma: Kayah Society As a Function of the Shan, Burma, Karen Context." In *Contemporary Change in Traditional Societies,* Vol. 2, J. H. Steward, ed. Urbana: University of Illinois Press. pp. 1–104.
   1967b "Ethnic Categories in Burma and the Theory of Social Systems." In *Southeast Asian Tribes, Minorities, and Nations,* Vol. 2, Peter Kunstadter, ed., Princeton, N.J.: Princeton University Press. pp. 93–124.
   1971 *Karen Ethno-History, Karen in Thailand: Comments from the Anthropology and Linguistics of the Kayah, the Shan and Burma.* Paper prepared for the symposium, "A Pivotal or Marginal People: The Place of the Karens in Southeast Asia." Mimegraphed.
   1973 personal communication
   n.d.-a *Kinship and Social Structure.* Ms.
   n.d.-b *Minority Peoples of Burma and The Theory of Social Systems.* Ms.

Lévi-Strauss
   1969 *The Elementary Structures of Kinship.* Boston: Beacon Press.

Luce, G. H.
  1959a "Introduction to the Comparative Study of Karen Languages." *Journal of the Burma Research Society* 42(1):-1–18.
  1959a "Old Kyaukse and the Coming of the Burmans." *Journal of the Burma Research Society* 42(1):73–109.

Marlowe, David H.
  1969 "Upland-Lowland Relationships: The Case of S'kaw Karen of Central Upland Western Chiang Mai." In *Tribesmen and Peasants in Northern Thailand*, Peter Hinton, ed. Chiang Mai: Tribal Research Center.
  1970 *The S'kaw Karen of Chiang Mai*. Paper presented at the annual meeting of the Association for Asian Studies, San Francisco, California.
  1971 *In the Mosaic: The Cognitive Bases of Karen North Thai Relationships*. Paper presented at the annual meeting of the Association for Asian Studies, Washington, D.C.

Marshall, Harry I., Rev.
  1922 *The Karen People of Burma: A Study in Anthropology and Ethnology*. Ohio State University Bulletin, vol. 26, no. 13. Columbus: Ohio State University Press.
  1945 *The Karens of Burma*. London: Longmans, Green and Co., Ltd.

McMahon, Alexander R.
  1876 *The Karens of the Golden Chersonese*. London: Harrison.

Maruyama, Magoroh
  1963 "The Second Cybernetics: Deviation-Amplifying Mutual Causal Processes." *American Scientist*, 51:164–79. Reprinted in *Modern Systems Research for the Behavioral Scientist*, Walter Buckley, ed. Chicago: Aldine Publishing Company. pp. 304–313.

Mintz, Sidney W.
  1959 "Internal Market Systems as Mechanisms of Social Articulation." In *Intermediate Societies, Social Mobility, and Communication: Proceedings of the 1959 Annual Spring*

Meeting of the American Ethnology Society, Verne F. Ray, ed. Seattle: University of Washington Press. pp. 20–30.

Mosel, James N.
    1957 "Thai-Administrative Behavior." In *Toward the Comparative Study of Public Administration*, William J. Stiffin, ed. Bloomington, Indiana: The Department of Government, Indiana University.

Murdock, George P.
    1949 *Social Structure*. New York: The Macmillan Co.

Polanyi, Karl, Conrad M. Arensberg, and Harry W. Pearson, eds.
    1957 *Trade and Market in the Early Empires*. New York: The Free Press.

Rajadhon, Anuman (Phya)
    1957 "Karen." *Thai Encylopedia, Manuscript of the National Bar Association*. Section 30:889–906. Original in Thai.

Sahlins, Marshall D.
    1961 "The Segmentary Lineage: An Organization of a Predatory Expansion." *American Anthropologist* 63:322–345.
    1962 Review of *Sociological Aspects of Economic Growth*, Bert F. Hoselitz. *American Anthropologist* 64:1063–1073.
    1965 "On the Sociology of Primitive Exchange." In *The Relevance of Models for Social Anthropology*, edited by M. Banton. London: Tavistock. (ASA Monograph, 1). pp. 139–236.
    1968 *Tribesmen*. Englewood Cliffs, N.J.: Prentice-Hall.
    1972 *Stone Age Economics*. Chicago: Aldine.

Scheffler, Harold W.
    1966 "Ancestor Worship in Anthropology, or, Observations on Descent and Descent Groups." *Current Anthropology*, 7(5):541–551.
    1973 "Kinship, Descent and Alliance." In *Handbook of Social and Cultural Anthropology*, John Honigman, ed. Chicago: Rand McNally. pp. 747–793.

Scott, J. G.
1900   *Gazetteer of Upper Burma and the Shan States.* Rangoon, Burma: Superintendent, Government Printing.

Seidenfaden, Erik (Major)
1958   *The Thai Peoples.* Bangkok, Thailand: The Siam Society.

Service, Elman
1962   *Primitive Social Organization.* New York: Random House.

Shafer, Robert
1955   "Classification of the Sino-Tibetan Languages." *Word* 11:94–111.

Skinner, G. William
1947   *Thailand Population Density* (map). Bangkok, Thailand: Cornell Research Center.

Sloan, Harold S., and Arnold J. Zurcher
1953   *Dictionary of Economics.* New York: Barnes and Noble, Inc.

Spencer, Joseph E.
1962   *Asia East by South.* New York: John Wiley and Sons.

Spicer, Edward H.
1971   "Persistent Cultural Systems." *Science* 174:795–800.

Spicer, Edward H., ed.
1961   *Perspectives in American Indian Culture Change.* Chicago: University of Chicago Press.

Stamp, L. D.
1973a "Karenni States." In *Encylopaedia Britannica.*
1973b "Karen State." In *Encylopaedia Britannica.*

Stern, Theodore
1965   *Research Upon Karen in Village and Town Upper Khwae Noi, Western Thailand.* Mimeographed.
1968   "Three Pwo Karen Scripts: A Study of Alphabet Formation." *Anthropological Linguistics* 10:1–39.

1970 *A People Between: The Pwo Karen of Western Thailand.* Paper presented at the annual meeting of the Association for Asian Studies, San Francisco, California.

Sternstein, Larry
    1964 "An Historical Atlas of Thailand." *The Journal of Siam Society* 52:7–20.

Trager, Frank N., ed.
    1956 *Annotated Bibliography of Burma.* New Haven: Human Relations Area Files.

U.S., Armed Forces
    1963 *Area Handbook for Thailand.* Washington, D.C.: American University.

Young, Oliver G.
    1962 *The Hill Tribes of Northern Thailand.* Bangkok: The Siam Society.

Index

Activities:
　domestic, 87–8
　of men, 21
　of women, 21
Administration, political, 282
Administrative divisions, Thailand, 146
Administrative headquarters, 18, 19
　of Amphur Hod, 34
Agriculture, techniques, 53–5, 56–8
Bamboo, 72–4
Ban Hong:
　demography, 26f
　description, 23f
Bazaar, 184
Blanchard, Wendell, 2, 5, 6, 10, 18, 50, 51
Blood brotherhood, 105ff
Boeke, J. H., 194
Brohm, John F., 245
Buddhist temples, 40
Burling, Robbins, 177
Bwe, 4

Cash crops, 207
Cash products, 207
Change, 230ff
　economic, 266–77
　evidence of, 234–36
　ideological-religious, 245
　political, 243
　social, 240
　techno-economic, 239

Chickens, 80–1
Climate, 49–51
Collecting, 83–4
Contact, external, 40
Content variation, 232
Construction, 89–90
Consumption:
　patterns of, 187f
　types of, 191–92
　units of, 187–91
Cousin sets, 98–9
Culture change, 231
Culture contact, 231
Curer, Thai, 35

Dalton, George, 177
Dam, 238
Dang relations, 98
Daughter village, 6, 44, 45, 157
de Young, John E., 18
Death, categories of, 29, 30
Demography, 257f
Descent, 92, 99–100
Distribution, 177f
Division of labor, 129ff
Divorce, 129
Dobby, E. H. G., 15, 50, 51
Dogs, 81–2
Dong Dam, 59
Dual economy, 194, 214
Duality, cause of, 218–27

INDEX

Economic organization, 173–74
Economic structure, 173–74
Economy, 173–74
Environment, Yanhee Dam and, 249
Exchange, 183
  medium of, 184

Fauna, 52–3
Fishing, 84–7
Flora, 51–2
Fortes, Meyer, 93
Friendships, 104ff

Gardens, 59
  fruit tree, 72–4
  tobacco, 72
  vegetable, 72–4
Gathering, 83

Hackett, William D., 9, 45
Hamilton, James W., 154, 167
Haudricourt, A. G., 8
Head elder, 152
Headman, 11, 44, 144
  economic authority of, 176
  "political headman", 147–48
  Thai appointed, 146–47
  traditional, 145, 148ff
Hinton, Peter, 5, 6, 7, 45, 54, 57, 60, 62, 92, 127, 259
History, traditional, 30ff
Hod, administrative center, 18, 19
House spirits, 138–39
Household, 119ff
  composition, 27, 120
  income, 213
  managerial, 66
  ritual, 138–39
Hui Sai, 59
Hunting, 82–3

Ijima, Shigeru, 5, 11
Inheritance, 61–2, 127–28
Irrigation, 55–6

Jones, Robert B., Jr., 8

Karen:
  dress:
    men, 21–2
    women, 21–2
  economy, 45
  history, 9
  kingdom, 10, 11
  language affiliation, 8
  location, 2ff, 15–6
  mannerisms, 22
  origin, 9
  population, 5
  religion, 45
  subgroups, distribution, 4
  village size, 6
"Karenness", 115–16
Keyes, Charles F., 7, 8
Kinship, 92f
  terminology, 95
Kunstadter, Peter, 53, 60

Labor boss, 176
Land speculation, 212
Law enforcement, 43
Leach, E. R., 10
Lebar, Frank M., 1, 8
Leclair, Edward E., Jr., 177
Lehman, F. K., 7, 8, 9, 11, 92, 93, 101–02
Lineage, 100ff
  ceremony, 182–83
  functions, 103–04
  head, 101
Lineage segment, 132ff
  functions, 134
Linkage:
  mechanical, 169
  organic, 170
Linguistic relations, 14
Luce, G. H., 8

Mang Meng, 59
Marriage, 124ff
  marital residence pattern, 28
Market, 196
Market economy, 194

INDEX

Marshall, Henry I., Rev., 2, 3, 4, 5, 6, 7, 11, 20, 44, 54, 56, 57, 63, 155, 239, 278
Medical clinic, 41
Middlemen:
  labor boss, 185–87
  salesmen, 185–87
  Thai, 42
  traders, 185–87
Midwifery, 41–2
Mintz, Sidney W., 183
Money:
  acquisition of, 206
  need for, 197f
  use of, 202f
Murdock, George P., 96

Oxen, 77–8

Paddy (wet rice), 65ff
  location, 58–9
  ownership, 61–2
  production, 66
Parent village, 6
Pigs, 78–80
Polanyi, Karl, 177
Political organization, of Karen village, 44
Pooling, 177–79
Population, 5
  of Amphur Hod, 33
  of Muban, 4
  density, 6
Pregnancy, beliefs concerning, 29
Pwo, 4
  villages, 5

Rajadhon, Anuman (Phya), 2, 5, 7, 9, 10
Reciprocity, 179–82
Redistribution, 182
Religion, 45
  changes in, 277–82
Relocation, government, 238
Residence, 119ff
  marital, 28, 120ff
Rice mill, 42

Ritual, 138ff
  family, 139
  lineage, 141–42

Sahlins, Marshall D., 177
Scheffler, Harold W., 97, 100
Schools, 40
Scott, J. G., 4
Seidenfaden, Erik (Major), 2, 5, 10
Sgaw, 4
Shafer, Robert, 8
Skinner, G. William, 6
Social organization, 44, 169f
Social structure, 173
Socio-economic class, 136–38
Soils, 50
Specialists, 91, 153–57
Spencer, Joseph E., 15, 50, 53
Spirit houses, 25, 31
Spirit medium, 35, 242, 278
Spirits, 25, 44, 46, 242
Sgaw villages, 5
Stern, Theodore, 45
Structural rearrangement, 232
Subsistence economy, 194
Subsistence products, sale of, 206
Swidden (dry rice), 62–5

Taxes, 61, 65
Tool manufacture, 88
Trading, long distance, 136
Transportation, 16, 38–40, 256
Turpentine factory, 42

Village:
  cluster, 18
  complex, 45, 157f
  daughter, 32–3
  dispersed, 18
  lower, 32
  size, 5
  spirit, 157f
  strip, 18
  structure, 144–45
  work, 90
Villages, restudied, 262

Wage labor, 136, 209
Wang Lung, 19, 34
Water buffalo, 75–7
Water control, 58
Water supply, 25
Water wheel, 59
Weaving, 87–8
Wet rice cycle, 69–71
"White Priest", 279–82

Work:
   distinguished from labor, 131
   management of, 175f
Work group, 67, 134ff

Yanhee Dam:
   environment, 249
   fishing, 252
   weather, 252
Young, Oliver G., 2, 4, 5, 6, 44, 45, 204

Notes

Notes

Notes

Notes